T0182040

Lecture Notes in Computer Science 14243

Founding Editors

Gerhard Goos
Juris Hartmanis

The series Lecture Notes in Computer Science (LNCS), including its subseries Lecture Notes in Artificial Intelligence (LNAI) and Lecture Notes in Bioinformatics (LNBI), has established itself as a medium for the publication of new developments in computer science and information technology research, teaching, and education.

LNCS enjoys close cooperation with the computer science R & D community, the series counts many renowned academics among its volume editors and paper authors, and collaborates with prestigious societies. Its mission is to serve this international community by providing an invaluable service, mainly focused on the publication of conference and workshop proceedings and postproceedings. LNCS commenced publication in 1973.

Wenjian Qin · Nazar Zaki · Fa Zhang · Jia Wu ·
Fan Yang · Chao Li
Editors

Computational Mathematics Modeling in Cancer Analysis

Second International Workshop, CMMCA 2023
Held in Conjunction with MICCAI 2023
Vancouver, BC, Canada, October 8, 2023
Proceedings

 Springer

Editors
Wenjian Qin
Shenzhen Institute of Advanced Technology,
Chinese Academy of Sciences
Shenzhen, China

Fa Zhang
Beijing Institute of Technology
Beijing, China

Fan Yang
Shenzhen Institute of Advanced Technology,
Chinese Academy of Sciences
Shenzhen, China

Nazar Zaki
College of Information Technology
United Arab Emirates University
Al Ain, United Arab Emirates

Jia Wu
Department of Imaging Physics
The University of Texas MD Anderson
Cancer Center
Houston, TX, USA

Chao Li
University of Cambridge
Cambridge, UK

ISSN 0302-9743   ISSN 1611-3349 (electronic)
Lecture Notes in Computer Science
ISBN 978-3-031-45086-0   ISBN 978-3-031-45087-7 (eBook)
https://doi.org/10.1007/978-3-031-45087-7

This Springer imprint is published by the registered company Springer Nature Switzerland AG
The registered company address is: Gewerbestrasse 11, 6330 Cham, Switzerland
Paper in this product is recyclable.

Preface

The 2nd Workshop on Computational Mathematics Modeling in Cancer Analysis (CMMCA 2023) was held in conjunction with the 26th International Conference on Medical Image Computing and Computer Assisted Intervention (MICCAI 2023) on October 8, 2023. It was with a sense of palpable anticipation that we gathered once more, this time within the captivating realm of Vancouver, to engage in a confluence of knowledge and insight.

Cancer is a complex and heterogeneous disease that often leads to misdiagnosis and ineffective treatment strategies. Pilot mathematical and computational approaches have been implemented in basic cancer research over the past few decades, such as the emerging concept of digital twins. These methods, rooted in rigorous math and biology, enable a profound computational exploration of cancer. They unveil connections between biological processes and computational insights across various omics data, including radiographics, pathology, genomics, and proteomics. These advanced computational techniques, with strong interpretability, synergize clinical data and algorithms within the realm of artificial intelligence, proving robust and clinically feasible.

CMMCA unites experts across mathematics, engineering, computer science, and medicine to explore novel mathematical approaches for multimodal cancer data analysis, with CMMCA 2023 emphasizing the discovery of cutting-edge techniques addressing trends and challenges in theoretical, computational, and applied aspects of mathematical cancer data analysis. All submissions underwent rigorous double-blind peer-review by at least two members (mostly three members) of the program committee, composed of 48 research experts in the field. The paper selection was based on methodological innovation, technical merit(s), relevance, significance of results, and clarity of presentation. Finally, we received 25 submissions, out of which 17 papers were accepted at the workshop and chosen to be included in this Springer LNCS volume.

In the aftermath of this intellectual rendezvous, we find ourselves compelled to extend heartfelt gratitude. We are grateful to the Program Committee for dedicating to reviewing the submitted papers and giving constructive comments and critiques, to the authors for submitting high-quality papers, and to the presenters for excellent presentations. Lastly, our appreciation extends to the attendees of CMCCA 2023, whose participation from all corners of the world enriched the collective intellectual tapestry.

October 2023

Wenjian Qin
Nazar Zaki
Fa Zhang
Jia Wu
Fan Yang
Chao Li

Organization

Organizing Chairs

Wenjian Qin	Shenzhen Institute of Advanced Technology, Chinese Academy of Sciences, China
Nazar Zaki	United Arab Emirates University, UAE
Fa Zhang	Beijing Institute of Technology, China
Jia Wu	University of Texas MD Anderson Cancer Center, USA
Fan Yang	Shenzhen Institute of Advanced Technology, Chinese Academy of Sciences, China
Chao Li	University of Cambridge, UK

Program Committee

Anusuya Baby	United Arab Emirates University, UAE
Eman Showkatian	University of Texas MD Anderson Cancer Center, USA
Erlei Zhang	Northwest A&F University, China
Harsh Singh	United Arab Emirates University, UAE
Hongrun Zhang	University of Cambridge, UK
Hulin Kuang	Central South University, China
Jiafeng Xu	China University of Geosciences, China
Jiahui He	Shenzhen Institute of Advanced Technology, Chinese Academy of Sciences, China
Jin Liu	Central South University, China
Jing Ke	Shanghai Jiao Tong University, China
Jinyun Chen	Chongqing Medical University, China
Kai Hu	Xiangtan University, China
Ken Chen	Shenzhen Institute of Advanced Technology, Chinese Academy of Sciences, China
Liangliang Liu	Henan Agricultural University, China
Lintao Liu	Houston Methodist Research Institute, USA
Ming Liu	Shenzhen Institute of Advanced Technology, Chinese Academy of Sciences, China
Morteza Salehjahromi	University of Texas MD Anderson Cancer Center, USA
Rafat Damseh	United Arab Emirates University, UAE

Contents

Virtual Contrast-Enhanced MRI Synthesis with High Model Generalizability Using Trusted Federated Learning (FL-TrustVCE): A Multi-institutional Study

Wen Li[1], Yiming Shi[2], Saikit Lam[1], Andy Lai-Yin Cheung[3], Haonan Xiao[1], Chenyang Liu[1], Tian Li[1], Shaohua Zhi[1], Bernie Liu[4], Francis Kar-Ho Lee[5], Kwok-Hung Au[5], Victor Ho-Fun Lee[3], and Jing Cai[1,6(✉)]

[1] The Hong Kong Polytechnic University, Hong Kong SAR, China
`jing.cai@polyu.edu.hk`
[2] School of Computer Science and Technology, Hainan University, Haikou, China
[3] Department of Clinical Oncology, The University of Hong Kong, Hong Kong SAR, China
[4] The Hong Kong University of Science and Technology, Hong Kong SAR, China
[5] Department of Clinical Oncology, Queen Elizabeth Hospital, Hong Kong SAR, China
[6] Research Institute for Smart Ageing, The University of Hong Kong, Hong Kong SAR, China

Abstract. In this study, we developed a trusted federated learning framework (FL-TrustVCE) for multi-institutional virtual contrast-enhanced MRI (VCE-MRI) synthesis. The FL-TrustVCE is featured with patient privacy preservation, data poisoning prevention, and multi-institutional data training. For FL-TrustVCE development, we retrospectively collected MRI data from 18 institutions, in total 438 patients were involved. For each patient, T1-weighted MRI, T2-weighted MRI, and corresponding CE-MRI were collected. T1-weighted and T2-weighted MRI were used as input to provide complementary information, and CE-MRI was used as the learning target. Data from 14 institutions were used for FL-TrustVCE model development and internal evaluation, while data from the other 4 institutions were used for external evaluation. The synthetic VCE-MRI was quantitatively evaluated using MAE and PSNR. The data poisoning prevention was visually assessed by reviewing the excluded images after training. Three single institutional models (separately trained with single institutional data), a joint model (jointly trained using multi-institutional data), and two popular federated learning frameworks (FedAvg and FedProx) were used for comparison. Quantitative results show that the proposed FL-TrustVCE outperformed all comparison methods in both internal and external testing datasets, yielding top-ranked average MAE and PSNR of 23.45 ± 4.93 and 33.23 ± 1.50 for internal datasets and 30.86 ± 7.20 and 31.87 ± 1.71 for external datasets. The poisoned data was successfully excluded. This study demonstrated that the proposed FL-TrustVCE is able to improve the VCE-MRI model generalizability and defend against data poisoning in the setting of multi-institutional model development.

Keywords: Data Poisoning · Federated Learning · Image Synthesis · MRI

W. Li and Y. Shi—Contributed equally to this work.

W. Qin et al. (Eds.): CMMCA 2023 (MICCAI Workshop), LNCS 14243, pp. 1–10, 2023.
https://doi.org/10.1007/978-3-031-45087-7_1

1 Introduction

Gadolinium-based contrast-enhanced MRI (CE-MRI) is an essential diagnostic tool in medical domain, which provides life-saving medical information through enhancing the visualization of lesions for disease diagnosis and MRI-assisted tumor delineation [1, 2]. However, the use of gadolinium-based contrast agents (GBCAs) during CE-MRI scanning can result in a fatal systemic disease known as nephrogenic systemic fibrosis (NSF) [3]. NSF can cause severe physical impairment, such as joint contractures of fingers, elbows, and knees, and can progress to involve critical organs such as the heart, diaphragm, pleura, pericardium, kidney, liver, and lung [4]. It was reported that the incidence rate of NSF is around 4% after GBCA administration in patients with severe renal insufficiency, and the mortality rate can reach 31% [5]. Currently, there is no effective treatment for NSF, making it crucial to find a CE-MRI alternative for patients at risk of NSF.

In recent years, deep learning-based virtual contrast enhanced MRI (VCE-MRI) has garnered attention from researchers as a promising substitute for gadolinium-based CE-MRI [6–9]. The VCE-MRI is typically generated from multi-parametric MRI sequences, such as T1-weighted (T1w) MRI and T2-weighted (T2w) MRI, and is capable of performing similar functions to gadolinium-based CE-MRI in disease diagnosis [6, 7, 10] and radiotherapy tumor delineation [11]. Despite its potential benefits, one major obstacle to the widespread adoption of VCE-MRI technique is the lack of large, diverse datasets to train a generalizable model that can capture the complexity and variability of real-world imaging data. Current deep learning models have mostly been trained and evaluated using intra-institutional data, as a result, these models may suffer from significant performance drop when applied to MRI data from external institutions due to the heterogeneous nature of MRI [12]. Therefore, improving the generalizability of VCE-MRI model is a critical priority before the bench-to-bedside application of VCE-MRI techniques. However, gathering MRI data from multiple institutions for model training is challenging due to patient privacy concerns. Federated learning (FL) provides a promising technique to facilitate multi-institutional model training without explicit patient data sharing, thus can mitigates confidentiality and privacy issues associated with clinical data [13].

Nevertheless, FL presents unique challenges for VCE-MRI synthesis. Due to the distributed nature of FL paradigm, the global model is vulnerable to outlier training data in local institutions (also known as data poisoning) [14]. Trained with poisoned data, the corrupted global model will make incorrect predictions on testing data indiscriminately [15] or make incorrect predictions on some specific testing data with similar pattern to the poisoned training data [16, 17]. In clinical practice, the training dataset of collaborative institutions are preprocessed locally by different operator, which always uncontrollably leads to inconsistent quality of the postprocessed data, such as inclusion of outliner image regions, misalignment between input and target image pairs, mislabeling between input and target data, etc., even with a standard preprocessing workflow. The low-quality training data may act as data poisonings, which can negatively affect the performance of global model.

To address the issue of FL-based data poisoning in medical domain, we propose a novel FL framework called FL-TrustVCE for VCE-MRI synthesis, which incorporates the FLTrust mechanism [18]. By developing this framework, we aim to bring this innovative technique from bench-to-bedside and make it more accessible for clinical applications. The main contributions of this work are threefold: (i) we have developed and validated a FL-TrustVCE framework, which is specifically designed to prevent locally-preprocessed data from introducing negative effects in VCE-MRI synthesis. To our knowledge, this is the first attempt to apply FL to VCE-MRI synthesis; (ii) our study incorporates MRI data from 18 institutions, which is the largest number of institutions included in the VCE-MRI synthesis study to date. This large and diverse dataset may lead to a more robust and high-performing model; (iii) the trained global VCE-MRI synthesis model holds promise to provide a general model that can be leveraged for further model development in the broader research community.

2 Methods and Materials

2.1 FL-TrustVCE

Base Network. This study employs two routine contrast-free MRI modalities (i.e., T1w and T2w MRI) to provide complementary information for model training. To synthesize VCE-MRI, we used a multi-modality guided synergistic neural network (MMgSN-Net) as the base network. The effectiveness of MMgSN-Net in multi-input VCE-MRI synthesis has been demonstrated in [11]. The MMgSN-Net consists of five main components: a multimodality learning module (for modality-specific features learning), a synergistic guidance system (for complementary features fusion), a self-attention module (for capturing large size information), a multi-level module (for edge detection), and a discriminator (for improving synthesis performance).

Basic Federated Learning Paradigm. The basic FL paradigm for each iteration consists of three main steps. Step 1: global model weights synchronizing; Step 2: local model training, and Step 3: local updates aggregation and global model updating. In Step 1, the central server sends the global model weights w_g to n local clients ($n > 1$). In Step 2, local clients initiate the local models via received global model weights w_g, then fine-tunes the received global weights using local dataset for one or more iterations. After fine-tuning, the ith client obtains the updated local model weights w_i. In Step 3, the central server aggregates the local model updates u_i ($u_i=w_i\text{-}w_g$ for i^{th} client) according to a certain aggregation rule $u_g = f(u_1, u_2, \ldots u_{n-1}, u_n)$, where $f(\cdot)$ represents the aggregation rule. Then updating the global model using the aggregated updates by $w_g = w_g + \alpha \cdot u_g$, where α is the learning rate.

FL-TrustVCE. The aggregation rule is a crucial aspect in FL paradigm, as it directly affects the performance of the final FL model [19–21]. In order to mitigate the potential data poisoning risks arising from uncontrollable local data preprocessing, we propose a FL-TrustVCE framework in this study. This framework was built on the basic FL paradigm and incorporated an additional central server model that is trained using a root dataset. The central server model is used to guide local model updates selection. It is worth noting that the root dataset is a critical component of the FL-TrustVCE framework, as it determines the selection of local MRI data for model training. In order to develop a generalizable global model, a heterogeneous root dataset is required for diverse local MRI data selection. In this study, we included the MRI data from 11 institutions to generate a heterogenous root dataset, which was then preprocessed using a standard data preprocessing strategy (as described in Sect. 2.1). The heterogeneous root dataset is used to prevent the central server model from eliminating the local model updates that were trained with heterogeneous MRI data, which is necessary to improve the generalizability of the VCE-MRI model. It worth noting that a small number of training samples in root dataset is sufficient for the FLTrust mechanism development, and the central server model update was only used for local model updates selection and not involved in updates aggregation, as suggested in [18].To guide eliminating of local model updates that trained with poisoned data, only the slices around nasopharynx were included in the root dataset. The FL-TrustVCE framework comprises three main components: 1) Trust score calculation, 2) Local model updates normalization, and 3) Normalized updates aggregation, as shown in Fig. 1.

(1) *Trust score calculation:* this operation uses the popular cosine similarity to measure the direction similarity of the local model update and the central server model update. A positive value indicates a similar direction, while a negative value indicates an opposite direction. A higher value is considered to be more similar to central server model update. To prevent negative updates in the opposite direction from negatively impacting the aggregated global model, *ReLU* operation was applied to clip the negative updates. The final trust score can be calculated as follows:

$$S_i = ReLU\left(\frac{\langle u_i, u_c \rangle}{\|u_i\| \cdot \|u_c\|}\right) \tag{1}$$

where S_i is the calculated trust score, u_i is the update of ith local model and u_c is the update of the central server model. $\langle A, B \rangle$ represents dot product of two updates, $\|\cdot\|$ means the l_2 norm of a specified update.

2) *Local model updates normalization:* In this operation, we normalize each local model update to have the same magnitude as the central server update. Considering the multi-institutional MRI datasets have inconsistent intensity distributions, the dataset with a larger intensity may dominate the global model update, so we normalize the update of each local model to ensure no local model update contributes too much or too little to the global model update. The normalization operation can be formulated as:

$$\overline{u_i} = \frac{\|u_c\|}{\|u_i\|} \cdot u_i \tag{2}$$

where $\overline{u_i}$ means the normalized update of ith local model.

3) *Aggregation of normalized local updates:* the normalized updates are aggregated with a factor of corresponding trust score S_i of each local model, which can be represented as:

$$u_g = \frac{\sum_{i=1}^{n} S_i \cdot \overline{u_i}}{\sum_{j=1}^{n} S_j} \tag{3}$$

where u_g is the final global update.

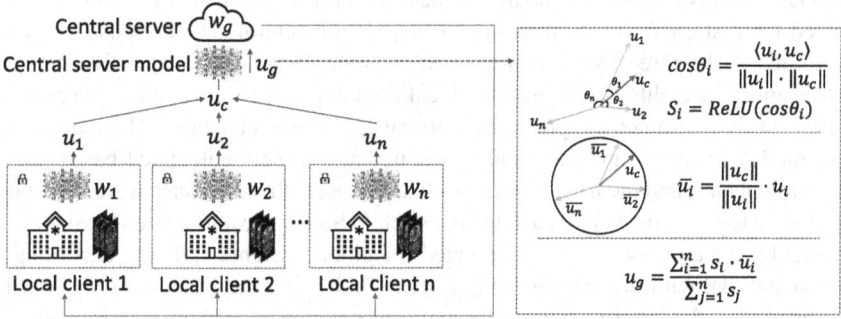

Fig. 1. Illustration of the developed FL-TrustVCE framework.

The final global weights could be updated with:

$$w_g = w_g + \alpha \cdot u_g \tag{4}$$

where w_g is the weights of the global model, α is the learning rate.

2.2 Data Description

The multi-institutional MRI data were retrieved from 18 institutions in Hong Kong, which were labelled as institution-1, institution-2, ..., institution-18, respectively. A total of 438 patients with biopsy-proven (stage I-IVB) nasopharyngeal carcinoma (NPC) were included in this study. For each patient, T1-weighted (T1w) MRI, T2-weighted (T2w) MRI, and CE-MRI were retrieved. Due to differences in MRI scanners, imaging parameters and patient characteristics, the MRI qualities are heterogeneous in terms of image contrast, resolution, and intensity distributions, etc. Prior to model training, all data were resampled to 256*224 using SimpleITK (V2.2.0) [22].Rigid registration was applied to register T1w MRI and T2w MRI to CE-MRI. After registration, all patients were normalized by z-score normalization [12] using mean value and standard deviation of each patient.

For the FL-TrustVCE development, data from 14 institutions were utilized, including three datasets for local clients' training (institution-1 to institution-3), four datasets for external evaluation to assess model generalizability (institution-4 to institution-7), and one root dataset for central server model training (institution-8 to institution-18). The local datasets consisted of 173, 134, and 71 patients, respectively, and 130, 105, and 53 patients were randomly split for training while the remaining 43, 29, and 18 patients were used for internal evaluation. The external evaluation datasets consisted of 18, 9, 9, and 7 patients, respectively. Due to the heterogeneous dataset is needed for the root dataset, datasets with less than five patients (institution-8 to institution-18) were included in root dataset to increase the data diversity, resulting in a total of 17 patients in the root dataset.

2.3 Implementation

Our study involved three local clients, and the global model was initialized randomly using Gaussian distribution. Compared to the basic FL paradigm, the FL-TrustVCE also involved three steps for each iteration: In Step 1, the central server sends the global weights w_g to the three local clients; In Step 2, the three local clients fine-tune the received global weights based on their local datasets while the central server model simultaneously fine-tuned the global weights based on the root dataset. Then the central server model update u_c and the local model updates u_i were calculated based on the global weights w_g, and the trust score as well as the normalized updates were calculated according to Eqs. (1) and (2) for each local model; In Step 3, the normalized local updates and calculated trust scores were aggregated for global weights updating according to Eqs. (3) and (4), with the learning rate α set to 0.001. For the base MMgSN-Net, L1 loss was used as the loss function of the synthesis network. The batch size was set as 1, and the Adam optimizer was used to optimize the base model. 200000 iterations were trained for the FL-TrustVCE framework.

2.4 Evaluations

The model generalizability was evaluated using four external datasets, which were not involved in training of any models. We trained six comparison models to assess the effectiveness of the FL-TrustVCE framework, including three single-institutional models that were separately trained with three local datasets based on MMgSN-Net, a joint model that was trained based on MMgSN-Net using all the training datasets involved in the development of FL-TrustVCE, and two popular FL frameworks, FedAvg [23] and FedProx [24], which were trained using three local client datasets. The three single-institutional models and the joint model were trained without FL. To quantitatively evaluate the performance of the models, we used two widely adopted evaluation metrics: mean absolute error (MAE) and peak signal-to-noise ratio (PSNR). Paired two-tailed t-test was applied to test if the synthetic VCE-MRI images were significantly different. Additionally, we qualitatively assessed the synthetic VCE-MRI of different models by visually comparing them with real CE-MRI. It is worth noting that the poisoning data was distributed randomly among data from different institutions, instead of deliberately added. To demonstrate the effectiveness of FL-TrustVCE in eliminating poisoning data, we recorded the clipped local model updates during training and saved the corresponding training image pairs that used for local model training and central server model training for evaluation.

3   Results and Discussion

3.1 Quantitative Results

Table 1 summarizes the quantitative comparisons between the proposed FL-TrustVCE framework and the six comparison models on the four external datasets and three internal datasets. As shown in Table 1, FL-TrustVCE outperformed all comparison models with top-ranked MAE and PSNR of 30.86 ± 7.20 and 31.87 ± 1.71, respectively. Among the single-institutional models, Individual-1 achieved the best average MAE and PSNR of 33.08 ± 7.05 and 31.34 ± 1.59 on external datasets, possibly because it had more training samples than the other two datasets. After including more institution datasets for training, the joint model outperformed the three single-institutional models (p < 0.05) on external datasets. This performance improvement may be due to the increased heterogeneity of the training data, which is consistent with the findings of Li et al. [12], who showed that joint models trained with more heterogeneous training data can achieve better generalizability, even with the same number of training samples. The joint model also achieved better quantitative performance than the classic FedAvg model. However, with tolerable accuracy sacrifice, FedAvg can address patient privacy concerns, making it possible to include more institutional datasets for model development. FL-TrustVCE obtained slightly better external results and significantly better internal results than Fed-Prox (p < 0.05). With similar quantitative results, FL-TrustVCE is able to alleviate a practical problem: eliminating data poisoning in local institutional data preprocessing during FL development. Individual-2 model obtained the best internal results, but it only performed well on the internal Individual-2 dataset, while FL-TrustVCE achieved a comparable internal results on all three internal datasets, with MAE and PSNR of 23.45 ± 4.93 and 33.23 ± 1.50, respectively.

Table 1. Quantitative evaluation of synthetic VCE-MRI from different models.

Model name	External results		Internal results	
	MAE ± SD (↓)	PSNR ± SD (↑)	MAE ± SD (↓)	PSNR ± SD (↑)
Individual-1	33.08 ± 7.05	31.34 ± 1.59	25.93 ± 5.41	32.11 ± 1.67
Individual-2	37.28 ± 7.75	30.41 ± 1.46	**23.42 ± 5.80**	**34.25 ± 1.93**
Individual-3	37.80 ± 8.51	30.22 ± 1.60	24.62 ± 4.42	32.36 ± 1.06
Joint model	31.85 ± 7.13	31.63 ± 1.64	24.35 ± 5.10	32.94 ± 1.51
FedAvg	32.25 ± 7.05	31.46 ± 1.63	27.26 ± 5.49	32.08 ± 1.45
FedProx	31.00 ± 7.19	31.80 ± 1.65	26.75 ± 5.32	32.26 ± 1.43
FL-TrustVCE	**30.86 ± 7.20**	**31.87 ± 1.71**	23.45 ± 4.93	33.23 ± 1.50

3.2 Qualitative Results

Figure 2 shows the qualitative results of VCE-MRI generated from different models. The three FL models and the joint model generated similar quality VCE-MRI with similar contrast enhancement in tumor regions (red boxes). However, the VCE-MRI generated from the three single-institutional models suffered from varying degrees of mis-enhancement, especially the images generated from Institution-1 and Institution-2 models, which showed blurring of overall image quality and incorrect black regions (indicated by yellow arrow). The Individual-3 model also exhibited unsatisfactory enhancement of tumor regions (indicated by the red arrow). These qualitative results suggest that both the joint model and FL models can achieve satisfactory contrast enhancement on external unseen dataset.

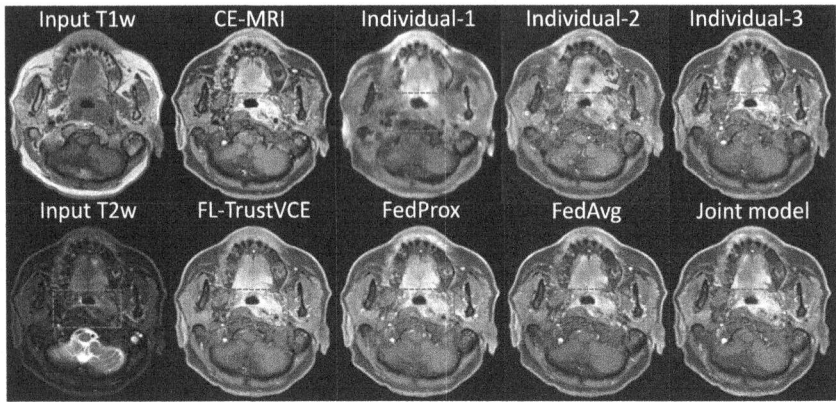

Fig. 2. Illustration of VCE-MRI images generated from different models.

Different from FedAvg and FedProx, FL-TrustVCE also has the ability to eliminate the potential data poisoning caused by inconsistent local institution data preprocessing. Specifically, using the central server model as a reference, the FL-TrustVCE can identify and eliminate local model updates that were trained with outlier images, as shown in Fig. 3, thereby avoiding the negative impact of such images on the global model performance.

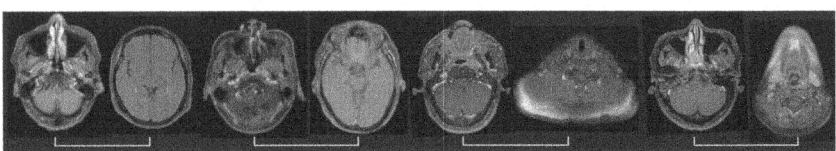

Fig. 3. Illustration of eliminated outlier images during FL-TrustVCE training. The left image and right image of each pair are training MRI in root dataset and corresponding eliminated local MRI.

4   Conclusion

In this study, we proposed a FL-TrustVCE framework to enable multi-institutional model training without data sharing. By addressing the practical issue of inconsistent data preprocessing, FL-TrustVCE demonstrated superior performance compared to the three single-institutional models, the joint model, and two state-of-the-art FL frameworks, both on internal and external datasets. The qualitative results also demonstrated that FL-TrustVCE successfully eliminated outlier images. The findings of this study suggest that FL-TrustVCE represents a promising approach to overcome data poisoning issues associated with multi-institutional model training.

Data Use Declaration: The use of this dataset was approved by the Institutional Review Board of the University of Hong Kong/Hospital Authority Hong Kong West Cluster (HKU/HA HKW IRB) with reference number UW21–412, and the Research Ethics Committee (Kowloon Central/Kowloon East) with reference number KC/KE-18–0085/ER-1. Due to the retrospective nature of this study, patient consent was waived.

Acknowledgement. This research was partly supported by research grants of General Research Fund (GRF 15102219, GRF 15103520), the University Grants Committee, and Project of Strategic Importance Fund (P0035421), Projects of RISA (P0043001), One-line Budget (P0039824, P0044474), The Hong Kong Polytechnic University, and Shenzhen-Hong Kong-Macau S&T Program (Category C) (SGDX20201103095002019), Shenzhen Basic Research Program (R2021A067), Shenzhen Science and Technology Innovation Committee (SZSTI).

References

1. Zahra, M.A., et al.: Dynamic contrast-enhanced MRI as a predictor of tumour response to radiotherapy. Lancet Oncol. **8**(1), 63–74 (2007)
2. Grossman, R.I., et al.: Multiple sclerosis: gadolinium enhancement in MR imaging. Radiology **161**(3), 721–725 (1986)
3. Sadowski, E.A., et al.: Nephrogenic systemic fibrosis: risk factors and incidence estimation. Radiology **243**(1), 148–157 (2007)
4. Thomsen, H.S.: Nephrogenic systemic fibrosis: a serious late adverse reaction to gadodiamide. Eur. Radiol. **16**(12), 2619–2621 (2006)
5. Schlaudecker, J.D., Bernheisel, C.R.: Gadolinium-associated nephrogenic systemic fibrosis. Am. Fam. Physician **80**(7), 711–714 (2009)
6. Kleesiek, J., et al.: Can virtual contrast enhancement in brain MRI replace gadolinium?: a feasibility study. Invest. Radiol. **54**(10), 653–660 (2019)
7. Gong, E., et al.: Deep learning enables reduced gadolinium dose for contrast-enhanced brain MRI. J. Magn. Reson. Imaging **48**(2), 330–340 (2018)
8. Li, W., et al., Gadolinium-free Contrast-enhanced MRI (GFCE-MRI) Synthesis via Generalizable MHDgN-Net for Patients with Nasopharyngeal Carcinoma
9. Li, W., et al., CE-Net: multi-inputs contrast enhancement network for nasopharyngeal carcinoma contrast enhanced T1-weighted MR synthesis
10. Zhao, J., et al.: Tripartite-GAN: synthesizing liver contrast-enhanced MRI to improve tumor detection. Med. Image Anal. **63**, 101667 (2020)
11. Li, W., et al.: Virtual contrast-enhanced magnetic resonance images synthesis for patients with nasopharyngeal carcinoma using multimodality-guided synergistic neural network. Int. J. Radiat. Oncol. Biol. Phys. **112**(4), 1033–1044 (2022). https://doi.org/10.1016/j.ijrobp.2021.11.007
12. Li, W., et al.: Multi-institutional investigation of model generalizability for virtual contrast-enhanced MRI synthesis. In: Wang, L., Qi Dou, P., Fletcher, T., Speidel, S., Li, S. (eds.) Medical Image Computing and Computer Assisted Intervention – MICCAI 2022: 25th International Conference, Singapore, September 18–22, 2022, Proceedings, Part VII, pp. 765–773. Springer Nature Switzerland, Cham (2022). https://doi.org/10.1007/978-3-031-16449-1_73
13. Rieke, N., et al.: The future of digital health with federated learning. NPJ Dig. Med. **3**(1), 119 (2020)

14. Biggio, B., Nelson, B., Laskov, P.: Poisoning attacks against support vector machines. arXiv preprint arXiv:1206.6389 (2012)
15. Fang, M., et al. Local model poisoning attacks to byzantine-robust federated learning. In: Proceedings of the 29th USENIX Conference on Security Symposium (2020)
16. Bagdasaryan, E., et al.: How to backdoor federated learning. In: International Conference on Artificial Intelligence and Statistics. PMLR (2020)
17. Xie, C., et al.: DBA: distributed backdoor attacks against federated learning. In: International Conference on Learning Representations (2020)
18. Cao, X., et al.: FLTrust: byzantine-robust federated learning via trust bootstrapping. arXiv preprint arXiv:2012.13995 (2020)
19. Li, X., et al.: FedBN: federated learning on Non-IID features via local batch normalization. arXiv preprint arXiv:2102.07623 (2021)
20. Kamp, M., Fischer, J., Vreeken, J.: Federated learning from small datasets. arXiv preprint arXiv:2110.03469 (2021)
21. Kamp, M., et al. Efficient decentralized deep learning by dynamic model averaging. In: Machine Learning and Knowledge Discovery in Databases: European Conference, ECML PKDD 2018, Dublin, Ireland, September 10–14, 2018, Proceedings, Part I 18. Springer (2019). https://doi.org/10.1007/978-3-030-10925-7_24
22. Yaniv, Z., et al.: SimpleITK image-analysis notebooks: a collaborative environment for education and reproducible research. J. Digit. Imaging 31(3), 290–303 (2018)
23. McMahan, B., et al.: Communication-efficient learning of deep networks from decentralized data. In: Artificial Intelligence and Statistics. PMLR (2017)
24. Li, T., et al.: Federated optimization in heterogeneous networks. Proc. Mach. Learn. Syst. 2, 429–450 (2020)

Label-Efficient Cross-Resolution Polyp Segmentation in Colonoscopy

Xiaozhou Shi[1], Youjian Zhang[2], Li Li[2], Yunxin Tang[2], Zezhou Li[2],
and Zhicheng Zhang[2(✉)]

[1] WELL-LINK, Beijing, China
[2] JancsiTech, Guangdong, China
zhangzhicheng13@mails.ucas.edu.cn

Abstract. Pixel-wise annotation is crucial but expensive for many deep-learning based application, especially for high-resolution (HR) image segmentation. Thus, lowering the burden of HR image annotation is a practical and cost-effective topic to save more human and material resources in the dataset preparation. In this work, we proposed a label-efficient cross-resolution polyp segmentation framework via unsupervised domain adaption with unlabeled HR images and labeled low-resolution (LR) images. The proposed framework consists of two workflows: super-resolution (SR) reconstruction and segmentation network. The SR network reconstructs LR image into HR image and the segmentation network is for polyp segmentation. We trained our framework using a hybrid training dataset, including CVC-ColonDB and CVC-ClinicDB (LR images) for supervised training, one-third of ETIS-LARIB (HR images) to be the unsupervised dataset, one-third as the validation dataset, and the remaining treated as the internal testing dataset. After the network training, to further evaluate the generalization of the proposed framework, we tested the well-trained model on CVC-PolypHD (an external testing dataset). The final experimental results demonstrate that our method achieves superior performance over other state-of-the-art methods in terms of performance and generalization.

Keywords: Polyp segmentation · Domain adaption · Super resolution

1 Introduction

Early screening is of great significance to Colorectal Cancer (CRC) since the five-year survival rate of CRC dramatically dropped down from more than 90% in stage I to 10% in stage IV [13]. Colonoscopy is the most commonly used CRC early screening device due to its convenience and directness, whose related technologies have attracted increasing attention [13]. Polyp segmentation is an essential step in the subsequent diagnosis and treatment of CRC [21]. With the

---

X. Shi and Y. Zhang—Contribute equally to this work.

© The Author(s), under exclusive license to Springer Nature Switzerland AG 2023
W. Qin et al. (Eds.): CMMCA 2023 (MICCAI Workshop), LNCS 14243, pp. 11–20, 2023.
https://doi.org/10.1007/978-3-031-45087-7_2

boost of high-resolution (HR) colonoscopy, colonoscopy images are becoming more and more clear, helping locate and segment lesions more accurately. While the HR colonoscopy brings convenience, it also brings technical challenges, one of which is the HR colonoscopy image segmentation due to the burden of massive pixel-wise annotations for HR images.

Recently, numerous high-performance deep learning (DL)-based polyp segmentation and detection algorithms have been proposed [4, 8, 16, 18], whose success lies in amounts of high-quality open released labeled datasets. For instance, [18] utilized text attention to exploit size-related and polyp number-related features, and employed an auxiliary classification task to weight the text-based embedding. While their training datasets have to be doped with a significant number of labeled HR images, which in reality is an unaffordable effort due to the requirement of huge pixel-wise annotation in scaled projects. Thus, to lower the burden of HR image annotations, making most of unlabeled HR images with labeled LR images to train a well-designed neural network is a valuable research.

In this paper, we proposed an label-efficient HR polyp image segmentation method with labeled LR image-guidance: Cross-resolution Domain Adaption Network (CreDA-Net). The motivation derives from our preliminary experiment that if we only used LR labeled training dataset to well-train the U-Net [17], the mean Dice coefficient on the testing dataset - ETIS (an HR image dataset) dramatically dropped down from 0.70 to 0.55 as shown in the Table 1, which is consistent with our intuition: the richer the diversity of the training dataset, the better the performance of the DL-based model. Thus, we argue that if we can synthesize corresponding HR images based on LR images to pull in the gap between HR and LR images, we can markedly improve the accuracy of the HR image segmentation with a virtual hybrid labeled training dataset. To be specific, we alternately trained the SR reconstruction network and the polyp segmentation network in each step. For the SR reconstruction network, we employed simulated paired images in the HR domain to train the SR network and then used the adversary domain adaption technology to pull in the gap between the real and virtual HR domain. Moreover, we utilized the real labeled LR images and virtual labeled HR images to train the segmentation network simultaneously.

In summary, our contributions are three-fold: 1) To the best of our knowledge, compared to other state-of-the-art (SOTA) methods, the proposed method is the first label-efficient HR polyp image segmentation trained on the labeled LR and unlabeled HR image, which will greatly lower the burden of pixel-wise HR image annotation. 2) We employ a SR reconstruction technique to generate virtual labeled HR dataset and then combine these HR dataset with real LR dataset to simultaneously train the HR polyp segmentation network using adversary domain adaption technique. 3) Experiments on both internal and external testing datasets have demonstrated the superiority of our method over other SOTAs in terms of performance and generalization.

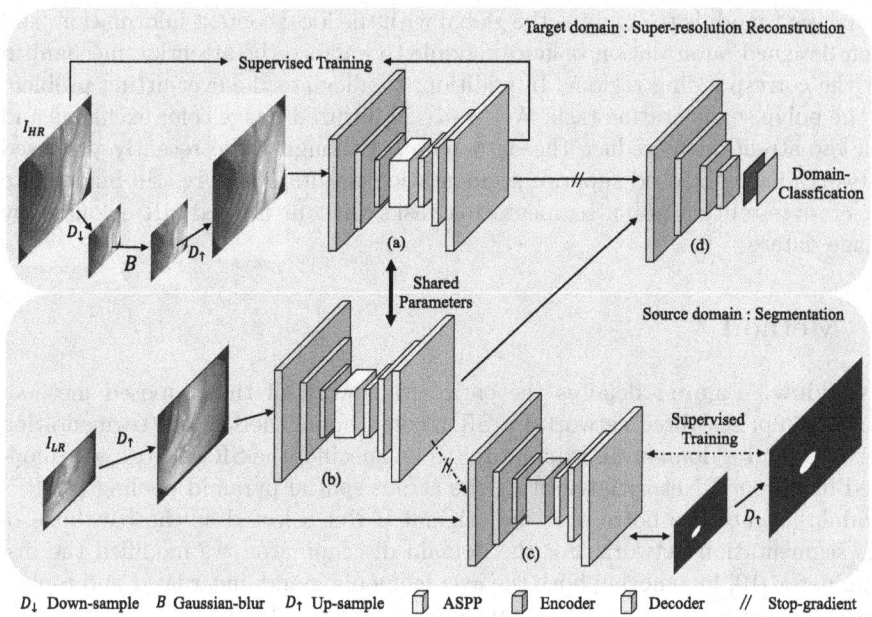

Fig. 1. The overview of the proposed framework. (a, b) SR reconstruction networks with shared parameters. They were trained in the HR domain and can generate virtual labeled HR images from labeled LR images for the following segmentation task. (c) Segmentation network. For LR images, we directly used their annotations as the ground truths. For virtual HR images (the outputs of SR network from LR images), we up-sampled corresponding LR labels as the ground truths. (d) Adversary domain discriminator that pulls the LR and HR domain distribution. During the network training, we used stop-gradient strategy to control the direction of gradient back-propagation. I_{HR} denotes the HR image, and I_{LR} is the LR image.

2   Related Work

For the medical image segmentation task, U-Net is undoubtedly the most classic neural network, which has been applied to polyp segmentation successfully and achieved excellent performance [17]. Inspired by the success of the U-Net in biomedical image segmentation, numerous networks have made advanced modifications based on U-Net for improving segmentation performance. For instance, U-Net++ was proposed derived from original U-Net with dense connection [23]. Also, ResUNet added the residual module to the original U-Net [22]. ResUNet++ combined the advantages of U-Net++ with ResUNet, further improving the performance of original U-Net [9]. However, these networks were not specially designed for the polyp segmentation task. To design a more suitable polyp segmentation model, Fan *et al.* [6] employed the reverse attention to locate the polyp areas and then refine object boundaries implicitly. To make segmentation results consistent at multi-image scales, Nguyen *et al.* [15] utilized a cascading context module to combine the global with the local context information, and then designed an attention balance module to balance the attention mechanism for the corresponding regions. In addition, to alleviate the over-fitting problem in the polyp segmentation task, Wei *et al.* [20] utilized image color exchange and shallow attention to reduce the data noise. Although these recently proposed networks have achieved superior segmentation results, they are still inadequate for cross-resolution polyp segmentation tasks without labeled HR colonoscopy image dataset.

3   Method

Overview. Figure 1 denotes the entire framework of the proposed method, which comprises three networks: a SR reconstruction network, a segmentation network, and a domain discriminator. To be specific, the SR network was modified based on U-Net by integrating the atrous spatial pyramid pooling (ASPP) module [5] into the bottom of the original U-Net selected as the backbone of the segmentation network. For the domain discriminator, we modified the discriminator [10] by ignoring both the average pooling and linear layer and replacing batch normalization with instance normalization. In the training stage, we employed HR images to simulated paired dataset for the SR network training, and then we used LR images and their corresponding virtual HR images to simultaneously train the segmentation network. In this work, all the related modules were trained in an end-to-end manner. In the testing step, we tested HR images using the well-trained segmentation network, and then outputted the final results.

Super-Resolution Networks. For the intuition: the diversity of the training dataset will immensely influence the performance of the DL-based methods. In other words, when we only employ LR images to train the segmentation networks, the well-trained networks are sensitive to the spatial resolution of testing samples with high probability, whose segmentation accuracy on HR images will drop dramatically. To address the above problem, the common idea is to re-collect amounts of HR images and make corresponding annotations, however, this practice is unaffordable due to the huge burden of data collection and annotation. Therefore, in this paper, we introduced a SR network to generate virtual labeled HR images. To make full of global information, for SR network, base on the original U-Net, we introduce the ASPP module, which can enable multi-scale contextual information extraction and enhance global representations in the super-resolution network. For the network training, according to the equation: $I_{LR} = B * D_{\downarrow}I_{HR}$, we first down-sampled the HR images I_{HR} and then adopted a gaussian filter with random derivation to imitate the image blurry process. Then, we up-sampled the virtual LR images I_{LR} as the SR network input and used the original HR images as the ground truths.

Adversary Domain Adaption. Adversarial domain adaptation aims to reduce the distance between the approximate domain discrepancies by using an adversarial objective *w.r.t.* a domain discriminator, which ensures that the neural network is unable to differentiate between the distributions of the source and target domains. In this work, to pull in the gap between these HR and LR domain, we introduced the adversary domain adaptation technique with a domain discriminator and treated HR and LR images as two different domains: source domain S and target domain T. The discriminator consists of several blocks. Each block includes two convolution layers. Since instance Normalization does not depend on batch size, which can provide more stable performance during training than. Here, each convolution layer is followed by an instance normalization layer and leaky rectified linear activation function. The size of all convolution layers is set at 3×3.

Segmentation Network. To demonstrate the effectiveness of our framework, we selected the original U-Net as the segmentation network. There were two inputs during the segmentation network training: real LR images and virtual HR images. Simultaneously, using labeled LR dataset can make the segmentation network more fine-grained for images detail. Moreover, using the virtual labeled HR images derived from the SR network on real LR images and the up-sampled annotations will increase the diversity of the training dataset and further improve the ability of polyp characterization at the HR scale.

Loss Function. For the SR network, we first used the joint loss function with the combination of L_1 loss and perception loss L_{pl} as the strong supervision. Then, to reduce the gap in appearance between domain T and S, adversarial domain adaptation loss was introduced to tell the domain category. To be specific, we designed a simple forward convolution neural network as the domain discriminator and used WGAN-GP loss as the adversarial loss [7]. The final goal is to help train a high-performance SR network that can generate virtual HR images with target HR style. The final loss function is as shown in *Eq.* 1

$$L_{G_{SR}} = L_1(I_{H_T}, I_{gt}) + \alpha L_{pl}(I_{H_T}, I_{gt}) - \beta \mathbb{E}[D(I_{H_S})]$$
$$L_D = \mathbb{E}[D(I_{H_S})] - \mathbb{E}[D(I_{H_T})] + \lambda L_{GP}. \tag{1}$$

where α, β and λ is the balance weight. I_{H_T} is the HR output of the SR network in the target domain, and I_{gt} is the corresponding ground truth. I_{H_S} denotes the HR output of the SR network in the source domain. L_{GP} is the gradient penalty [7]. For the segmentation network, we used focal loss L_f [11] and dice loss L_d [14] as the segmentation loss function $L_{seg} = L_d + L_f$. To train the entire framework effectively, in each step, we alternately trained SR and discriminator joint network and segmentation network in an end-to-end manner.

Implementation Details. We implemented our method using PyTorch with 4
NVIDIA V100 GPUs. For network input, we randomly cropped LR images into
patches of size 256×256, as well as corresponding annotations. We also cropped
HR images into patches of 512×512. As to network training, we employed the
AdamW [12] optimization algorithm to train the relevant parameters using a
cosine decay learning strategy from 10^{-4} to 10^{-5}. We trained the proposed
whole network in an end-to-end manner, which is trained 500 epochs with a
batch size of 64. We will release our code at https://github.com/xiaozhoushi/
CreDA-Net.git.

4   Experimental Results

4.1   Datasets and Evaluation.

Datasets. In this work, we employed four open released polyp segmentation datasets: CVC-ClinicDB/CVC-612 [1], CVC-ColonDB [2], ETIS-LARIB [3],
CVC-PolypHD [19]. In our training dataset, there are 912 labeled LR images
and 66 unlabeled HR images. Specifically, we used CVC-ClinicDB/CVC-612 and
CVC-ColonDB to compose a labeled LR dataset of 912 images. Also, we randomly and evenly divided ETIS-LARIB into three parts: one was for the training dataset as the unlabeled HR dataset, one was for the validation dataset, the
remaining was for the testing dataset. After the network training, we primarily
tested the proposed model on the internal testing dataset: ETIS-LARIB. Also,
we employed CVC-PolypHD as the external testing dataset to further evaluate
the efficiency of the proposed method.

Comparison with SOTAs. To evaluate the efficiency of the proposed
method, we selected U-Net [17], U-Net++ [23], ResUNet [22], ResUNet++ [9],
PraNet [6], CCBANet [15], and SANet [20] as the SOTA comparison methods.
We selected their open released codes for a fair comparison and re-trained all
these methods on our training dataset without any pre-training strategy.

4.2   Experimental Results

Quantitative Results. After the network training on our hybrid training
dataset, we directly evaluated all the related methods on the two testing datasets:
ETIS-LARIB and CVC-PolypHD. The results are shown in the Table 1. The
results in the first row from U-Net can be treated as the lower bound, which
was trained with only 912 labeled LR images. The second row denoted the
upper bound from U-Net, which was trained with 912 labeled LR and 66 labeled
HR images. Although the performance of ResUNet, ResUNet++, PraNet, and
CCBANet is inferior to that of the lower bound on the ETIS-LARIB, all the
comparison methods can obtain superior performance over the lower bound on
the CVC-PolypHD. In the given experimental setting: 912 labeled LR and 66
unlabeled HR images, our method can achieve superior performance over all the

other SOTAs on the two testing datasets in terms of two metrics: the mean IoU (mIoU) and the mean Dice (mDice). To be specific, our method can achieve a performance improvement by 36.18% (mIoU) and 31.27% (mDice) on the ETIS-LARIB, 60.69% (mIoU) and 46.94% (mDice) on the CVC-PolypHD over the lower bound. Note that our performance exceeds that of the upper bound on the internal testing dataset (ETIS-LARIB). The potential reason is that the training dataset for the segmentation network including both 912 labeled LR images and their corresponding virtual labeled HR images from the SR reconstruction network trained on the ETIS-LARIB dataset.

Table 1. Performance comparison with the Sota polyp segmentation methods.

Methods	ETIS-LARIB		CVC-PolypHD	
	mIoU	mDice	mIoU	mDice
U–Net w/o HRs	0.4740	0.5530	0.3701	0.4570
U–Net w HRs	0.6238	0.7035	0.6308	0.7045
U–Net++	0.5057	0.5845	0.5633	0.6322
ResUNet	0.4483	0.5370	0.4959	0.5983
ResUNet++	0.3399	0.4122	0.4834	0.5710
PraNet	0.3523	0.4091	0.4846	0.5884
CCBANet	0.3626	0.4232	0.4804	0.5762
SANet	0.5394	0.6297	0.5294	0.6228
CreDA-Net (Ours)	0.6455	0.7259	0.5947	0.6715

Qualitative Results. For visual inspection, we selected three samples from both ETIS-LARIB and CVC-PolypHD, respectively. The qualitative results are shown in Fig. 2. Compared with other SOTAs, the segmentation results from the proposed method were closer to the ground truths. Even for the challenging scenarios in rows 3 and 4, our model could handle and generate an accurate segmentation mask.

Ablation Study. To thoroughly investigate the effectiveness of our method, we conducted several ablation studies by removing specific components for comparison. Framework A: Train the SR network and segmentation network separately and remove all the components as the benchmark. Framework B: Employ the end-to-end strategy to train the SR and segmentation networks alternately in each step. Framework C: Introduce the ASPP module to modify the SR network. Framework D: Add the perceptual loss into the final loss function. Framework E: Use the domain discriminator to reduce the source and target domain gap. The results are shown in Table 2. With the addition of components, the performance has been gradually improved from Framework A to E.

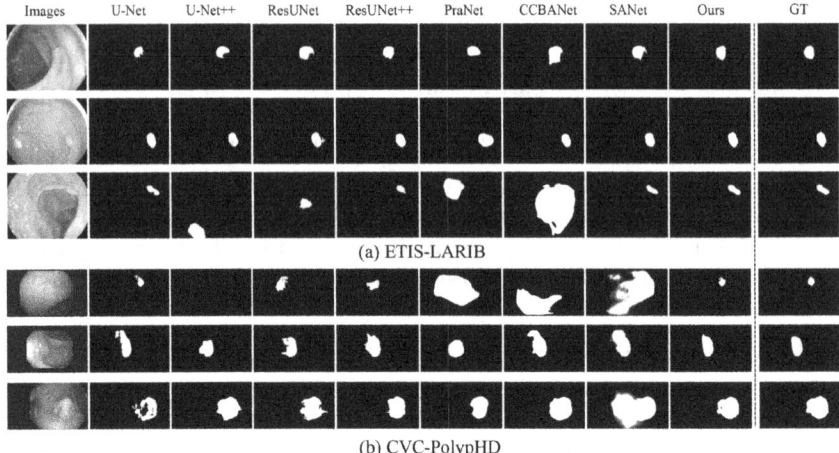

(a) ETIS-LARIB

(b) CVC-PolypHD

Fig. 2. Visual results from all the related methods. GT denotes the ground truth

Table 2. Ablation study

Framework	End-To-End	ASPP	Perceptual-Loss	Domain-Adaption	mIoU	mDice
A	×	×	×	×	0.5195	0.5955
B	√	×	×	×	0.5513	0.6295
C	√	√	×	×	0.5855	0.6612
D	√	√	√	×	0.6111	0.6910
E	√	√	√	√	0.6455	0.7259

5   Conclusion

Due to the huge burden of HR image pixel-wise annotations, in this work, we discarded annotating the HR images and then employed amounts of labeled LR images to train a well-designed neural network with the assistance of unlabeled HR images. We employed a SR network to generate a virtual HR labeled dataset to help well-train the following segmentation network. In the training stage, we adopted the adversary domain adaption technique to reduce the gap between HR and LR domains. Through various experiments, we proved the effectiveness of our method and the superior segmentation performance and generalization over other SOTAs. In the future, we will investigate if there are more applicable neural networks to instead U-Net as the segmentation network and obtain better segmentation performance in this particular scenario.

Acknowledgements. This work was partially supported by the National Natural Science Foundation of China (62001464, 82202954) and Chongqing Science and Technology Innovation Foundation (CYS23693).

References

1. Bernal, J., Sánchez, F.J., Fernández-Esparrach, G., Gil, D., Rodríguez, C., Vilariño, F.: WM-DOVA maps for accurate polyp highlighting in colonoscopy: validation vs. saliency maps from physicians. Comput. Med. Imaging Graph. **43**, 99–111 (2015)
2. Bernal, J., Sánchez, J., Vilarino, F.: Towards automatic polyp detection with a polyp appearance model. Pattern Recogn. **45**(9), 3166–3182 (2012)
3. Bernal, J., et al.: Comparative validation of polyp detection methods in video colonoscopy: results from the MICCAI 2015 endoscopic vision challenge. IEEE Trans. Med. Imaging **36**(6), 1231–1249 (2017)
4. Chen, C., Wang, J., Pan, J., Bian, C., Zhang, Z.: GraphSKT: graph-guided structured knowledge transfer for domain adaptive lesion detection. IEEE Trans. Med. Imaging **42**, 507–518 (2022)
5. Chen, L.C., Papandreou, G., Schroff, F., Adam, H.: Rethinking Atrous convolution for semantic image segmentation. ArXiv Preprint ArXiv:1706.05587 (2017)
6. Fan, D.-P., et al.: PraNet: parallel reverse attention network for polyp segmentation. In: Martel, A.L., et al. (eds.) MICCAI 2020. LNCS, vol. 12266, pp. 263–273. Springer, Cham (2020). https://doi.org/10.1007/978-3-030-59725-2_26
7. Gulrajani, I., Ahmed, F., Arjovsky, M., Dumoulin, V., Courville, A.C.: Improved training of Wasserstein GANs. In: Advances in Neural Information Processing Systems, vol. 30 (2017)
8. Guo, Y., Bernal, J., J. Matuszewski, B.: Polyp segmentation with fully convolutional deep neural networks—extended evaluation study. J. Imaging **6**(7), 69 (2020). https://doi.org/10.3390/jimaging6070069
9. Jha, D., et al.: ResuNet++: an advanced architecture for medical image segmentation. In: 2019 IEEE International Symposium on Multimedia (ISM), pp. 225–2255. IEEE (2019)
10. Ledig, C., et al.: Photo-realistic single image super-resolution using a generative adversarial network. In: Proceedings of the IEEE Conference on Computer Vision and Pattern Recognition, pp. 4681–4690 (2017)
11. Lin, T.Y., Goyal, P., Girshick, R., He, K., Dollár, P.: Focal loss for dense object detection. In: Proceedings of the IEEE International Conference on Computer Vision, pp. 2980–2988 (2017)
12. Loshchilov, I., Hutter, F.: Decoupled weight decay regularization. ArXiv Preprint ArXiv:1711.05101 (2017)
13. Martin, J.W., et al.: Enabling the future of colonoscopy with intelligent and autonomous magnetic manipulation. Nat. Mach. Intell. **2**(10), 595–606 (2020)
14. Milletari, F., Navab, N., Ahmadi, S.A.: V-Net: fully convolutional neural networks for volumetric medical image segmentation. In: 2016 Fourth International Conference on 3D Vision (3DV), pp. 565–571. IEEE (2016)
15. Nguyen, T.-C., Nguyen, T.-P., Diep, G.-H., Tran-Dinh, A.-H., Nguyen, T.V., Tran, M.-T.: CCBANet: cascading context and balancing attention for polyp segmentation. In: de Bruijne, M., et al. (eds.) MICCAI 2021. LNCS, vol. 12901, pp. 633–643. Springer, Cham (2021). https://doi.org/10.1007/978-3-030-87193-2_60
16. Pan, J., Bi, Q., Yang, Y., Zhu, P., Bian, C.: Label-efficient hybrid-supervised learning for medical image segmentation. In: Proceedings of the AAAI Conference on Artificial Intelligence (2022)
17. Ronneberger, O., Fischer, P., Brox, T.: U-Net: convolutional networks for biomedical image segmentation. In: Navab, N., Hornegger, J., Wells, W.M., Frangi, A.F.

(eds.) MICCAI 2015. LNCS, vol. 9351, pp. 234–241. Springer, Cham (2015). https://doi.org/10.1007/978-3-319-24574-4_28

18. Tomar, N.K., Jha, D., Bagci, U., Ali, S.: TGANet: text-guided attention for improved polyp segmentation. In: Wang, L., Dou, Q., Fletcher, P.T., Speidel, S., Li, S. (eds.) Medical Image Computing and Computer Assisted Intervention – MICCAI 2022. MICCAI 2022. Lecture Notes in Computer Science, vol. 13433, pp. 151–160. Springer, Cham (2022). https://doi.org/10.1007/978-3-031-16437-8_15

19. Vázquez, D., et al.: A benchmark for endoluminal scene segmentation of colonoscopy images. J. Healthc. Eng. **2017**, 4037190 (2017)

20. Wei, J., Hu, Y., Zhang, R., Li, Z., Zhou, S.K., Cui, S.: Shallow attention network for polyp segmentation. In: de Bruijne, M., et al. (eds.) MICCAI 2021. LNCS, vol. 12901, pp. 699–708. Springer, Cham (2021). https://doi.org/10.1007/978-3-030-87193-2_66

21. Wu, H., Chen, G., Wen, Z., Qin, J.: Collaborative and adversarial learning of focused and dispersive representations for semi-supervised polyp segmentation. In: Proceedings of the IEEE/CVF International Conference on Computer Vision, pp. 3489–3498 (2021)

22. Zhang, Z., Liu, Q., Wang, Y.: Road extraction by deep residual U-Net. IEEE Geosci. Remote Sens. Lett. **15**(5), 749–753 (2018)

23. Zhou, Z., Rahman Siddiquee, M.M., Tajbakhsh, N., Liang, J.: UNet++: A Nested U-Net Architecture for Medical Image Segmentation. In: Stoyanov, D., Taylor, Z., Carneiro, G., Syeda-Mahmood, T., Martel, A., Maier-Hein, L., Tavares, J.M.R.S., Bradley, A., Papa, J.P., Belagiannis, V., Nascimento, J.C., Lu, Z., Conjeti, S., Moradi, M., Greenspan, H., Madabhushi, A. (eds.) DLMIA/ML-CDS -2018. LNCS, vol. 11045, pp. 3–11. Springer, Cham (2018). https://doi.org/10.1007/978-3-030-00889-5_1

G-CNN: Adaptive Geometric Convolutional Neural Networks for MRI-Based Skull Stripping

Yifan Li[1], Chao Li[2], Yiran Wei[2], Stephen Price[2], Carola-Bibiane Schönlieb[3], and Xi Chen[1,4(✉)]

[1] Department of Computer Science, University of Bath, Bath, UK
{yl3548,xc841}@bath.ac.uk
[2] Division of Neurosurgery, Department of Clinical Neurosciences, University of Cambridge, Cambridge, UK
{cl647,yw500,sjp58}@cam.ac.uk
[3] Department of Applied Mathematics and Theoretical Physics, University of Cambridge, Cambridge, UK
cbs31@cam.ac.uk
[4] Department of Physics, University of Cambridge, Cambridge, UK
xc253@mrao.cam.ac.uk

Abstract. Skull stripping in MRI-based brain imaging involves extraction of brain regions from raw images. While some Convolutional Neural Nets (CNNs) models have been successful in automating this process, the reliance on local textures can negatively impact model performance in the presence of pathological conditions such as brain tumors. This study presents a novel yet practical approach to offer supplementary texture-invariant spatial information of the brain as a geometric prior to enhance shape representations to further enable informed segmentation decisions. Our numerical results demonstrate that the new method outperforms competing algorithms in skull stripping tasks for both healthy and pathological inputs. These findings underscore the potential of incorporating geometric information in deep learning models to enhance the accuracy of brain segmentation.

Keywords: Skull stripping · Deep learning · Convolutional neural networks · Geometric information

1 Introduction

Brain segmentation, also referred to as skull stripping, is an essential preprocessing step in neuroimaging research [19,24]. It involves extracting the brain region and removing non-cerebral tissues such as skull, dura, and scalp from brain MRI [3,12]. Various automated skull stripping tools have been proposed, including the Brain Extraction Tool (BET), Advanced Normalization Tools (ANTs), and Robotic Exploration for Extreme Environments

W. Qin et al. (Eds.): CMMCA 2023 (MICCAI Workshop), LNCS 14243, pp. 21–30, 2023.
https://doi.org/10.1007/978-3-031-45087-7_3

(ROBEX) [2,7,13,20,21,26]. However, these traditional processes can be time-consuming and subject to variability, given the complexity of the human brain, intra-patient variability, and differences in scanning protocols.

In recent years, deep learning-based techniques are emerging as promising tools, notably improving the outcomes in brain tissue segmentation [6,9,17,25]. Despite the proposal of complex deep learning methods, such as vision transformer (ViT) [18] and hybrid models that incorporate transformer blocks in the bottleneck [16], their effectiveness in the field of skull stripping remains limited due to their reliance on large training datasets. In contrast, the mainstream methods remain CNN-based models.

There are various CNN models for skull-stripping, including voxel-wise neural networks and fully connected CNNs [1,10,17,23]. Recently, Chen et al. [4] and Kamnitsas et al. [8] proposed 2D VoxResNet and 3D CNNs with conditional random fields (CRFs) for brain segmentation, respectively. Dey et al. [5] presented complementary segmentation networks for brain extraction, leveraging the complementary parts of brain tissues to infer pathological inputs. Besides, 3D U-Net has been proposed to utilize spatial information among MRI slices more thoroughly for skull stripping [6]. Furthermore, a recent work [15] proposed ensemble neural network (EnNet) which is a 3D convolutional neural network based method to achieve state-of-the-art (SOTA) performance in skull stripping. These CNN-based models have shown promising results in skull stripping; however, challenges remain due to the variability of brain structures and pathological conditions. Particularly, CNN-based networks tend to focus on local textures and lack global geometry information, rendering them susceptible to subject variability.

To offer supplementary spatial information and texture-invariant features, we propose a brain geometric information (GI) enhanced CNN framework in this work, termed G-CNN, which integrates GI derived from raw MRI images to enhance skull stripping performance. The GI representation is a compact yet effective means of encapsulating critical image features such as 3D spatial location, surface normals, and curvature information. Thus, G-CNN captures potential abnormal information and geometric structures that are often overlooked by standard CNN models, leading to improved segmentation performance. The primary contributions of our work are summarized as follows:

- We presents an efficient approach (termed as geometric point filtering) for extracting GI from raw MRI images and MNI152 brain template for training and inference, respectively.
- We design a G-CNN architecture that utilize GI as texture-invariant features to aid in skull-stripping tasks as a plug-in module for CNN segmentation models.
- We conducted experiments using a public dataset, consisting entirely of healthy subjects, and our in-house pathological dataset, achieving enhanced performance on skull-stripping tasks across both datasets.

The rest of the paper is organized as follows. The proposed approach is detailed in Sect. 2, and the experimental setup is described in Sect. 3. Section 4 shows the numerical results and is followed by the conclusion in Sect. 5.

2 Methodology

As depicted in Fig. 1, the G-CNN approach consists of two steps: first, extracting texture-invariant GI prior using geometric point (GP) filtering, and second, integrating this into the GI-encoded segmentation model. The GP filtering acts as a unique, non-repetitive preparatory procedure, extracting GI from the raw MRI image for training, and from the MNI152 brain template for inference.

Considering MRI data $\{\mathbf{X}_n\}_{n=1}^N$ and their corresponding ground-truth brain masks (or labels) $\{\mathbf{Y}_n\}_{n=1}^N$ for N patients, GP filtering scheme to efficiently extract brain GI (denoted as $\{\alpha_n\}_{n=1}^N$) from the given raw MRI data. This process involves transforming the labeled 3D images into a brain reference structure, denoted as γ, and subsequently generating a brain mesh from it using meshing algorithms, which facilitates the computation of geometric features such as 3D spatial coordinates, surface normals, and curvatures. The resultant features are then aligned to produce a GI prior α. Both the original MRI data $\mathbf{X}$ and the GI prior α serve as inputs to the designed GI encoded segmentation model. Ultimately, utilizing the GI prior, the model generates a prediction $\hat{\mathbf{Y}}$ as the desired skull stripping segmentation outcomes.

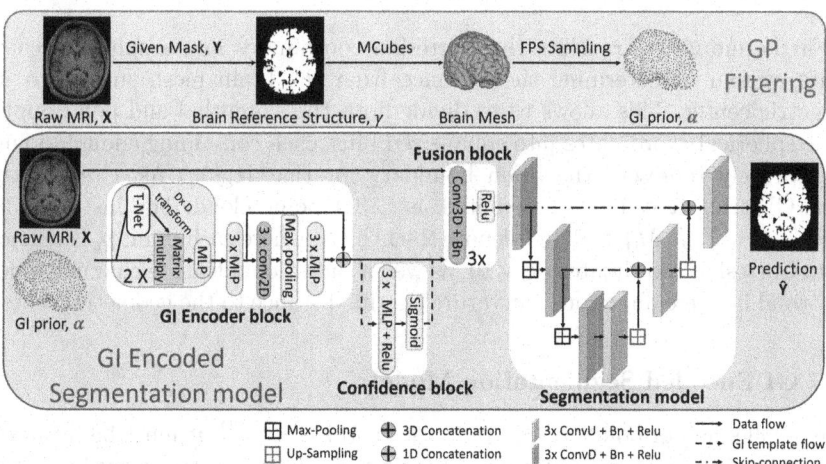

Fig. 1. Workflow of G-CNN. The approach comprises two main components, namely GP filtering and GI encoded segmentation model. Initially, GP filtering is performed on the MRI image to extract GI priors α, which is highlighted in red. These GI priors are then utilized as inputs to the GI encoded segmentation model, along with the MRI images, to produce accurate brain mask predictions $\hat{\mathbf{Y}}$. Within the GI encoder block, the T-Net consists of multiple shared Multilayer perceptrons (MLPs) that serve as a point-independent feature extraction module, incorporating max pooling and fully connected layers. The resultant output of T-Net is an $D \times D$ affine transformation matrix, which is used to apply transformation to the $M \times D$ input point cloud. After GI encoder, a confidence block is applied to the concatenated features, depending on whether α is from the MNI152 brain template or the raw MRI data, before being fused with the input image in the fusion block.

2.1   GP Filtering

We develop a new GP filtering scheme to extract geometric representation of raw MRI $\{\mathbf{Y}_n\}_{n=1}^N$, which extends its utility beyond mere pixel value analysis. Specifically, as illustrated in the GP filtering block in Fig. 1, we employ the Marching Cubes (MCubes) algorithm [11] to convert γ derived from $\{\mathbf{Y}_n\}_{n=1}^N$ or the MNI152 brain template into brain meshes. The MCubes technique is a well-established technique for constructing triangular models of constant density surfaces from 3D medical data, with O(n) complexity where n represents the number of voxels. It produces brain surface meshes that are free from distortions resulting from pathological abnormalities or variations in imaging parameters.

GP filtering is a one-off data processing step. In GP filtering, we employ the Farthest Point Sampling (FPS) method to sample M points from the D-dimensional GI point cloud for each of the N patients, further reducing computational costs for subsequent training. This results in a set of point clouds denoted as $\{\alpha_n\}_{n=1}^N$, where $\alpha_n \in \mathbb{R}^{M \times D}$. FPS algorithm randomly selects an initial point and then iteratively adds the farthest point from the previously selected points until the desired number of points is obtained. By using FPS, we can effectively reduce the size of point clouds while preserving their inherent shape.

Furthermore, we translate the Cartesian coordinates into a spherical coordinate system to determine the distance from the brain mesh surface to its geometric center. This allows us to divide both the azimuthal and polar angles of the spherical coordinates into equal-sized bins, each containing enough points to accurately represent the brain boundary for that region. As a result, the brain GI prior α can be represented as a 3D point cloud. For instance, let $\alpha_n = \{p_i | i = 1, ..., M\} \in \mathbb{R}^{M \times 8}$ denote the nth GI, where each point p_i is defined by its Cartesian coordinates (x, y, z), as well as additional feature channels, such as normal in three directions, curvature and its distance to the geometric center.

2.2   GI Encoded Segmentation Model

Give a collection of points $\alpha_n = \{p_i | i = 1, ..., M\} \in \mathbb{R}^{M \times D}$, it must be invariant to permutations of its members, necessitating certain symmetrizations in the net computation and transformation invariance.

GI encoder block comprises three critical components: two joint feature (point) transform modules (the orange square highlighted one in GI Encoder block in Fig. 1) to maintain the transformation invariance, a max pooling layer as a symmetric function to consolidate information from all points, and a local and global combination concatenation that integrates point-wise and global features. Specifically, the feature transform modules learn an affine transformation matrix $\mathbf{T}$ (with dimension $D \times D$) from the aggregated information of all points, which is subsequently applied to transform the point cloud inputs, as $\mathbf{T}(\alpha_n) \in \mathbb{R}^{M \times D}$. We adopt similar operation to higher-dimensional local features. These operations ensure that both input points and point features remain stable under transformations such as rotating and translating. Then, we then employ a symmetric function g and h to approximate a general function f that is intended to operate on a point cloud set.

$$f(\{p_1, .., p_M\}) \approx g(h(p_1), ..., h(p_M)) \tag{1}$$

where $f : 2^{\mathbb{R}^M} \to \mathbb{R}$, $h : \mathbb{R}^M \to \mathbb{R}^K$ and $g : \underbrace{\mathbb{R}^K \times \cdots \times \mathbb{R}^K}_{M} \to \mathbb{R}$ is a symmetric function. The GI encoder approximates h by MLPs and g by a composition of a single variable function and a max pooling function.

Confidence block governs the extent to which GI guidance is employed, particularly if α is from brain template. This block utilizes a learnable probability and is implemented via a fully connected layer with a Sigmoid activation function. GI ($\alpha : \mathbb{R}^{M \times D}$) processed by GI encoder and confidence blocks can be represented as $p_c(\omega_n | \alpha_n) \in \mathbb{R}^{M \times K}$.

Fusion block maps the learned $p_c(\omega_n | \alpha_n)$ to its original coordinates and process it through multiple convolutional layers. This serves to expand the influence region and learn the relationships between image pixels and the highlighted points. Consequently, this enables the highlighting of ambiguous regions as additional channels in the input MRIs. The training process is depicted in Algorithm 1.

Algorithm 1: G-CNN Model Training

// GI prior extraction by GP filtering
Generate γ from $\{\mathbf{Y}_n\}_{n=1}^N$ and the brain template.
Convert γ into meshes and calculate relevant geometric features for each vertex.
Generate point cloud $\{\alpha_n\}_{n=1}^N$ using FPS algorithm.
// Train GI enhanced segmentation model
for $epoch = 1, 2, \cdots,$ do
    Generate a random number $p \sim \mathcal{U}(0, 1)$.
    if $p \leq 0.8$ then
        Set the confidence block untrainable.
        Train with dataset $\{\mathbf{X}_n, \mathbf{Y}_n\}_{n=1}^N$ and $\{\alpha_n\}_{n=1}^N$.
    else
        Set the confidence block trainable.
        Train with dataset $\{\mathbf{X}_n, \mathbf{Y}_n\}_{n=1}^N$ and the specific α from brain template.
    end if
end for

2.3 Design of Loss Function

The proposed segmentation model (denoted by function $\phi(\cdot)$) is trained by the input features $\mathbf{X}$ and α and their corresponding brain masks $\mathbf{Y}$. We make use of the Dice similarity coefficient (or Dice score) to construct the loss function for the proposed model. The Dice score quantifies the degree of overlap between images. The segmentation model's loss function, denoted by $\mathcal{L}_s$, is established based on the Dice score as:

$$\mathcal{L}_s = 1 - \frac{2|\phi(\mathbf{X}, \alpha) \cap \mathbf{Y}|}{|\phi(\mathbf{X}, \alpha)| + |\mathbf{Y}|} \tag{2}$$

where the operator $\cap$ indicate the overlap area between two images and $|\cdot|$ denotes computed area of the underlying images.

3   Experiments

Our study adopted two distinct brain imaging datasets: the Calgary-Campinas-359 (CC359) dataset, containing 359 healthy adults aged 29-80 years, including 176 males [22], and our in-house dataset consisting of 125 glioblastoma-diagnosed patients (age range: 22-75 years, 78 males). To ensure consistency with the proposed experiments, we exclusively used T1-weighted images, normalized via Z-score, and cropped to $228 \times 228 \times 228$ for Unet and G-Unet, and $160 \times 192 \times 128$ for EnNet and G-EnNet experiments, respectively.

The one-off GI extraction process was implemented on a 2.3 GHz Intel Core i9 CPU using the PyMcubes library, taking about 7 s per patient. The G-CNN models were developed on Pytorch platform [14] under Python 3.8 on an NVIDIA GeForce RTX 3090 with a batch size of 1. We used the Adam optimizer with an initial learning rate of $r_0 = 0.0001$ that decayed per epoch according to $r_i = r_0(1 - \frac{i}{E})^{0.9}$, where i denotes the index of epoch and E represents the total number of epochs. We set E equal to 100 for the training phase, which on average took 16 h. Finally, we employed metrics of Dice score, precision, recall, false positive rate (FPR), and false negative rate (FNR) to evaluate performance.

4   Results and Discussions

4.1   Overall Performance of G-CNN Framework

We applied our framework directly on 3D Unet and the SOTA EnNet to test whether we could further improve their performance with our geometrically enhanced framework. Initially, we included 17 pathological patients in the training phase for all models, reserving the remaining 108 for testing. The training set thus comprised 70% healthy patients (251) from the CC-359 dataset along with 17 in-house pathological patients, while the test set was made up of the remaining 30% healthy patients (108) and 108 pathological patients. As shown in table Table 1, various degrees of improvement were observed across the average values of the dice coefficient, precision, recall, FPR, and FNR metrics for both G-Unet and G-EnNet compared with original 3D Unet and EnNet. The enhanced EnNet (G-EnNet) achieves the best performance under all evaluation matrices.

Table 1. Overall improvement for G-CNN framework. ↑ indicates higher values being more accurate, vice versa. The improved results are highlighted in bold. All the results are tested on the test dataset including 108 healthy and 108 pathological patients.

Model	Dice ↑ (%)	Precision ↑ (%)	Recall ↑ (%)	FPR ↓ (%)	FNR ↓ (%)
BET	81.77 ± 10.9	74.85 ± 15.62	92.39 ± 5.45	5.15 ± 4.40	7.61 ± 5.45
ROBEX	93.56 ± 3.98	94.68 ± 3.13	92.63 ± 6.04	0.74 ± 0.49	7.37 ± 6.04
3D Unet	96.68 ± 0.93	97.29 ± 0.21	97.18 ± 1.15	3.80 ± 0.31	2.82 ± 0.12
G-Unet (ours)	**97.62 ± 1.17**	**97.63 ± 1.38**	**97.66 ± 1.63**	**0.33 ± 0.21**	**2.34 ± 1.63**
EnNet	97.42 ± 1.20	97.87 ± 1.49	97.86 ± 1.57	1.19 ± 0.94	2.14 ± 1.57
G-EnNet (ours)	**97.94 ± 1.07**	**97.88 ± 1.35**	**98.02 ± 1.45**	1.17 ± 0.85	1.98 ± 1.45

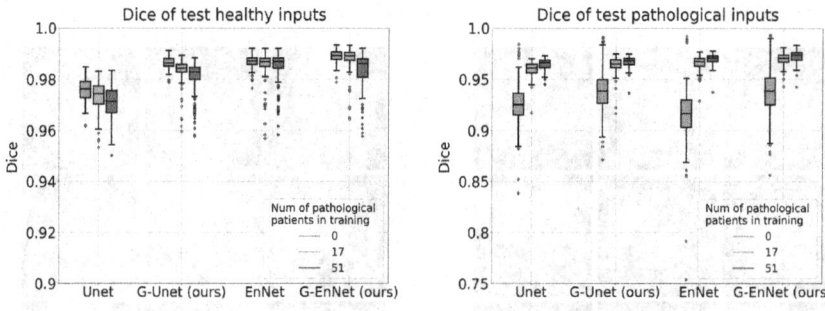

Fig. 2. The error-bar performance of various competing models under distinct experimental cohorts. Each cohort incorporates a varying number of pathological patients in the training phase, represented as 0 (orange boxplot), 17 (blue boxplot), and 51 (green boxplot). The left figure shows the performance tested on data of healthy subjects, while the right figure depicts the performance tested on data of subjects with tumor. (Color figure online)

4.2 Ablation Study: Pathological Patients in Training

To assess the influence of integrating pathological patients within the training process, we crafted a series of experimental cohorts. These cohorts were composed of 0, 17, and 51 patients respectively in the training phase, with the remaining patients designated for the testing. A clear comparison among models for healthy inputs and pathological inputs was facilitated by setting different scales for the y-axis, as shown in Fig. 2.

The Fig. 2 illustrates that our G-CNN models outperformed the original models in predicting both healthy and pathological inputs across all experiments. It is also noteworthy that when the training set did not include any patients with tumors, both G-CNN models excelled in predicting unseen pathological inputs. This superior performance may be attributed to the geometric shape prior incorporated into the G-CNN model, as indicated by the orange boxes in the right graph of the figure.

4.3 Clinical Case Study

Figure 3 demonstrates the enhanced performance of our model with both healthy and pathological inputs. Notably, the inclusion of 17 pathological patients in the training process has influenced the outcomes. As demonstrated in the left panel of Fig. 3, the Unet has inaccurately classified some regions as brain (indicated in green), whereas our improved G-Unet exhibits relatively superior performance. Moreover, as depicted in the right panel of Fig. 3, Unet fails to predict brain regions accurately in a scenario where a tumor is in close proximity to the brain boundary (marked in blue). Conversely, our G-Unet successfully predicts this particular region accurately, illustrating the effectiveness of the G-CNN approach for clinical scenarios.

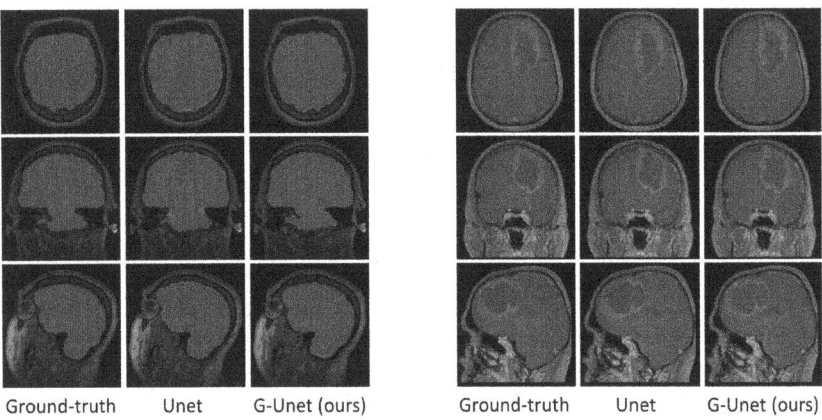

Ground-truth   Unet   G-Unet (ours)   Ground-truth   Unet   G-Unet (ours)

Fig. 3. Performance comparison of Unet and G-Unet on two clinical cases. The left panel depicts a healthy case, while the right panel presents a pathological one. From top to bottom, the views displayed are Axial, Coronal, and Sagittal respectively. Regions marked in red signify accurate brain predictions, those in blue represent missed brain regions, and those highlighted in green show regions inaccurately classified as brain tissue. (Color figure online)

5 Conclusions

We have developed a pipeline that exploits texture-invariant geometric features derived from brain structures as supplementary spatial information. In addition, we have proposed a G-CNN approach to integrate this information, thereby enhancing the representation for more accurate segmentation. The G-CNN approach is adaptable across various CNN architectures and has exhibited enhanced performance in predicting both healthy and pathological brain regions. Exploiting texture-invariant geometric interrelationships among image pixels emerges as a promising avenue for improving segmentation accuracy.

References

1. Atlason, H.E., Love, A., Sigurdsson, S., Gudnason, V., Ellingsen, L.M.: Unsupervised brain lesion segmentation from MRI using a convolutional autoencoder. In: Medical Imaging 2019: Image Processing, vol. 10949, pp. 372–378. SPIE (2019)
2. Avants, B.B., Tustison, N., Song, G., et al.: Advanced normalization tools (ants). Insight J **2**(365), 1–35 (2009)
3. Chaddad, A., Tanougast, C.: Quantitative evaluation of robust skull stripping and tumor detection applied to axial MR images. Brain Inf. **3**(1), 53–61 (2016)
4. Chen, H., Dou, Q., Yu, L., Qin, J., Heng, P.A.: VoxResNet: deep voxelwise residual networks for brain segmentation from 3D MR images. Neuroimage **170**, 446–455 (2018)
5. Dey, R., Hong, Y.: CompNet: complementary segmentation network for brain MRI extraction. In: Frangi, A.F., Schnabel, J.A., Davatzikos, C., Alberola-López, C., Fichtinger, G. (eds.) MICCAI 2018. LNCS, vol. 11072, pp. 628–636. Springer, Cham (2018). https://doi.org/10.1007/978-3-030-00931-1_72
6. Hwang, H., Rehman, H.Z.U., Lee, S.: 3D U-Net for skull stripping in brain MRI. Appl. Sci. **9**(3), 569 (2019)
7. Iglesias, J.E., Liu, C.Y., Thompson, P.M., Tu, Z.: Robust brain extraction across datasets and comparison with publicly available methods. IEEE Trans. Med. Imaging **30**(9), 1617–1634 (2011)
8. Kamnitsas, K., et al.: Efficient multi-scale 3D CNN with fully connected CRF for accurate brain lesion segmentation. Med. Image Anal. **36**, 61–78 (2017)
9. Kleesiek, J., et al.: Deep MRI brain extraction: a 3D convolutional neural network for skull stripping. Neuroimage **129**, 460–469 (2016)
10. Long, J., Shelhamer, E., Darrell, T.: Fully convolutional networks for semantic segmentation. In: Proceedings of the IEEE conference on computer vision and pattern recognition, pp. 3431–3440 (2015)
11. Lorensen, W.E., Cline, H.E.: Marching cubes: a high resolution 3D surface construction algorithm. ACM Siggraph Comput. Graph. **21**(4), 163–169 (1987)
12. Nilakant, R., Menon, H.P., Vikram, K.: A survey on advanced segmentation techniques for brain MRI image segmentation. Int. J. Adv. Sci. Eng. Inf. Technol. **7**(4), 1448–1456 (2017)
13. Park, J.G., Lee, C.: Skull stripping based on region growing for magnetic resonance brain images. Neuroimage **47**(4), 1394–1407 (2009)
14. Paszke, A., et al.: PyTorch: an imperative style, high-performance deep learning library. Adv. Neural. Inf. Process. Syst. **32**, 8026–8037 (2019)
15. Pei, L., et al.: A general skull stripping of multiparametric brain MRIs using 3D convolutional neural network. Sci. Rep. **12**(1), 10826 (2022)
16. Rao, V.M., et al.: Improving across-dataset brain tissue segmentation for MRI imaging using transformer. Front. Neuroimaging **1**, 46 (2022)
17. Rehman, H.Z.U., Hwang, H., Lee, S.: Conventional and deep learning methods for skull stripping in brain MRI. Appl. Sci. **10**(5), 1773 (2020)
18. Sagar, A.: ViTBIS: vision transformer for biomedical image segmentation. In: Oyarzun Laura, C., et al. (eds.) DCL/PPML/LL-COVID19/CLIP -2021. LNCS, vol. 12969, pp. 34–45. Springer, Cham (2021). https://doi.org/10.1007/978-3-030-90874-4_4
19. Shen, D., Davatzikos, C.: Hammer: hierarchical attribute matching mechanism for elastic registration. IEEE Trans. Med. Imaging **21**(11), 1421–1439 (2002)

20. Smith, S.M.: Fast robust automated brain extraction. Hum. Brain Mapp. **17**(3), 143–155 (2002)
21. Somasundaram, K., Kalavathi, P.: Automatic skull stripping of magnetic resonance images (MRI) of human head scans using image contour. In: NCIMP2010: Proceedings of the National Conference on Image Processing, pp. 147–151 (2010)
22. Souza, R., et al.: An open, multi-vendor, multi-field-strength brain MR dataset and analysis of publicly available skull stripping methods agreement. Neuroimage **170**, 482–494 (2018)
23. Thakur, S.P., et al.: Skull-stripping of glioblastoma MRI scans using 3D deep learning. In: Crimi, A., Bakas, S. (eds.) BrainLes 2019. LNCS, vol. 11992, pp. 57–68. Springer, Cham (2020). https://doi.org/10.1007/978-3-030-46640-4_6
24. Thompson, P., Toga, A.W.: A surface-based technique for warping three-dimensional images of the brain. IEEE Trans. Med. Imaging **15**(4), 402–417 (1996)
25. Yogananda, C.G.B., Wagner, B.C., Murugesan, G.K., Madhuranthakam, A., Maldjian, J.A.: A deep learning pipeline for automatic skull stripping and brain segmentation. In: 2019 IEEE 16th International Symposium on Biomedical Imaging (ISBI 2019), pp. 727–731. IEEE (2019)
26. Zhang, H., Liu, J., Zhu, Z., Li, H.: An automated and simple method for brain MR image extraction. Biomed. Eng. Online **10**(1), 1–12 (2011)

The Value of Ensemble Learning Model Based on Conventional Non-Contrast MRI in the Pathological Grading of Cervical Cancer

Zhimin He[1,2], Fajin Lv[1], Chengwei Li[1], Yang Liu[1], and Zhibo Xiao[1(✉)]

[1] Department of Radiology, The First Affiliated Hospital of Chongqing Medical University, Chongqing 400016, China
5894526@qq.com

[2] Department of Radiology, The First Hospital of Putian City, Putian 351100, Fujian, China

Abstract. Purpose: To investigate the value of an stacking ensemble learning model based on conventional non-enhanced MRI sequences in the pathological grading of cervical cancer. **Methods:** We retrospectively included 98 patients with cervical cancer (54 well/moderately differentiated and 44 poorly differentiated). Radiomics features were extracted from T2WI Axi and T2WI Sag. Feature selection was performed by intra-class correlation coefficients (ICC), t-test, least absolute shrinkage and selection operator (LASSO). Logistic Regression (LR), Support Vector Machine (SVM), k-Nearest Neighbor (kNN), and Extreme Gradient Boosting (XGB) were used as the first-layer base classifier, and LR as the second-layer meta-classifier in stacking ensemble learning model. The model performance was evaluated by the area under the curve (AUC) and accuracy. **Results:** In the basic classifiers, the XGB model showed the best performance, the average AUC was 0.74(0.69,0.76) and the accuracy was 0.73. It was followed by SVM, LR and KNN models, and the average AUC were 0.73(0.66,0.80), 0.71(0.62,0.78) and 0.66(0.61,0.72), respectively. The performance of stacking ensemble model showed effective improvement, with an average AUC of 0.77(0.67,0.84), and the accuracy was 0.83. **Conclusions:** The ensemble learning model based on conventional non-enhanced MRI sequences could identify poorly differentiated cervical cancer from well/moderately differentiated cervical cancer, and can provide more references for preoperative non-invasive assessment of cervical cancer.

Keywords: Cervical cancer · Grade · Radiomics · Ensemble learning · Magnetic resonance imaging

1 Introduction

Cervical cancer ranks fourth in morbidity and mortality among female malignant tumors, posing a serious threat to the life and health of women around the world [1]. Numerous studies have shown that tumor stage, pathological subtypes and grades of cervical cancer are the main factors affecting the prognosis of patients, and are also the key factors for formulating clinical treatment plans [2–5]. Magnetic resonance imaging (MRI) plays a

© The Author(s), under exclusive license to Springer Nature Switzerland AG 2023
W. Qin et al. (Eds.): CMMCA 2023 (MICCAI Workshop), LNCS 14243, pp. 31–41, 2023.
https://doi.org/10.1007/978-3-031-45057-7_4

crucial role in the diagnosis and staging of cervical cancer, but routine sequences have limited utility in assessing pathological subtypes and grades [6]. Previous research on classifying pathological subtypes of cervical cancer has achieved favorable outcomes [7, 8]. For the pathological grading of cervical cancer, various MRI technologies have been explored, such as diffusion weighted imaging (DWI), dynamic contrast enhanced magnetic resonance imaging (DCE-MRI), etc. However, their wide application in clinical practice is hindered by lengthy scanning and post-processing times, low repeatability, and the cost and potential health risks associated with gadolinium contrast agents used in DCE-MRI [9–12]. If preoperative prediction of pathological grade of cervical cancer can be achieved by non-enhanced MRI sequence alone, it can effectively reduce the cost of examination and the risk of contrast adverse reactions for patients, and it can be easily promoted clinically.

Radiomics, an innovative image analysis method, can provide deep-level features that are not discernible to the naked eye [13–15]. Numerous previous studies have demonstrated excellent predictive performance of radiomics in cervical cancer diagnosis, subtypes, and lymph node metastasis [16–18]. However, in cervical cancer pathology grading, radiomics models based on a single classifier seems to be less than ideal, and the model performance still needs to be further improved to meet the needs of clinical applications [2]. Ensemble learning combines multiple weak classifiers to obtain a strong classifier with significantly enhanced generalization capability [19]. The stacking ensemble learning algorithm uses the predictions of the base classifier as new features, and trains the meta-classifier with these new features to obtain the prediction results, and this algorithm can effectively improve the model performance [20].

Therefore, this study aims to explore the value of an ensemble learning model based on conventional non-contrast MRI sequences for cervical cancer pathological grading. The goal is to provide a non-invasive, efficient, and accurate preoperative pathological grading prediction method for cervical cancer patients.

2   Materials and Methods

2.1 Study Population

In this retrospective study, patients with cervical cancer admitted to the First Affiliated Hospital of Chongqing Medical University from January 2018 to September 2021 were enrolled, and the inclusion criteria were radical hysterectomy and postoperative pathological confirmation of cervical cancer. Exclusion criteria included: (1) chemotherapy, conization, radiotherapy or any other treatments before surgery; (2) stage IA cervical cancer; (3) rare histological types; (4) lack of preoperative clinical data, such as serological examination; (5) lack of preoperative MRI, such as CT enhancement, out-of-hospital consultation, and poorly displayed lesions. Finally, a total of 98 cases were included. The specific selection process is shown in Fig. 1. This study was ethically approved (No.2021–395) and a waiver of informed consent was obtained from the subjects. This study was conducted in accordance with the guidelines of the Declaration of Helsinki.

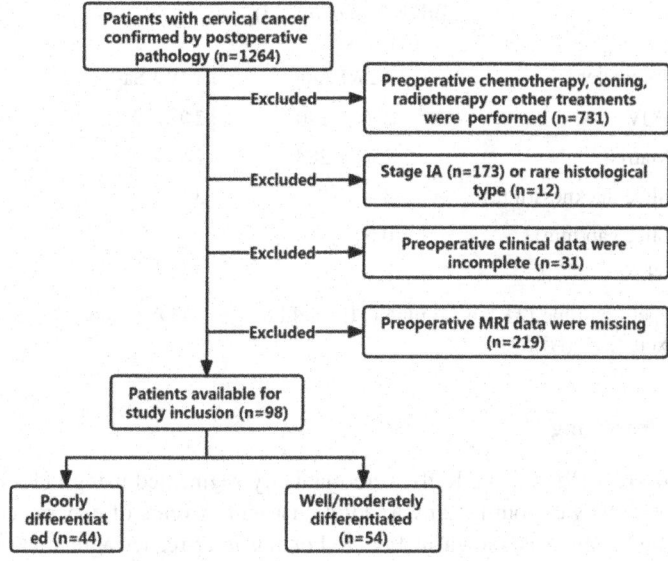

Fig. 1. Patient enrollment flowchart.

2.2 Grouping

The samples were divided into two groups based on postoperative pathology: the well/moderately differentiated group and the poorly differentiated group. Clinical data and MRI were obtained before radical hysterectomy. The clinical data included age, body mass index (BMI), red blood cell count (RBC), white blood cell count (WBC), platelet count (PLT), squamous cell carcinoma antigen (SCCAg), carbohydrate antigen 125 (CA125), carbohydrate antigen 199 (CA19–9), and carcino-embryonic antigen (CEA). MRI include two non-enhanced conventional sequences of Axial T2-weighted imaging (T2WI Axi) and Sagittal T2-weighted imaging (T2WI Sag).

2.3 MRI Protocol

In the study, all patients underwent MRI scans prior to surgery with a 3.0T MRI (Signa HD Excite, GE healthcare, USA), using an 8-channel phased-array abdominal coil. The MRI protocol included T2WI Axi and T2WI Sag. See Table 1.

Table 1. Imaging parameters of all MRI sequences.

Parameter	T2WI Axi	T2WI Sag
TR(ms)	3740	3440
TE(ms)	110.9	106.3

(continued)

Table 1. (*continued*)

Parameter	T2WI Axi	T2WI Sag
FOV	240 × 240	240 × 240
Matrix	256 × 288	224 × 288
Slice thickness(mm)	3	3
Slice gap(mm)	0.5	1
NEX	2	2

repetition time (TR), echo time (TE), field of view (FOV), number of excitations (NEX).

2.4   Image Processing

Region of Interest (ROI). The ROIs were manually segmented using ITK-SNAP 3.8 software. The ROIs were outlined by a radiologist with 3 years of experience in MRI diagnosis. The example is shown in Fig. 2. For the inter-reader agreement analysis, 30% of the cases were randomly selected and outlined by a radiologist with 10 years of experience. The second reader was unaware of the first reader's segmentation results, and both readers were blinded to the pathological results.

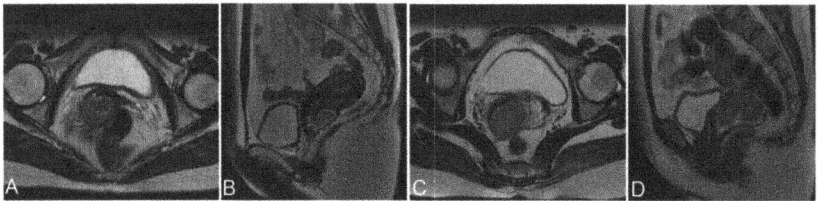

Fig. 2. A-B shows the T2WI Axi and T2WI Sag of a patient of poorly differentiated cervical cancer; C-D shows that of a patient of well/moderately differentiated.

Radiomic Feature Extraction. The radiomics package (PyRadiomics 3.0.1) was used to extract radiomics features. Radiomics features were extracted from T2WI Axi and T2WI Sag, respectively, including: shape features, first-order histogram features, texture features, Laplacian-of-Gaussian filter domain (LoG, 0.5–4.0 mm kernel) texture matrix features, and wavelet filtered domain texture matrix features.

Feature Reproducibility Analysis and Selection. Features with ICC $\geq$ 0.75 are generally considered to exhibit good consistency [21]. To ensure the stability of the radiomics features extracted, only features with ICC $\geq$ 0.75 were retained in this study. Subsequently, we employed the t-test and LASSO for feature selection.

2.5 Model Establishment

The samples were randomly divided into training and testing sets at a ratio of 7:3. In this study, we utilized a stacking ensemble algorithm consisting of two layers. The first layer comprised basic classifiers (LR, SVM, kNN, and XGB) that learned from the training data. The results generated by these classifiers were then used to train the second-layer meta-classifier, which needed to possess strong generalization ability while remaining simple enough to correct biases introduced by the first-layer machine learning algorithms on the training set, thereby avoiding overfitting. Consequently, we employed LR as the meta-classifier in the second layer. See Fig. 3.

2.6 Model Evaluation and Statistical Methods

The model performance was evaluated on the testing set using Python 3.8.5. The receiver operating characteristic (ROC) curve with cross-validation and AUC with 95% confidence interval (95% CI) were used to reflect the model performance. The cross-validation method was quadratic 3-fold cross-validation. Additionally, accuracy, precision, recall, and F1 score were calculated. Statistical analysis was performed using SPSS 22.0 software. The two independent sample t-test was used for normally distributed continuous variables and the Mann-Whitney U test was used for non-normally distributed continuous variables. The chi-square test was used for categorical variables. $P < 0.05$ was considered as a statistically significant difference.

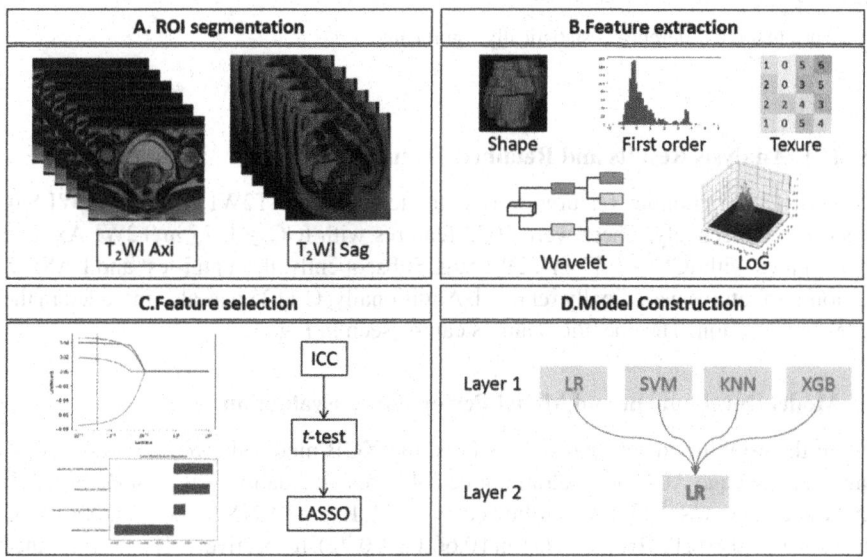

Fig. 3. Radiomics flow chart.

3 Results

3.1 Demographic Characteristics

The CA125 level was 19.1(12.5, 42.3) U/ml in the poorly differentiated group and 14.4(10.7, 19.4) U/ml in the well/moderately differentiated group, and the difference was statistically significant (P = 0.002). There were no statistically significant differences in other clinical indicators between the two groups. See Table 2.

Table 2. The demographic and clinical characteristic of patients.

	Poorly differentiated	Well/moderately differentiated	P	Training set	Test set	P
Age	49(43,59)	51(46,58)	0.529	50(46,59)	52(41,58)	0.899
BMI	23.49 ± 3.10	23.48 ± 3.22	0.995	22.7(21.4,25.8)	23.4(21.4,26.1)	0.847
RBC	4.0(3.7,4.4)	4.0(3.8,4.4)	0.546	4.0(3.8,4.4)	4.0(3.8,4.4)	0.893
WBC	5.5(4.7,6.6)	5.1(4.1,6.2)	0.170	5.3(4.1,6.4)	5.4(4.4,6.4)	0.945
PLT	193(158,235)	204(175,261)	0.093	216 ± 68	193 ± 48	0.104
SCCAg	1.4(0.9,2.6)	1.8(1.0,4.0)	0.202	1.6(0.9,3.2)	1.7(1.2,3.9)	0.400
CA125	19.1(12.5,42.3)	14.4(10.7,19.4)	0.002*	16.7(11.2,29.0)	15.4(11.5,19.0)	0.520
CA19–9	13.4(7.5,26.4)	13.0(8.0,18.3)	0.355	12.0(7.1,22.0)	15.6(9.2,22.0)	0.345
CEA	2.6(1.6,6.2)	2.2(1.6,3.4)	0.150	2.2(1.6,4.5)	2.3(1.6,5.0)	0.883

* indicates that the difference is statistically significant

3.2 ICC Analysis Results and Retained Features

A total of 1288 radiomics features were extracted from the T2WI Axi and T2WI Sag sequences, respectively. There were 1072 features with ICC ≥ 0.75 in T2WI Axi and 1100 features with ICC ≥ 0.75 in T2WI Sag. Subsequently, through t-test and LASSO, 8 radiomics features were finally retained. Additionally, CA125 was also included in the model construction. The specific features can be seen in Fig. 4.

3.3 Model Development and Model Performance Evaluation

Among the established four basic classifiers, the XGB model showed the best performance, the average AUC of quadratic three-fold cross-validation was 0.74 (0.69, 0.76) and the accuracy was 0.73. It was followed by SVM, LR and KNN models, and the AUC was 0.73(0.66,0.80), 0.71(0.62,0.78) and 0.66(0.61,0.72), respectively. The performance of the stacking ensemble model showed effective improvement, with an average AUC of 0.77(0.67, 0.84) based on the quadratic three-fold cross-validation, and the accuracy, precision, recall, and F1 score were all 0.83. The detailed performance of each model can be found in Table 3. Additionally, ROC curves with confidence intervals for each model were plotted, as shown in Fig. 5.

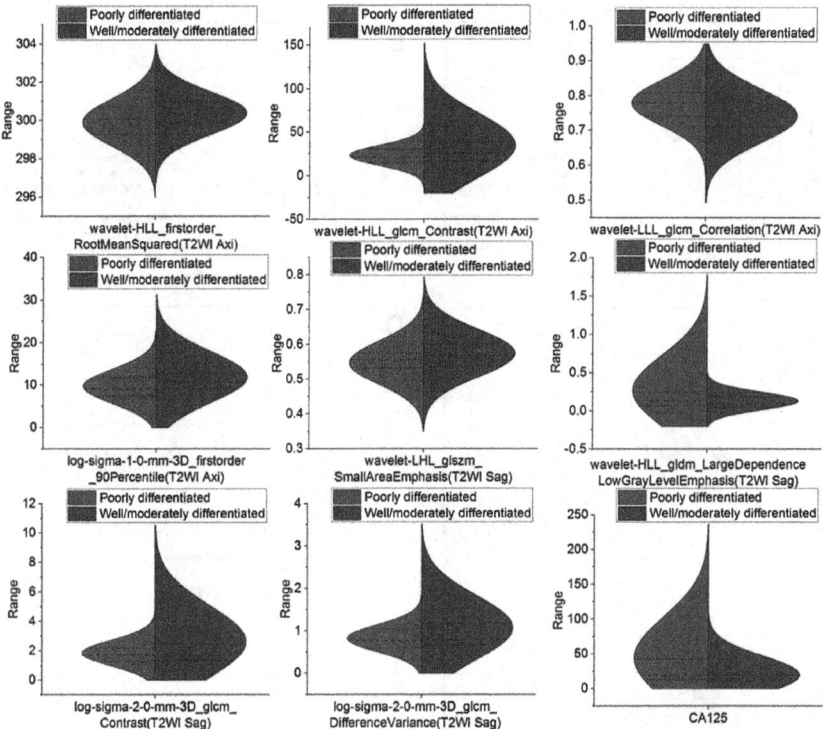

Fig. 4. The split violin plot shows the differences in retained features between poorly differentiated group and well/moderately differentiated group.

Table 3. Performance of each model.

	AUC	Accuracy	Precision	Recall	F1 score
LR (layer 1)	0.71(0.62,0.78)	0.70	0.70	0.70	0.69
SVM (layer 1)	0.73(0.66,0.80)	0.63	0.62	0.63	0.62
KNN (layer 1)	0.66(0.61,0.72)	0.66	0.66	0.67	0.65
XGB (layer 1)	0.74(0.69,0.76)	0.73	0.73	0.73	0.73
LR (layer 2)	0.77(0.67,0.84)	0.83	0.83	0.83	0.83

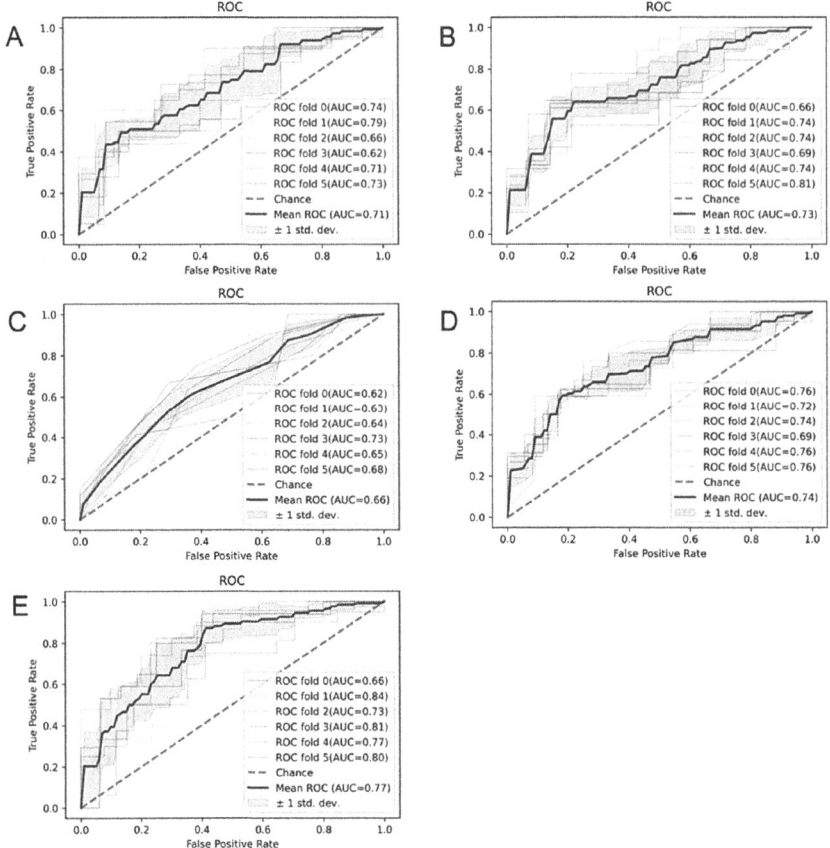

Fig. 5. A-E represents ROC curves for LR, SVM, kNN, XGB, LR (layer 2) models.

4 Discussion

The individualized treatment is closely related to tumor aggressiveness, and histological grading is an important factor reflecting the aggressiveness, which affects the treatment and prognosis of patients [22]. In clinical work, patients with the same stage of cervical cancer have different prognosis using the same treatment plan, considering that it should be related to the heterogeneity of the tumor [23]. The poorer differentiated the tumor, the more complex the composition and the higher the heterogeneity [24]. Meanwhile, poorly differentiated tumors have more aggressiveness, earlier metastatic ability, and lower survival rates compared to well/moderately differentiated tumors [22, 25]. Therefore, the classification of the two groups is closely related to the prognosis of patients.

In previous studies, Xie YL et al. classify the two groups by texture analysis of DCE-MRI with an AUC of 0.705 [2]. Lin Y et al. used ADC histogram analysis to identify the two groups and found that skewness had the best discriminatory performance with an AUC of 0.71 [26]. Poorly differentiated tumors have increased cell density and curvature of the extracellular space, which may account for the different ADC distribution between different grades. However, it has also been suggested that the identification of the two by ADC values has yielded mixed results [27, 28]. Therefore, it is important to explore new identification options. Radiomics provides a more informative basis for tumor assessment through high-throughput extraction of deep quantitative features [13–15]. In machine learning, the prediction of a single classifier has a high bias. In contrast, ensemble learning is a combinatorial decision based on base classifiers, by training multiple base classifiers and combining them to accomplish the learning task. In general, stacking ensemble learning algorithms have better performance than single machine learning algorithms [19, 29].

In this study, we modeled CA125 and 8 radiomics features based on T2WI Axi and T2WI Sag, and achieved good discriminative results. CA125 is a glycoprotein which presents a high expression status in the malignant organism [30]. In present study, we found that the CA125 level was significantly higher in poorly differentiated cervical cancer than that in well/moderately differentiated cervical cancer, which may be associated with the more aggressive, earlier metastatic ability, and lower survival rate of poorly differentiated tumors [22, 25]. In the radiomics features, we found that most of the features that can better distinguish between the two groups were related to signal intensity. For example, the Root_Mean_Squared is a measure of the magnitude of the image signal values. The Contrast is a measure of local intensity variation, with larger values associated with larger differences in intensity values between neighboring voxels. The Large_Dependence_Low_Gray_Level_Emphasis is applied to measure the joint distribution that is more correlated with lower gray level values. In general, the overall mean signal intensity of well/moderately differentiated cervical cancer was higher than that of poorly differentiated cervical cancer, and there was less variation in signal intensity between adjacent voxels in well/moderately differentiated cervical cancer. These phenomena may be associated with the more complex composition and greater heterogeneity of poorly differentiated tumors [24].

Of course, there are some limitations in this study: (1) the external data are needed to further validate the model performance; (2) DWI were not included in this study, which could be explored in the future.

In conclusion, the stacking ensemble learning model based on conventional non-enhanced MRI sequences has a strong classification ability in identifying poorly differentiated cervical cancer and well/moderately differentiated cervical cancer.

References

1. Sung, H., et al.: Global cancer statistics 2020: GLOBOCAN estimates of incidence and mortality worldwide for 36 cancers in 185 countries. CA Cancer J. Clin. **71**(3), 209–249 (2021)
2. Xie, Y.L., et al.: The value of texture analysis based on dynamic contrast-enhanced MRI for differentiating cervical adenocarcinoma from squamous cell carcinoma and its prediction of stages. Radiol. Pract. **34**(08), 835–840 (2019). (in Chinese)
3. Zhu, M., et al.: Pretreatment neutrophil-lymphocyte and platelet-lymphocyte ratio predict clinical outcome and prognosis for cervical Cancer. Clin. Chim. Acta **483**, 296–302 (2018)
4. Horn, L.C., et al.: Prognostic relevance of low-grade versus high-grade FIGO IB1 squamous cell uterine cervical carcinomas. J. Cancer Res. Clin. Oncol. **145**(2), 457–462 (2019)

5. Zhou, J., et al.: The prognostic value of histologic subtype in node-positive early-stage cervical cancer after hysterectomy and adjuvant radiotherapy. Int. J. Surg. **44**, 1–6 (2017)
6. Vincens, E., et al.: Accuracy of magnetic resonance imaging in predicting residual disease in patients treated for stage IB2/II cervical carcinoma with chemoradiation therapy: correlation of radiologic findings with surgicopathologic results. Cancer **113**(8), 2158–2165 (2008)
7. Zhang, Q., et al.: Whole-tumor texture model based on diffusion kurtosis imaging for assessing cervical cancer: a preliminary study. Eur. Radiol. **31**(8), 5576–5585 (2021)
8. He, Z., et al.: The value of HPV genotypes combined with clinical indicators in the classification of cervical squamous cell carcinoma and adenocarcinoma. BMC Cancer **22**(1), 776 (2022)
9. Wang, C., et al.: Application of DCE-MRI combined with DWI in the evaluation of clinical staging of patients with cervical squamous cell carcinoma. Pract. J. Cancer. **37**(03), 492–494+500 (2022) (in Chinese)
10. Liu, J.R., et al.: Multiparametric magnetic resonance imaging to characterize pathological grading and stage of cervical squamous cell carcinoma. Chin. J. Magn. Reson. Imaging **12**(12), 29–33 (2021). (in Chinese)
11. Rogosnitzky, M., Branch, S.: Gadolinium-based contrast agent toxicity: a review of known and proposed mechanisms. Biometals **29**(3), 365–376 (2016)
12. Prince, M.R., et al.: Incidence of immediate gadolinium contrast media reactions. AJR Am. J. Roentgenol. **196**(2), W138–W143 (2011)
13. Lambin, P., et al.: Radiomics: extracting more information from medical images using advanced feature analysis. Eur. J. Cancer **48**(4), 441–446 (2012)
14. Gillies, R.J., Kinahan, P.E., Hricak, H.: Radiomics: images are more than pictures. Data. Radiol. **278**(2), 563–577 (2016)
15. Lambin, P., et al.: Radiomics: the bridge between medical imaging and personalized medicine. Nat. Rev. Clin. Oncol. **14**(12), 749–762 (2017)
16. Wang, W., et al.: Multiparametric MRI-based radiomics analysis: differentiation of subtypes of cervical cancer in the early stage. Acta Radiol. **63**(6), 847–856 (2022)
17. Wang, T., et al.: Preoperative prediction of pelvic lymph nodes metastasis in early-stage cervical cancer using radiomics nomogram developed based on T2-weighted MRI and diffusion-weighted imaging. Eur. J. Radiol. **114**, 128–135 (2019)
18. Xiao, M., et al.: Multiparametric MRI-based radiomics nomogram for predicting lymph node metastasis in early-stage cervical cancer. J. Magn. Reson. Imaging **52**(3), 885–896 (2020)
19. Xu, J.W., Yang, Y.: Ensemble learning methods: a research review. J. Yunnan Univ. **40**(6), 1082–1092 (2018). (in Chinese)
20. Wolpert, D.H.: Stacked generalization. Neural Netw. **5**(2), 241–259 (1992)
21. Koo, T.K., Li, M.Y.: A guideline of selecting and reporting intraclass correlation coefficients for reliability research. J. Chiropr. Med. **15**(2), 155–163 (2016)
22. Matsuo, K., et al.: Association of tumor differentiation grade and survival of women with squamous cell carcinoma of the uterine cervix. J. Gynecol. Oncol. **29**(6), e91 (2018)
23. Cui, Y.Q., et al.: Advances in radiomics of cervical cancer. Chin. J. Magn. Reson. Imaging **11**(06), 477–480 (2020). (in Chinese)
24. Ciolina, M., et al.: Texture analysis versus conventional MRI prognostic factors in predicting tumor response to neoadjuvant chemotherapy in patients with locally advanced cancer of the uterine cervix. Radiol. Med. **124**(10), 955–964 (2019)
25. Costantini, M., et al.: Diffusion-weighted imaging in breast cancer: relationship between apparent diffusion coefficient and tumour aggressiveness. Clin. Radiol. **65**(12), 1005–1012 (2010)
26. Lin, Y., et al.: Correlation of histogram analysis of apparent diffusion coefficient with uterine cervical pathologic finding. AJR Am. J. Roentgenol. **204**(5), 1125–1131 (2015)

27. Payne, G.S., et al.: Evaluation of magnetic resonance diffusion and spectroscopy measurements as predictive biomarkers in stage 1 cervical cancer. Gynecol. Oncol. **116**(2), 246–252 (2010)
28. Kuang, F., et al.: The value of apparent diffusion coefficient in the assessment of cervical cancer. Eur. Radiol. **23**(4), 1050–1058 (2013)
29. Zhou, G., Guo, F.L.: Research on ensemble learning. Comput. Technol. Autom. **37**(04), 148–153 (2018). (in Chinese)
30. Liu, Y., Sun, J.F., Ding, S.: Diagnostic value of routine inflammatory markers combined with squamous cell carcinoma associated antigen and carbohydrate antigen 199 in cervical adenocarcinoma. Lab. Med. Clin. **18**(07), 869–873 (2021). (in Chinese)

Federated Multi-organ Dynamic Attention Segmentation Network with Small CT Dataset

Li Li, Yunxin Tang, Youjian Zhang, Zezhou Li, Guanqun Zhou, Haotian Zhou, and Zhicheng Zhang$^{(\boxtimes)}$

JancsiTech, Guangdong, China
`zhangzhicheng13@mails.ucas.edu.cn`

Abstract. Multi-organ segmentation, as an upstream task for many medical tasks, has been applied to many real clinical scenarios with great success. However, the existing multi-organ segmentation algorithms, which require either amount of real patient datasets or centralized storage of the patient data, neither meet the requirements of modern patient privacy regulations nor bring a heavy burden of data collection to hospitals. Inspired by federated learning, in this work, an abdominal multi-organ segmentation framework based on dynamic attention has been proposed with the assistance of a federated framework to aggregate weights among clients in the server. Besides, the segmentation model adopts a weight adaptive approach to dynamically select convolutional kernels internally. After the network training federally, we evaluated the well-trained model on both the internal testing dataset from all the clients and the unseen external testing dataset from the center server. The experimental results show that the proposed federated aggregation scheme improves the generalization ability of the model in a smaller training dataset and partially alleviates the problem of class imbalance.

Keywords: Multi-organ Segmentation · Federal Learning · Small Dataset · Class Imbalance

1 Introduction

Multi-organ segmentation for computed tomography (CT) images is an important and challenging task in medical image analysis, that has to be compelled to accurately delineate the contours of internal organs [10] like the liver, kidneys, pancreas, spleen, *etc.* Though pixel-wise organ segmentation will give valuable anatomical info for several downstream tasks, like computer-aided diagnosis [13], surgery planning [7], and other clinical applications [6] [8], their success depends on giant amounts of the high-quality labeled training dataset, which is an unaffordable effort in many scenarios: 1) For one hospital, aggregation of enough high-quality CT information and annotation is time-consuming. 2) The distribution of the training dataset collected by one hospital is insufficient, limiting

W. Qin et al. (Eds.): CMMCA 2023 (MICCAI Workshop), LNCS 14243, pp. 42–50, 2023.
https://doi.org/10.1007/978-3-031-45087-7_5

the generalization ability of models. 3) To stop revealing patient privacy, centralized storage of patient datasets from multiple hospitals is impractical. Thus, to lower the burden of collecting and annotating multi-organ training information and decrease the quantity of training information, training distributed multi-organ segmentation models to avoid centralized information storage may be a long-standing and necessary topic.

For multi-organ segmentation in CT, many deep learning-based methods [10,12,17] have been proposed, which can obtain comparable performance in the certain testing dataset. U-Net, as a common medical image segmentation network, has been widely used in many tasks [12]. In recent years, amounts of Unet-based transformer models have been proposed for abdominal multi-organ segmentation to establish long-distance dependency relationships between multiple organs [15]. TransUNet [5] and TransClaw U-net [16] capture feature information by combining transformer structures with convolutions in the encoder. UCTransNet [14] replaces the original skip connection with transformer structures. These models have achieved excellent segmentation performance on the Synapse [3] dataset. However, due to the large number of trainable parameters, the transformer model requires a large dataset for the network training. Since the burden of multi-organ annotation, preparing the entire training dataset inside only one hospital is over-stressed. Thus, how to promote the collaborative preparation of datasets by multiple hospitals is a direction worth exploring, thereby reducing the burden on individual hospitals and then protecting patient privacy. Besides, abdominal multi-organ segmentation also faces many difficulties, such as category imbalance, *etc.* The performance of the pancreas in multi-organ segmentation is far inferior to that of the spleen and liver, due to the high variability of pancreatic morphology and small targets.

Inspired by the multi-client aggregation capability of federated learning in data quantity and distribution [11], we proposed a U-shaped dynamic attention-based federated learning framework trained simultaneously on different datasets from several hospitals without sharing data. Moreover, the proposed U-based dynamic attention model can be well combined with the federated framework to solve the problems of low data volume and imbalanced abdominal multi-organ segmentation categories. Specifically, the decoder can dynamically select convolutional kernels through weight adaptation. To verify its effectiveness, this work collected four different datasets, three of which are used in the federated clients, and the remaining one is used as an external testing set. In summary, our contributions are three-fold:

1. In the case of small datasets, the proposed model framework achieved excellent performance in abdominal multi-organ segmentation tasks.
2. To protect patient privacy and lower the burden of collecting and labeling data for a single hospital, the paradigm of federal learning is employed so that we can spread the burden of labeling across several hospitals and get the following benefits from this method: a) Accelerate the data preparation process; b) Protect patient privacy and prevent data breaches; c) Expand the statistical distribution of training data through multi-center clinical data aggregation

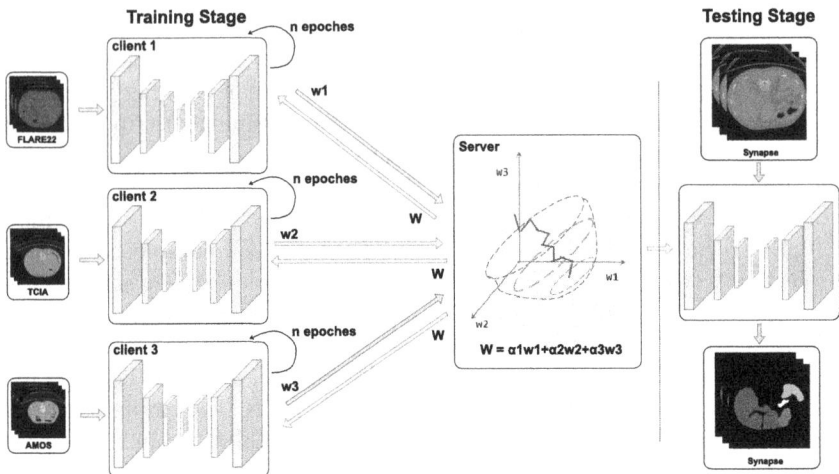

Fig. 1. Federated Aggregation Scheme. On the left is the training stage, and on the right is the testing stage. Each client employs their special dataset. α is to balance the weight of each client. After federal training, we can test the well-trained model on the external dataset (Synapse).

to explore whether federated aggregation can improve model generalization on external testing datasets.
3. Experiments on both internal and external testing datasets have demonstrated the superiority of our method. Notably, the combination of federated learning and the proposed U-shaped dynamic attention model has proved to be more effective in pancreas segmentation tasks.

2   Method

Inspired by FedAvg [11], a dynamic attention-based federated learning framework is proposed for multi-organ segmentation, which consists of a federated aggregation scheme with a segmentation model. In the proposed framework, we can employ several clients to simulate several hospitals, we use three clients as an example, each of which possesses multi-organ datasets from different hospitals, respectively. The federated framework and segmentation model are described in the following section.

Federated Aggregation Scheme. Figure 1 illustrates the overall framework of this work, including the training stage and testing stage. To begin with, the three hospitals use their training dataset to respectively train segmentation models locally for 20 epochs and then upload their weights to the central server, where the three weights are combined through aggregation to obtain a weighted average, and the new weights are redistributed to the three hospitals for the next

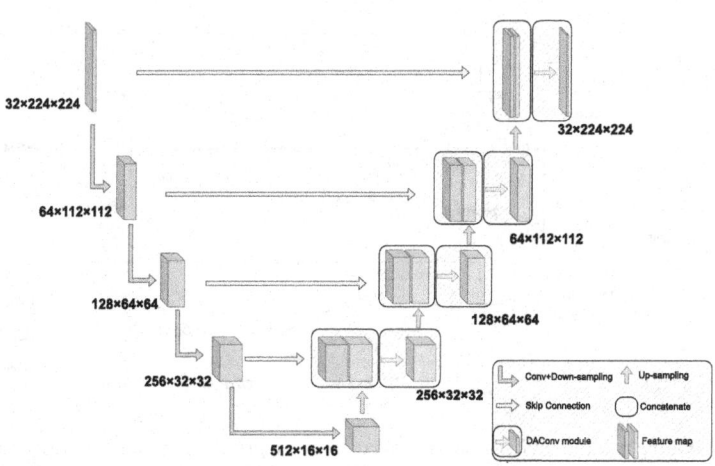

Fig. 2. U-DANet: a schematic diagram of the segmentation network, consisting of encoders, decoders, and skip connections. DAConv module is the dynamic attention module.

round of training. This training process is referred to as one communication round. Synapse [3], as an unseen dataset, serves as an external testing set. The weighted average method is calculated by the following equation:

$$W = \alpha_i w_i = \frac{N_i}{\sum_{i=1}^{C_N} N_i} w_i \tag{1}$$

where W represents the new weight after the weights aggregation in a central server. $i = 1, 2, 3$ and C_N indicates the number of clients, and w_i shows the weight of the i-th client. N_i shows the number of data from the i-th client.

Segmentation Network. Inspiration from U-Net [12] and SKNet [9], this work proposes a U-shaped dynamic attention segmentation model for the federated framework, named U-DANet. The network structure is shown in Fig. 2. In the encoder stage, continuously multiple 3×3 convolutions are used for channel amplification to capture rich semantic information. In addition, max pooling is used to reduce the size of feature maps. In the decoder stage, feature maps are upsampled and concatenated with the semantic feature maps obtained from the encoder, followed by convolutional operations using the dynamic attention module (DAConv module). The specific structure of the DAConv module is shown in Fig. 3. Firstly, feature maps $x_1 \in \mathbb{R}^{B \times C \times W \times H}$ is convolved by a 3×3 group convolution and a 5×5 group convolution. Then concatenate these two feature maps in a higher dimensional space to obtain a new feature map $x_2 \in \mathbb{R}^{B \times 2 \times C \times W \times H}$. Where B represents the batch size, C indicates channel numbers, and H/W shows the size of feature maps. The mathematical expression for the above process is as follows:

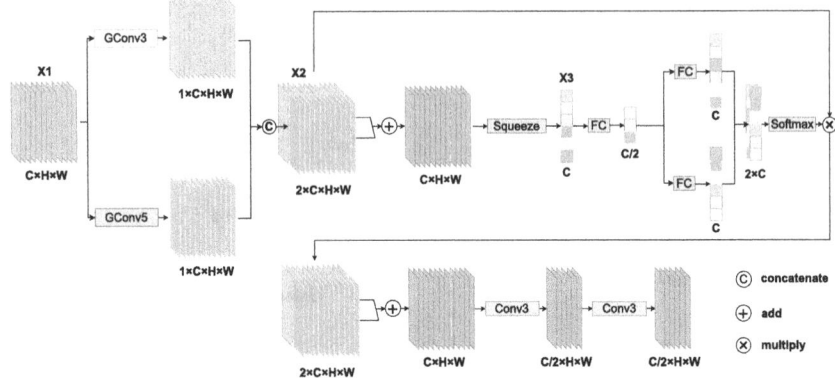

Fig. 3. DAConv module. GConvn shows an n × n group convolution (groups = 8), Conv3 indicates a 3 × 3 convolution and FC represents full connections. C: Channel; H: Hight; W: Width

$$x_2 = \text{Concat}((\text{unsq}(\text{GConv3}(x_1), dim = 1), \text{unsq}(\text{GConv5}(x_1), dim = 1))) \quad (2)$$

where $GConv3$ represents a 3 × 3 group convolution, $GConv5$ shows a 5 × 5 group convolution, and $unsq(x, dim = 1)$ indicates expanding the dimension on the first dimension. $Concat(,)$ represents concatenating two sets of feature maps on the first dimension. The feature map x_2 is added according to the elements in the first dimension. Subsequently, spatial information is embedded into the channel to generate one-dimensional vectors $x_3 \in \mathbb{R}^C$. After that, two one-dimensional vectors are obtained through fully connected layers. After concatenating these two one-dimensional vectors, use softmax to obtain the probability value, and then multiply them by x_2 to dynamically select convolutions. Using this approach, the weights of feature maps in x_2 can be adjusted dynamically. Finally, after two 3 × 3 convolution layers, the final feature map can be outputted. The mathematical expression for x_2 to x_3 is as follows:

$$x_3 = \text{Mean}(\text{Sum}(x_2, dim = 1), dim = 3, 4) \quad (3)$$

where $Sum(x, dim = 1)$ represents adding elements on the first dimension. $Mean(x, dim = 3, 4)$ shows squeezing feature maps by average values in both height and width dimensions.

Implementation Details. This work for abdominal multi-organ segmentation is constructed with NVIDIA 3090 using PyTorch. All experiments are trained using Adam optimizer, with a learning rate of 1e-5 and a batch size of 8. In addition, this work uses Dice loss and focal loss for backpropagation. In the data processing phase, the original dataset is cut into slices and resized into 224 × 224. Data augmentation is essential, including random rotation, random flipping, and random contrast enhancement. We will release our code as soon as possible.

Table 1. Datasets include both internal and external datasets. Internal datasets participate in training and testing, and external datasets only participate in testing.

	Internal Data			External Data
Data_name	FLARE22	TCIA	AMOS	Synapse
client	client_1	client_2	client_3	unseen
train_num	304	300	301	0
test_num	76	75	75	71

3 Experimental Results

Dataset. This work has four publicly available datasets, including FLARE22 [1], TCIA [4], AMOS [2] and Synapse [3]. The CT data is processed into slices and the original CT values are retained. The testing set and training set are divided by patients, without data breach. The specific quantity is shown in Table 1.

Quantitative Analysis. In the experimental section, this work is divided into three parts: localized, centralized, and federated parts. Quantitative indicators adopt Dice indicators commonly used in segmentation tasks. Throughout the experiment, three hospitals are simulated. The A dataset comes from client 1, the B dataset comes from client 2, and the C dataset comes from client 3.

In local training, different clients use their own datasets for independent training. Local training is conducted using the U-Net model. From the results of the trained model in both internal and external testing sets, it can be seen that the results of external testing are unacceptable. It is worth noting that in client_2, although the average Dice of the internal test set is higher than that of the external test set. However, for the stomach, the Dice in the internal test set is lower than that in the external test set, the potential explanation is that the stomach is difficult to segment in dataset B. This phenomenon prompts us to propose a new method to alleviate the problem of category imbalance in multi-organ segmentation. For centralized network training with mixed data sets from all clients, due to the expansion of the number of data sets and the richness of the data distribution in the dataset, The test result on the external dataset have been improved greatly, but still lower than those of the internal mixed dataset. For the federated network training, the federated framework is trained with distributed dataset. We can see that the Dice coefficient are superior to centralized training and local training, which demonstrated that the dynamic attention federation framework proposed in this work exhibits excellent segmentation performance for multi organ segmentation. For difficult objects to be segmented such as the stomach and pancreas, our proposed method led to significant improvements. The quantitative results are shown in the Table 2.

CT images   Label   Centra_UNet   Fed_UNet   Ours

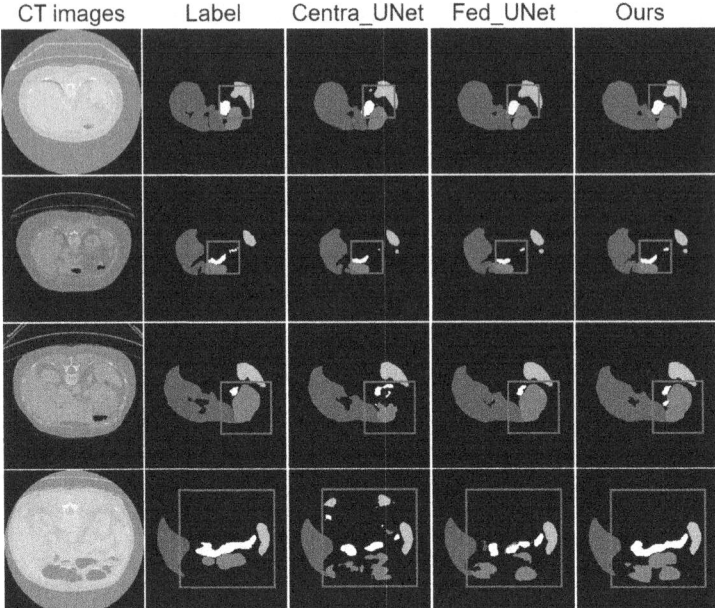

Fig. 4. Qualitative results. The first column is the CT image, and the second column is the ground truth. Centra_UNet shows the visualization results of the UNet model on external test set D, using a mixed ABC dataset during training. Fed_UNet represents the visualization results on external dataset D after training using the UNet model in a federated manner. The last column is our proposed method.

Qualitative Analysis. Figure 4 shows the qualitative results of different methods, ground truth, and CT images. In mask images, rose red represents the spleen, green shows the liver, deep yellow indicates the stomach, and white represents the pancreas. The red box identifies areas where other methods not perform well, which indicates that the stomach and pancreas are difficult points in multi organ segmentation.

Ablation Study. From the perspective of ablation, combining the proposed U-DANet with the federated framework can achieve significant improvements in external datasets, especially in balancing different types of organs. In the centralized network training, U-DANet can obtain a better average Dice value than U-Net. To be specific, in segmenting the pancreas, the proposed model can achieve by 13.4% improvement over U-Net on the external testing dataset and 6.9% on the internal testing dataset. In federated learning, the effect of the integration of U-DANet is far better than that of U-Net, which further indicates that the proposed federated framework has stronger adaptability.

Table 2. Quantitative results. The red font represents the best average Dice value, and bold font indicates qualitative results on the external dataset. A is the FLARE22 dataset. B is the TCIA dataset. C is the AMOS dataset. D is the Synapse dataset. ABC represents mixing ABC datasets together.

| | | Train_data | Test_data | Dice | | | | |
				Spleen	Liver	Stomach	Pancreas	AVG
Localized	client_1	A	A	90.20	95.53	73.74	63.24	80.68
			D	**58.26**	**87.22**	**48.06**	**46.95**	**60.12**
	client_2	B	B	94.01	93.45	20.27	54.61	65.59
			D	**59.90**	**88.84**	**50.83**	**44.61**	**61.04**
	client_3	C	C	77.10	89.70	65.85	48.35	70.25
			D	**60.99**	**89.19**	**53.75**	**39.64**	**60.89**
Centralized	UNet	ABC(Mixed)	ABC	84.69	88.85	72.41	56.46	75.60
			D	**73.06**	**94.57**	**69.45**	**60.33**	**74.35**
	U-DANet	ABC(Mixed)	ABC	90.18	92.97	73.29	56.54	78.25
			D	**83.71**	**94.67**	**61.20**	**64.10**	**75.92**
Federated	UNet	Distributed Data	A	95.57	96.06	84.79	74.69	87.78
			B	96.63	95.11	73.14	66.12	82.75
			C	71.49	84.87	65.20	50.91	68.11
			D	**90.42**	**95.19**	**75.89**	**71.09**	**83.15**
	U-DANet	Distributed Data	A	95.32	96.32	84.77	70.01	86.61
			B	96.96	95.34	72.34	65.36	82.50
			C	82.83	91.18	66.95	52.97	73.48
			D	**89.75**	**95.89**	**78.48**	**77.22**	85.34

4 Conclusion

Due to the huge burden of large-scale of CT image collection and pixel-wise annotations for a single hospital, as well as patient privacy concerns, in this work, we made most of the multi-client aggregation capability of federated learning in data quantity and data distribution and then proposed a U-based dynamic attention model-based federal learning framework. The proposed framework can run in several clients simultaneously and leverage multi-client training data, which can deal with extremely small data sets. After network testing, a superior performance has been achieved on the external testing dataset, which demonstrates multi-client federated aggregation training can greatly improve the generalization ability of the model. As well, we have also achieved satisfactory performance in pancreatic segmentation, which is a weakness in other multi-organ segmentation methods. In further, on the basis of the segmentation ability of the existing model, it is worth exploring to increase the number of classification organs of the model.

Acknowledgements. This work was partially supported by the National Natural Science Foundation of China (62001464, 82202954) and Chongqing Science and Technology Innovation Foundation (CYS23693).

References

1. MICCAI FLARE22 challenge dataset (2022). https://zenodo.org/record/7860267#.ZFm_oXZBxrq
2. Multi-modality abdominal multi-organ segmentation challenge 2022 dataset (2022). https://amos22.grand-challenge.org/
3. Synapse dataset (2023). https://www.synapse.org/#!Synapse:syn3193805/wiki/89480
4. TCIA dataset (2023). https://wiki.cancerimagingarchive.net/display/Public/Pancreas-CT
5. Chen, J., et al.: TransUNet: transformers make strong encoders for medical image segmentation. arXiv preprint arXiv:2102.04306 (2021)
6. Fu, Y., Lei, Y., Wang, T., Curran, W.J., Liu, T., Yang, X.: A review of deep learning based methods for medical image multi-organ segmentation. Physica Med. **85**, 107–122 (2021)
7. Howe, R.D., Matsuoka, Y.: Robotics for surgery. Annu. Rev. Biomed. Eng. **1**(1), 211–240 (1999)
8. Li, Q., Song, H., Chen, L., Meng, X., Yang, J., Zhang, L.: An overview of abdominal multi-organ segmentation. Curr. Bioinform. **15**(8), 866–877 (2020)
9. Li, X., Wang, W., Hu, X., Yang, J.: Selective kernel networks. In: Proceedings of the IEEE/CVF Conference on Computer Vision and Pattern Recognition, pp. 510–519 (2019)
10. Liang, X., Li, N., Zhang, Z., Xiong, J., Zhou, S., Xie, Y.: Incorporating the hybrid deformable model for improving the performance of abdominal CT segmentation via multi-scale feature fusion network. Med. Image Anal. **73**, 102156 (2021)
11. McMahan, B., Moore, E., Ramage, D., Hampson, S., y Arcas, B.A.: Communication-efficient learning of deep networks from decentralized data. In: Artificial intelligence and statistics, pp. 1273–1282. PMLR (2017)
12. Ronneberger, O., Fischer, P., Brox, T.: U-Net: convolutional networks for biomedical image segmentation. In: Navab, N., Hornegger, J., Wells, W.M., Frangi, A.F. (eds.) MICCAI 2015. LNCS, vol. 9351, pp. 234–241. Springer, Cham (2015). https://doi.org/10.1007/978-3-319-24574-4_28
13. Van Ginneken, B., Schaefer-Prokop, C.M., Prokop, M.: Computer-aided diagnosis: how to move from the laboratory to the clinic. Radiology **261**(3), 719–732 (2011)
14. Wang, H., Cao, P., Wang, J., Zaiane, O.R.: Uctransnet: rethinking the skip connections in u-net from a channel-wise perspective with transformer. In: Proceedings of the AAAI Conference on Artificial Intelligence, vol. 36, no. 3, pp. 2441–2449 (2022)
15. Xiao, H., Li, L., Liu, Q., Zhu, X., Zhang, Q.: Transformers in medical image segmentation: a review. Biomed. Signal Process. Control **84**, 104791 (2023)
16. Yao, C., Hu, M., Li, Q., Zhai, G., Zhang, X.P.: TransClaw U-Net: claw U-Net with transformers for medical image segmentation. In: 2022 5th International Conference on Information Communication and Signal Processing (ICICSP), pp. 280–284. IEEE (2022)
17. Zhou, Z., Rahman Siddiquee, M.M., Tajbakhsh, N., Liang, J.: UNet++: a nested U-Net architecture for medical image segmentation. In: Stoyanov, D., et al. (eds.) DLMIA/ML-CDS -2018. LNCS, vol. 11045, pp. 3–11. Springer, Cham (2018). https://doi.org/10.1007/978-3-030-00889-5_1

A 3D Inverse Solver for a Multi-species PDE Model of Glioblastoma Growth

Ali Ghafouri$^{(\boxtimes)}$ ⓘ and George Biros

Oden Institute, University of Texas at Austin, 201 E. 24th Street, Austin, TX, USA
ghafouri@utexas.edu biros@oden.utexas.edu

Abstract. We propose and evaluate fitting a multi-species go-or-grow tumor-growth partial differential equation (PDE) model for glioblastomas to a multi-parametric, single-snapshot magnetic resonance imaging (mpMRI) scan. We model the dynamics of proliferative, infiltrative, and necrotic tumor cells and their coupling to oxygen concentration. Fitting the PDE to the data is a formidable inverse problem as we need an estimate of the healthy subject anatomy, the tumor initial location, and the PDE parameters that control the evolution dynamics. Inverting for these quantities using a single mpMRI is an ill-posed problem. To address this ill-posedness, we use a single-species inverse solver to estimate the initial location of the tumor. Then, we estimate the multi-species model parameters using a derivative-free optimization. We evaluate our model on 24 subjects from the BraTS20 dataset. We compare with the single-species models in terms of Dice coefficients for the tumor core (proliferative + necrotic). The single-species model achieves a median dice score of 0.792 whereas the multi-species model achieves the median of 0.810. Additionally, our multi-species model can also reconstruct necrotic and proliferative and cells, and edema, achieving median dice scores of 0.435, 0.518, and 0.484, respectively.

Keywords: Glioblastoma · Multi-species · Tumor growth models · Inverse problems

1 Introduction

Glioblastomas (GBMs) are malignant brain tumors with a poor prognosis. GBM MRI scans typically comprise a single pre-treatment multi-parametric scan, which makes the quantification of tumor infiltration beyond the visible margin difficult. Biophysical models hold the promise of aiding scan interpretation and ultimately improving clinical diagnosis, patient stratification, and therapy strategies [10]. Here we are interested in creating a subject-specific biophysical model using a single snapshot mpMRI. Our hypothesis is that multi-species

Supplementary Information The online version contains supplementary material available at https://doi.org/10.1007/978-3-031-45087-7_6.

W. Qin et al. (Eds.): CMMCA 2023 (MICCAI Workshop), LNCS 14243, pp. 51–60, 2023.
https://doi.org/10.1007/978-3-031-45087-7_6

tumor growth models that are fitted to the scan phenotype have the potential to provide useful clinical information. However, as shown in other works [12,19], this task is highly ill-posed and requires regularization even for single-species models. Here, using the multi-species GBM growth model introduced in [17], we propose a reconstruction algorithm for model parameters and the initial condition of the tumor. The PDE model includes interactions between three tumor species, proliferative, necrotic, and infiltrative, and has ten coefficients that need to be fitted to the patient data–in addition to the tumor initiation location.

Contributions: First, we introduce a reconstruction algorithm in which we recover the tumor initiation locations, in other words, the initial condition (IC) for the PDE, and the model parameters. Our algorithm leverages an existing single-species approximation to reconstruct the IC [4,14,19], followed by an appropriately regularized parameter reconstruction. Second, we present a preliminary evaluation of our scheme on 24 clinical cases from the BraTS20 dataset [2]. We report the performance of our solver and show that the multi-species model reconstructions are stable and match the single-species Dice coefficients. At the same time, the model also matches necrotic, non-necrotic and the edema regions, something that the single-species model cannot do, while also solving for infiltrative tumor cells that are not observable in scans. To the best of our knowledge, our work is the first approach to calibrating a multi-species tumor growth model from a single mpMRI.

Related Work: The single-species reaction diffusion model is the most commonly used mathematical model for quantifying tumor growth at the organ level, as demonstrated by several prior studies [3,4,7,14–16,18,19]. However, this widely studied model does not differentiate necrotic, non-necrotic, and edematous tissue. While there have been numerous studies on multi-species models, they have mostly focused on forward problems aimed at simulating the biological process of tumor growth [13,17]. In [8], the authors employ a two-species model with longitudinal data to calibrate for tumor growth in which the reconstruction of the initial condition is not required. However, pretreatment longitudinal data is less commonly available for GBMs whereas with post-treatment scans we need to account for the treatment effects, which complicates the analysis. Our goal is to try to extract as much patient-specific biophysical information as possible from the first pretreatment scan, and then use it for downstream clinical tasks.

2   Methods

We present our model using the following notation. Our model consists of three distinct tumor species, necrotic ($n = n(\mathbf{x}, t)$), proliferative ($p = p(\mathbf{x}, t)$), and infiltrative ($i = i(\mathbf{x}, t)$) cells, where $\mathbf{x}$ denotes a voxel and t denotes time. The total tumor concentration is represented as $c = n + p + i$. A BraTS20 image segmentation yields enhancing, non-enhancing, necrotic tumor and edema. Here we group enhancing and non-enhancing labels together and we view them as proliferative cells. We don't have direct observations for infiltrative cells. We also need the healthy tissue segmentation in white matter $(w(\mathbf{x},t))$, gray matter $(g(\mathbf{x},t))$, cerebrospinal fluid (CSF)/ventricles (VT) $(f(\mathbf{x},t))$. We denote the observed tumor data as p_d, n_d, and l_d, which respectively denote the observed proliferative, necrotic, and edema labels.

Multi-species Tumor Growth Model: Our go-or-grow model builds upon previous works [13,17]. The model defines three states for tumor cells: proliferative, infiltrative, and necrotic. In the presence of sufficient oxygen, tumor cells undergo mitosis and continue to proliferate. In the absence of sufficient oxygen, tumor cells switch to an invasive state and begin to migrate towards areas with higher oxygen levels. Once they locate sufficient oxygen, these invasive cells switch back to a proliferative state and continue to divide. Hypoxia ultimately leads to necrosis for both infiltrative and proliferative cells. The multi-species PDE is given below.

$$\partial_t p - \mathcal{R}p + \alpha p(1-i) - \beta i(1-p) + \gamma p(1-n) = 0 \quad \text{in } \Omega \times (0,1] \quad \text{(1a)}$$
$$\partial_t i - \mathcal{D}i - \mathcal{R}i - \alpha p(1-i) + \beta i(1-p) + \gamma i(1-n) = 0 \quad \text{in } \Omega \times (0,1] \quad \text{(1b)}$$
$$\partial_t n - \gamma(i+p)(1-n) = 0 \quad \text{in } \Omega \times (0,1] \quad \text{(1c)}$$
$$\partial_t o + \delta_c op - \delta_s(1-o)(w+g) = 0 \quad \text{in } \Omega \times (0,1] \quad \text{(1d)}$$
$$\partial_t w + \frac{w}{w+g}(\mathcal{D}i + \mathcal{R}p + \mathcal{R}i) = 0 \quad \text{in } \Omega \times (0,1] \quad \text{(1e)}$$
$$\partial_t g + \frac{g}{w+g}(\mathcal{D}i + \mathcal{R}p + \mathcal{R}i) = 0 \quad \text{in } \Omega \times (0,1] \quad \text{(1f)}$$
$$p(\mathbf{x},0) - p_0 = 0 \quad \text{in } \Omega \quad \text{(1g)}$$
$$i(\mathbf{x},0) = 0 \quad \text{in } \Omega \quad \text{(1h)}$$
$$n(\mathbf{x},0) = 0 \quad \text{in } \Omega \quad \text{(1i)}$$
$$o(\mathbf{x},0) - 1 = 0 \quad \text{in } \Omega \quad \text{(1j)}$$
$$g(\mathbf{x},0) - g_0 = 0 \quad \text{in } \Omega \quad \text{(1k)}$$
$$w(\mathbf{x},0) - w_0 = 0 \quad \text{in } \Omega \quad \text{(1l)}$$
$$f(\mathbf{x},0) - f_0 = 0 \quad \text{in } \Omega \quad \text{(1m)}$$

The current study presents a framework that involves the initial segmentation of white matter $(w_0(\mathbf{x}))$, gray matter $(g_0(\mathbf{x}))$, and CSF/VT $(f_0(\mathbf{x}))$. The tumor concentration's initial condition is represented by $p_0(\mathbf{x})$, under the assumption that the tumor initiates as a proliferative cell type. The model comprises of various components, including transition terms (γ, β, α), a diffusion (migration) operator $\mathcal{D}$, and proliferation/consumption terms $(\mathcal{R}, \delta_s, \delta_c)$. The diffusion term $\mathcal{D}i$ is defined as $\mathcal{D}i = \text{div}(k\nabla i)$ where k is the inhomogeneous diffusion rate $k = \kappa w + \kappa_g g$ where κ is the diffusion coefficient; following the literature we take

$\kappa_g = 0.2\kappa$ [5,9]. The reaction operator $\mathcal{R}$ for a species s is defined as:

$$\mathcal{R}s = \begin{cases} \rho_m s(1-c), & o > o_i \\ (\dfrac{o-o_m}{o_i-o_m})\rho_m s(1-c), & o_i \geq o \geq o_m \\ 0, & o < o_i \end{cases} \quad (2)$$

where o_m is the mitosis oxygen threshold, o_i is the invasive oxygen threshold and $\rho_m = \rho w + \rho_g g$ and similarly to diffusion term, we assume $\rho_g = 0.2\rho$ where ρ is the reaction coefficient. We also assume $o_m = \frac{o_i + o_h}{2}$ where o_h is the hypoxic oxygen threshold [13,17]. The transition terms α, β and γ are defined as:

$$\alpha(o) = \alpha_0 \mathcal{H}(o_i - o), \quad (3)$$
$$\beta(o) = \beta_0 \mathcal{H}(o - o_i), \quad (4)$$
$$\gamma(o) = \gamma_0 \mathcal{H}(o_h - o), \quad (5)$$

where α_0, β_0 and γ_0 are scalar positive coefficients in which controls the transitioning of species. We define three observation operators to compare the species concentrations (p, n, i) generated by our multi-species model to the observed MRI segmentation (p_d, n_d, l_d). These operators map the model-predicted fields to a binary segmentation per tissue type, which can then be compared to the MRI segmentation. To this end, observation operators are defined below.

$$\mathcal{O}c = \mathcal{H}(c-w)\mathcal{H}(c-g)\mathcal{H}(c-f), \quad (6)$$
$$\mathcal{O}p = \mathcal{H}(p-n)\mathcal{H}(p-i)\mathcal{O}c, \quad (7)$$
$$\mathcal{O}n = \mathcal{H}(n-p)\mathcal{H}(n-i)\mathcal{O}c, \quad (8)$$
$$\mathcal{O}l = (1 - \mathcal{O}p - \mathcal{O}n)\mathcal{H}(i - i_e). \quad (9)$$

The observed quantities of total tumor, proliferative, necrotic, and edema cells are denoted by $\mathcal{O}c, \mathcal{O}p, \mathcal{O}n$, and $\mathcal{O}l$, respectively. The Heaviside step function is represented by $\mathcal{H}$. We use a smooth version of the Heaviside function noted as $\mathcal{H}(x) = \frac{1}{1+\exp(-\omega x)}$ where ω is a shape factor determining the smoothness of the function. Throughout the remainder of this paper, the initial healthy brain segmentation is denoted as $\Omega_0 = (w_0, g_0, f_0)$ and the model coefficients vector is denoted by $\mathbf{q}$. The model consists of ten scalar coefficients ($\mathbf{q} \in \mathbb{R}^{10}_+$) that dictate the tumor species' migration, proliferation, and necrosis. Specifically, the unknown parameters are ρ in $\mathcal{R}$, κ in $\mathcal{D}$, β_0, α_0, and γ_0, the invasive oxygen threshold o_i, a hypoxic oxygen threshold o_h, an oxygen consumption rate δ_c, an oxygen source rate δ_s, and an edema invasive threshold i_e.

Inverse Problem: The unknown fields and parameters are $(\Omega_0, p_0, \mathbf{q})$. To estimate these quantities, we employ an inversion scheme consisting of three stages. First, we introduce an approximation to Ω_0. Next, we estimate p_0 using a simplified single-species model. Finally, we invert for the growth model parameters $\mathbf{q}$ using the inverse problem formulation presented below:

$$\min_{\mathbf{q}} \mathcal{J} := \frac{1}{2}\|\mathcal{O}p - p_d\|^2_{L_2} + \frac{1}{2}\|\mathcal{O}n - n_d\|^2_{L_2} + \frac{1}{2}\|\mathcal{O}l - l_d\|^2_{L_2} + \frac{\lambda}{2}\|\mathbf{U}^T\mathbf{q}\|^2, \quad (10)$$

subject to the go-or-grow model $\mathcal{F}(\Omega_0, p_0, \mathbf{q})$ given by Eq. (1) and λ is the regularization factor. The objective function consists of two parts. The first three terms represent the L_2 mismatch between simulated observed species and data species. The last term is the biophysical regularization, which is based on Hessian sampling. This regularization is based on a simplified multi-species model in 1D, which we computed the Hessian of the inverse problem for a large number of parameters. We identified the combination of common model coefficients $\mathbf{q}$ that induce ill-posedness and enforce this term into the objective function to avoid such ill-posed directions. The regularization is proposed to alleviate the ill-posedness of the parameters for the model coefficients $\mathbf{q}$. Details on that will be reported elsewhere.

2.1 Inversion Algorithm

S.1 To derive the pretumor anatomy Ω_0 and the tumor data, we use three steps: (Tumor Segmentation:) First, we perform an affine registration of the mpMRI scans to a template atlas. Then, we use a deep neural network [11] trained on the BraTS dataset [2] to segment the scans into tumor regions of proliferative, necrotic, and edema. (Healthy tissue Segmentation:) Next, we register (using ANTs [1]) multiple templates (normal brain scans with known segmentation) to the patient's scan and use an ensemble-atlas-based segmentation to create healthy tissue labels for the patient. (Pretumor anatomy:) Finally, we replace the tumorous regions of the brain with white matter, creating an approximation of the healthy anatomy Ω_0.

S.2 To estimate the initial condition of the tumor, we use an adjoint based method developed for single-species reaction diffusion model [14,19]. In this model, the goal is to reconstruct the tumor core (proliferation + necrotic data) using a single-species reaction diffusion model. This inversion scheme includes an ℓ_0 constraint to enforce sparsity in the initial location of the tumor, tacitly assuming that the tumor originates on a small number of locations.

S.3 The final step involves estimating the model coefficients by utilizing a gradient-free optimizer known as CMA-ES [6]. Given the healthy precancerous anatomy Ω_0 and the initial condition of the brain (p_0), the coefficients vector $\mathbf{q} \in \mathbb{R}_+^{10}$ is estimated, which determines the proliferation, migration, and necrosis of the tumor species.

In **S.**1, we perform the preprocessing step for ten different atlases. In **S.**2, the IC inversion employs an iterative scheme to enforce sparsity constraints on the solution. Specifically, the scheme uses a quasi-Newton optimization method (L-BFGS) globalized by Armijo linesearch, with gradient-based convergence criteria. In **S.**3, the regularization is based on a simplified 1D model of the multi-species model. The regularization aims to find the common ill-posedness weighted based on the strength of the ill-posedness in the parameter space, and the directions are penalized in the objective function. Our solver operates in parallel and for an image resolution of 160^3, it takes approximately 6 h on 4 GPUs.

The most expensive step of the overall algorithms is the derivative free optimization for the ten model parameters in which we have to solve a large number of forward problems. In the future we will replace this step with a derivative based scheme.

3   Results

We pose the following research questions to investigate our results:

Q1 How does the multi-species model compare to the single species? The metric here is the Dice coefficient for the whole tumor.

Q2 How well can the model reconstruct individual species observed in the MRI scans, i.e. necrotic tissue and edema?

To answer these questions, we utilize the Dice score, which for species s is defined as $\pi_s = \frac{2|s^{\mathrm{rec}} \cap s^*|}{|s^{\mathrm{rec}}| + |s^*|}$ where s^{rec} and s^* represent the observed species from the inversion and data, respectively, and $|\cdot|$ denotes the cardinality of the corresponding set. To address **Q1**, we compare the Dice scores for the tumor core obtained from the single-species model ($\pi_{\mathrm{tc}}^{\mathrm{ss}}$) and the multi-species model ($\pi_{\mathrm{tc}}^{\mathrm{ms}}$). Additionally, to answer **Q2**, we report the Dice scores for proliferative (π_p), necrotic (π_n), and edema (π_l) species.

We report the results of our proposed inversion scheme on a cohort of patients selected from the BraTS20_Training dataset. The effectiveness of our approach in accurately reconstructing tumor regions is indicated by the inversion metrics presented in Table 1, with a summary of the reconstruction measures expressed as Dice scores. Additionally, we visually assess the accuracy of our reconstruction by presenting the corresponding segmentation results for five patients in Fig. 1. To obtain the data, we used the algorithm described in 2.1 for healthy brain segmentation and tumor segmentation. We present the reconstructed segmentation from our multi-species algorithm, and we also visualize the single-species reconstruction.

Our algorithm enables us to identify and distinguish different cell types and their distribution within tumor regions. The multi-species reconstruction is more informative in comparison to single-species reconstruction, as it provides segmentation for all species rather than only tumor core. In order to gain further insight into the performance of our model, we have included the reconstruction results for 24 patients from the BraTS20 dataset algorithm in the appendix. We report the Dice scores for both single-species and multi-species reconstruction, as well as for each individual tumor species. The single-species reconstruction yielded an average Dice score of 0.790 ± 0.057, with a median of 0.792, while the multi-species algorithm achieved an average Dice score of 0.743 ± 0.203, with a median of 0.810. Regarding the necrotic, proliferative, and edema cells, the multi-species model achieved an average Dice score of 0.410 ± 0.244 with a median of 0.435, 0.464 ± 0.217 with a median of 0.518, and 0.445 ± 0.267 with a median of 0.484, respectively.

Our inversion scheme has demonstrated good results in reconstructing tumor regions for patients from the BraTS20 dataset. Nevertheless, multi-species reconstructions present certain challenges. For example, in the case of patient Train-

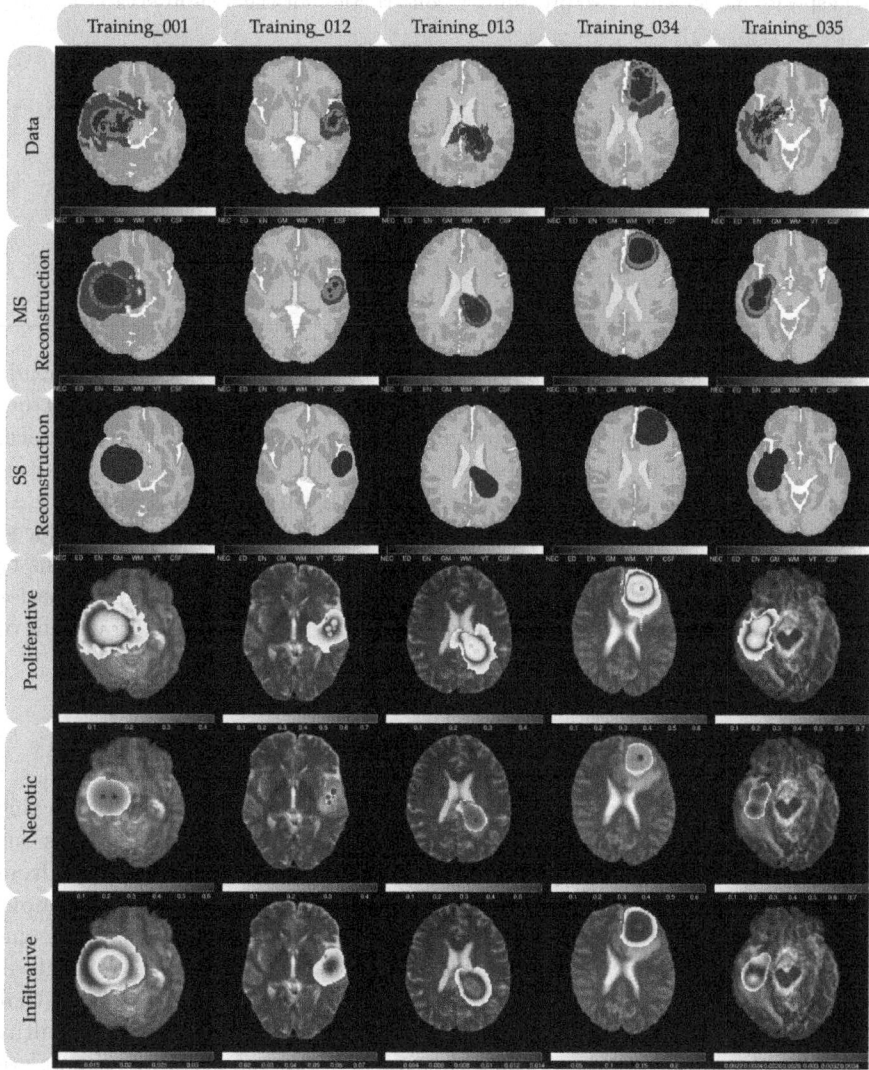

Fig. 1. Here we summarize the reconstructions for the single and multi-species models. Each column corresponds to a patient from the BraTS Training dataset [2], and includes the segmented tumor from the mpMRI scans and the affinely registered template in the first row. The second row displays the results of our multi-species reconstruction (MS Reconstruction), while the third row shows the results of a single-species model reconstruction (SS Reconstruction). The last three rows present the underlying species of the proliferative, necrotic, and infiltrative cells, respectively.

Table 1. Dice scores for tumor segmentation using multi-species and single-species models. The Dice scores for the proliferative, necrotic, and edema cells are denoted as π_p, π_n, and π_l, respectively. The reconstruction of tumor core (proliferative+necrotic) using multi-species and single-species models is denoted as π_{tc}^{ms} and π_{tc}^{ss}, respectively. Our results demonstrate that our model achieves similar reconstruction quality as the single-species model while also providing reconstruction for the non-observable species.

Patient's ID	π_p	π_n	π_l	π_{tc}^{ms}	π_{tc}^{ss}
Training_001	3.28E-1	5.53E-1	7.60E-1	7.87E-1	8.14E-1
Training_012	6.94E-1	3.23E-1	4.72E-1	8.61E-1	7.61E-1
Training_013	1.80E-1	6.31E-1	4.07E-1	6.68E-1	7.52E-1
Training_034	5.32E-1	7.23E-1	9.16E-2	8.92E-1	8.78E-1
Training_035	3.40E-1	5.05E-1	2.71E-1	7.40E-1	7.12E-1

ing_005, our model exhibits some error in reconstructing the tumor core, while providing good reconstruction of edema. Additionally, the heterogeneous structure of the tumorous region in the brain can affect the algorithm's performance. As can be observed in Fig. 1 for patient Training_001, the multi-species reconstruction failed to capture the heterogeneous structure of the necrotic species. We are working on developing models that take into account the mass-induced deformation of the tumor (mass effect), in which the brain anatomy deforms to potentially capture this heterogeneous structure. Overall the Dice coefficients for the subspecies are somewhat low pointing to a need for further improvement of biophysical models of tumor growth.

4   Conclusions

We presented a preliminary evaluation of a multi-species inverse solver, which operates in a black box fashion and requires no manual preprocessing. It is one of the first solvers that can invert for the observable abnormal tissue type from mpMRI scans and provide biophysical model output that closely resembles input data. Our study demonstrates our solver produces reconstructions that are comparable with a single-species for the whole tumor, while being more informative. This is something to be confirmed in future investigations, but we assume that the signficant sources of error in our reconstruction are our estimate healthy precancerous anatomy and our using the tumor initial condition inversion algorithm using the single-species model. Furthermore the edema model is perhaps too simple. Despite these shortcomings, we illustrated the feasibility of our algorithm through its calibration on a few clinical cases. With only a small number of calibration parameters, our solver can reconstruct a brain tumor from a single snapshot of a patient. Our model allows for the quantification of the multi-species of the brain tumor, including the brain vascularization, without any assumptions of the symmetry or location of the tumor. Our future goals include combining our solver with mass deformation and testing it on the complete patient dataset. Ultimately, we aim to integrate our model with biophysical features to explore correlations between patient survival and tumor recurrence regions.

References

1. Avants, B.B., Tustison, N., Song, G., et al.: Advanced normalization tools (ants). Insight J. **2**(365), 1–35 (2009)
2. Bakas, S., et al.: Identifying the best machine learning algorithms for brain tumor segmentation, progression assessment, and overall survival prediction in the brats challenge. arXiv preprint arXiv:1811.02629 (2018)
3. Gholami, A., Mang, A., Biros, G.: An inverse problem formulation for parameter estimation of a reaction-diffusion model of low grade gliomas. J. Math. Biol. **72**(1), 409–433 (2016)
4. Gholami, A., et al.: A novel domain adaptation framework for medical image segmentation. In: Crimi, A., Bakas, S., Kuijf, H., Keyvan, F., Reyes, M., van Walsum, T. (eds.) BrainLes 2018. LNCS, vol. 11384, pp. 289–298. Springer, Cham (2019). https://doi.org/10.1007/978-3-030-11726-9_26
5. Gooya, A., et al.: GLISTR: glioma image segmentation and registration. IEEE Trans. Med. Imaging **31**(10), 1941–1954 (2012)
6. Hansen, N., Ostermeier, A.: Adapting arbitrary normal mutation distributions in evolution strategies: the covariance matrix adaptation. In: Proceedings of IEEE International Conference on Evolutionary Computation, pp. 312–317. IEEE (1996)
7. Hogea, C., Davatzikos, C., Biros, G.: Brain-tumor interaction biophysical models for medical image registration. SIAM J. Sci. Comput. **30**(6), 3050–3072 (2008)
8. Hormuth, D.A., Al Feghali, K.A., Elliott, A.M., Yankeelov, T.E., Chung, C.: Image-based personalization of computational models for predicting response of high-grade glioma to chemoradiation. Sci. Rep. **11**(1), 1–14 (2021)
9. Lipková, J., et al.: Personalized radiotherapy design for glioblastoma: integrating mathematical tumor models, multimodal scans, and Bayesian inference. IEEE Trans. Med. Imaging **38**(8), 1875–1884 (2019)
10. Mang, A., Bakas, S., Subramanian, S., Davatzikos, C., Biros, G.: Integrated biophysical modeling and image analysis: application to neuro-oncology. Annu. Rev. Biomed. Eng. **22**, 309 (2020)
11. Myronenko, A.: 3D MRI brain tumor segmentation using autoencoder regularization. In: Crimi, A., Bakas, S., Kuijf, H., Keyvan, F., Reyes, M., van Walsum, T. (eds.) BrainLes 2018. LNCS, vol. 11384, pp. 311–320. Springer, Cham (2019). https://doi.org/10.1007/978-3-030-11726-9_28
12. Ozisik, M.N.: Inverse Heat Transfer: Fundamentals and Applications. Routledge, Abingdon (2018)
13. Saut, O., Lagaert, J.B., Colin, T., Fathallah-Shaykh, H.M.: A multilayer grow-or-go model for GBM: effects of invasive cells and anti-angiogenesis on growth. Bull. Math. Biol. **76**(9), 2306–2333 (2014)
14. Scheufele, K., Subramanian, S., Biros, G.: Fully automatic calibration of tumor-growth models using a single MPMRI scan. IEEE Trans. Med. Imaging **40**(1), 193–204 (2020)
15. Scheufele, K., Subramanian, S., Mang, A., Biros, G., Mehl, M.: Image-driven biophysical tumor growth model calibration. SIAM J. Sci. Comput. Publ. Soc. Ind. Appl. Math. **42**(3), B549 (2020)

16. Subramanian, S., Ghafouri, A., Scheufele, K., Himthani, N., Davatzikos, C., Biros, G.: Ensemble inversion for brain tumor growth models with mass effect. IEEE Trans. Med. Imaging (2022)
17. Subramanian, S., Gholami, A., Biros, G.: Simulation of glioblastoma growth using a 3D multispecies tumor model with mass effect. J. Math. Biol. **79**(3), 941–967 (2019)
18. Subramanian, S., Scheufele, K., Himthani, N., Biros, G.: Multiatlas calibration of biophysical brain tumor growth models with mass effect. In: Martel, A.L., et al. (eds.) MICCAI 2020. LNCS, vol. 12262, pp. 551–560. Springer, Cham (2020). https://doi.org/10.1007/978-3-030-59713-9_53
19. Subramanian, S., Scheufele, K., Mehl, M., Biros, G.: Where did the tumor start? An inverse solver with sparse localization for tumor growth models. Inverse Prob. **36**(4), 045006 (2020)

Domain Knowledge Adapted Semi-supervised Learning with Mean-Teacher Strategy for Circulating Abnormal Cells Identification

Huajia Wang, Yinglan Kuang, Xianjun Fan, Yanling Zhou, Xin Ye, and Xing Lu[✉]

Sanmed biotech Inc., Zhuhai, Guangdong, China
lv.xing@sanmedbio.com

Abstract. The number of signals in each signal channel in the nucleus of a four-color FISH image is the basis for distinguishing between normal cells, deletion signal cells, and CACs. In previous studies, we adopted deep learning for signal detection, which required a relatively large number of voxel-level labeled cells and signal images for training. In this study, we introduce a mean teacher mechanism into the training process and propose an end-to-end semi-supervised object detection method to detect the signal. We also propose Domain-Adaptive Pseudo Labels as a false positive filtering based on the prior knowledge of CAC signal. The experimental results show that the strategies proposed is simple and effective. On the four-color FISH image, when using only 8% of labeled data is used, it can all achieve 0.15% 0.41% 0.55% and 0.85% F1 score improvements compared to the supervised baseline.

Keywords: Circulating Abnormal Cells Detection · Deep Learning · Semi-Supervised learning · Prior Knowledge

1 Introduction

In the field of early lung cancer diagnosis, liquid biopsy [1] has been increasingly recognized for its non-invasive or minimal invasive, convenient and highly reproducible characteristics. Genetically circulating abnormal cells or circulating tumor cells (CACs or CTCs) [2–5], ctDNA or cfDNA, and exosomes are the main detection targets for liquid biopsy. Katz et al. [7] developed a antigen-independent, four-color fluorescence in situ hybridization (FISH)-based method to detect CACs in 207 lung cancer patients with an accuracy of 94.2%, a sensitivity of 89%, and a specificity of 100%. Ye et al. [6] lunched a multiple centers cohort in China, which combined clinical characteristics, radiological characteristics of pulmonary nodules, artificial intelligence analysis of LDCT data, and liquid biopsy(CACs) achieved the best diagnostic performance compared with the Mayo Clinic Model and Veterans' Affairs Model. These studies demonstrated that Lung Cancer could be diagnosed with high precision by CACs. However, CACs are rare in blood samples, the CAC identification based on FISH is very labor-intensive and time-consuming.

© The Author(s), under exclusive license to Springer Nature Switzerland AG 2023
W. Qin et al. (Eds.): CMMCA 2023 (MICCAI Workshop), LNCS 14243, pp. 61–70, 2023.
https://doi.org/10.1007/978-3-031-45087-7_7

The research in the paper carried out on the FISH-based image with four-color fluorescent. A typical FISH image is shown in Fig. 1, which consisted of five-channels, DAPI, aqua, gold, green, red. We get the cell boundary based on the DAPI image, and perform signal detection on the four-color image. The signals in each cell are counted to determine the cell's category.

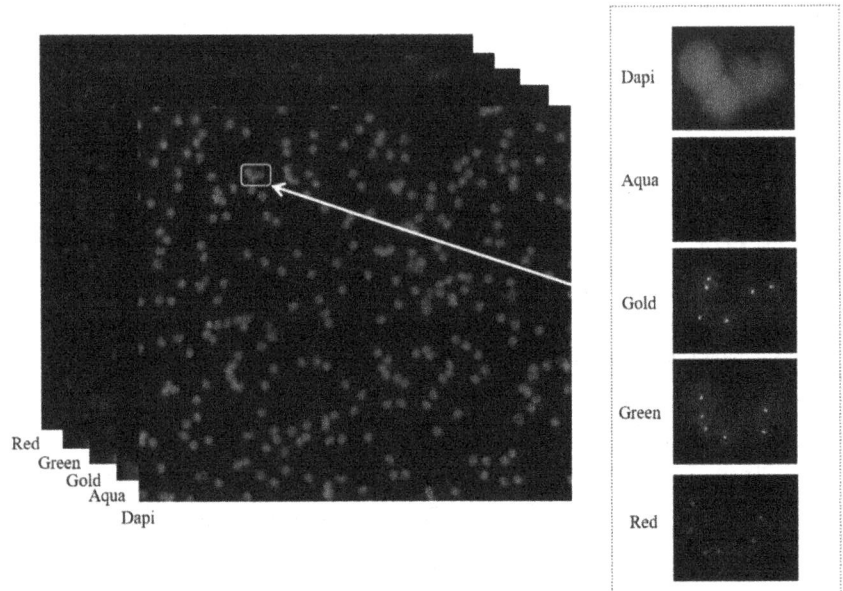

Fig. 1. FISH-based Image. The image contain five channels which are DAPI, Aqua, Gold, Green, Red. (Color figure online)

With the application of CTCs identification in early lung cancer diagnosis, researchers have begun to utilize computer-based methods for the automatic identify of CTCs. Ligthart et al. [8] classify cells by using features extracted techniques which included the standard deviation of the signal in the CK-PE channel, peak signal values in the DNA-DAPI and CD45-APC channels, and object size. Lannin et al. [9] performed feature extraction on images and experimented with four machine learning methods random forest, k-nearest neighbors, Bayesian classifier, and support vector machine for cell classification. Xu et al. [10] utilized You Only Look Once (YOLO)-V4 to detect signals in FISH images and enhanced the small targets detection capability by using a larger scale feature map.

However, deep learning model training requires a large amount of labeled data, which the pixel level cells and signal labeling is enormous in the field of CACs. As depicted in Fig. 1, each image typically contains 200 to 400 cells, with each cell usually having two or three signals for each channel. Consequently, labeling a single set four-color image requires labeling over 1600 signal. Semi-supervised learning [11] offers a potential solution to minimize the amount of labeling required. One approach within semi-supervised learning is the mean teacher [12]. This method utilizes a small set of labeled data to train the model and subsequently employs the model to predict labels for unlabeled data, generating pseudo labels. The model is then trained using both labeled and unlabeled data. By leveraging unlabeled data, this approach enhances the model's performance and reduces the reliance on labeled data.

In our research, we have employed the mean teacher approach to develop an end-to-end semi-supervised learning network architecture for signal detection. We have utilized yolov5 as our example detector and incorporated semi-supervised learning to enhance the model's detection performance by training it with unlabeled data. Furthermore, we have designed a false positive filtering method based on prior knowledge of the signal to improve the accuracy of pseudo-labeling. By leveraging this method, we can enhance the quality of the generated pseudo-labels. Experimental results have demonstrated that our designed framework, with the aid of unlabeled data, can significantly improve the model's effectiveness in signal detection.

2   Related Work

Many people have tried to combine semi-supervised learning with deep learning to reduce the need for labeled data. Semi-supervised learning methods for medical images are more applied to segmentation tasks. Xu et al.[13] proposed SegPL, which was a medical image segmentation method of semi-supervised learning based entirely on original pseudo labels. Moreover, the EM framework is introduced to get the generalization form of SegPL, and different thresholds are used to generate pseudo-labels at different periods to further improve the segmentation effect of the model. Wang et al. [14] developed Annotation-effIcient Deep lEarning. By adding constraints to pseudo-labeled samples, updating pseudo labels, using cross-model collaborative optimization learning and other strategies, the model trained on 10% of the labeled data has comparable results to the fully supervised model.

Signal detection falls under the domain of object detection tasks; however, the existing semi-supervised object detection methods proposed by researchers have primarily focused on natural images [15–20]. Sohn et al. [21] introduced self-training to the field of object detection and put forth a straightforward and efficient semi-supervised learning approach called STAC. Liu et al. [15] proposed the unbiased teacher method, which incorporated the mean teacher concept into the object detection task. Additionally, Liu et al. [20] developed unbiased teacherV2, which extended semi-supervised learning to anchor-free detectors.

3   The Proposed Method

3.1   Problem Statement

To develop semi-supervised learning object detection algorithm applied to the signal detection in FISH-based images, labeled data $D_s = \{x_i^s, y_i^s\}_{i=1}^{N_s}$ and unlabeled data $D_u = \{x_i^u\}_{i=1}^{N_u}$ is used for model training, where x^s is labeled image data. x^u is unlabeled image data. y^s is annotation including categories, coordinates, and dimensions. N_s and N_u are the number of labeled data and unlabeled data.

3.2 End-to-End Semi-supervised Learning Signal Detect Framework

Yolo v5 is used as signal detector. Then, semi-supervised learning framework is designed based on the mean teacher paradigm, and the entire architecture is shown in Fig. 2. Although it is an end-to-end framework, the entire training process is divided into two stages. The first stage is training the model with labeled data, which is fully supervised learning. The second stage is training the model with both labeled data and unlabeled data, which is semi-supervised learning.

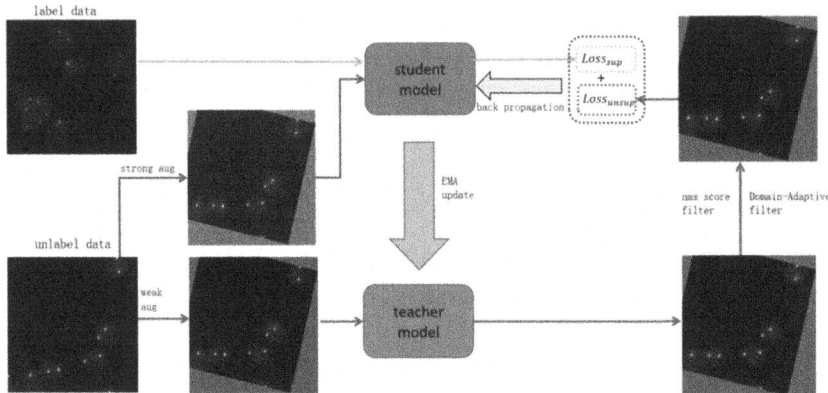

Fig. 2. Overview of End-to-End semi-supervised learning signal detect Framework.

For the first stage, the model is mainly trained through the supervised loss function, the loss function is as follows.

$$loss_{sup} = \sum_i L_{box}\left(x_i^s, y_i^s\right) + L_{obj}\left(x_i^s, y_i^s\right) + L_{cls}\left(x_i^s, y_i^s\right) \tag{1}$$

L_{box} is location loss, L_{obj} is objectness loss, L_{cls} is classes loss. After the stage, copy the parameters of the model into teacher model and student model respectively.

For the second stage, weak data augmentation and strong data augmentation were implemented on the unlabeled data respectively. The teacher model predicts the unlabeled data with weak data augmentation, and then performs NMS and threshold filtering false positives based on the prediction result to obtain the pseudo label of the unlabeled data. In this way, unlabeled data will have pseudo label, that allow unlabeled data to participate in model training. We combine unlabeled data with strong data augmentation and labeled data to train the student model, the loss function is as follows.

$$loss_{unsup} = \sum_i L_{box}(x_i^u, y_i^u) + L_{obj}(x_i^u, y_i^u) + L_{cls}(x_i^u, y_i^u) \tag{2}$$

$$loss_{semi} = loss_{sup} + \lambda_u loss_{unsup} \tag{3}$$

We set λ_u as 1. We update the parameters of the student model based on the $loss_{semi}$, as shown in Eq. 4.

$$\theta_s = \theta_s + \gamma \frac{\partial loss_{semi}}{\partial \theta_s} \tag{4}$$

In order to obtain reliable pseudo labels, we adopt the Exponential Moving Average to update the teacher model iteration by iteration, as shown in Eq. 5. The teacher model can be regarded as an ensemble of the student model of different iterations.

$$\theta_t = \alpha\theta_t + (1 - \alpha)\theta_s \tag{5}$$

3.3 Domain-Adaptive Pseudo Label

With semi-supervised learning, the noisy pseudo labels that generated by the teacher model are difficult to avoid. If the pseudo labels are too noisy, it will downgrade the training performance of the student model. Some studies [15, 21] have employed a high confidence threshold to filter out false positives and improve the quality of pseudo-labeling. However, while a high confidence threshold enhances the precision of pseudo-labeling, it can also result in a lower recall rate, thereby affecting the overall performance of the model.

In the paper, we leveraged the prior knowledge of the signal to improve quality of pseudo labels. We used the traditional image processing method to extract the maximum pixel value and the average intensity value from image base the bounding box of the pseudo labels. And we compare the signal features value with max features value of all signal. If this value is too small, discard the pseudo label of this signal. The equation is as follows. We think that the signal point features of the same input image are relatively close.

$$threshold_{maxpixel} = \mu * \max(ROI^u) \tag{6}$$

$$threshold_{aveintensity} = \nu * max(AveInt(ROI^u)) \tag{7}$$

we set μ is 0.5 and ν is 0.5. ROI^u is bounding box of pseudo labels of the unlabeled image. AveInt is the average intensity of the signal. If the maximum pixel value or the average intensity value of the signal's pseudo label is lower the $threshold_{maxpixel}$ or $threshold_{aveintensity}$, the signal's pseudo label will be abandoned.

4 Experiments and Result

4.1 Data Set

The sample data is composed of 4 healthy people and 18 cancer patients, which is collected from 5 hospitals and one genetic company. We generate data through the following steps. We draw 10 ml of peripheral blood from people, and then use the Ficoll-Hypaque density gradient separation method, Cytospin system, and four-color FISH technology to visualize chromosomes 3 and 10 in order to detect whether the chromosome is abnormal. The number of FISH images per sample is mostly between 140 and 200. The dimension of image is 4128 * 3600, and the number of channels is 5, which are DAPI, aqua, gold, red, and green. This paper mainly focuses on signal detection on four-color images.

In the study, 50 images are selected from 22 samples, and each sample take 1–4 images. The selection standard is mainly based on the cell counts of each image. Five experienced FISH image diagnostic experts annotated signal images with Labelme, and then 2 diagnostic experts reviewed the annotated results.

In subsequent experiments, we divided the labeled data set into three set, 2 images as the training labeled set, 23 images as the training unlabeled set, and 25 images as the test set.

4.2 Experiments Setup

We trained yolov5s in supervised training with 8% labeled data and 100% labeled data respectively as our control group. Then, unlabeled data with 8% labeled data train yolov5s using the mean teacher, which is semi-supervised learning. Domain-Adaptive Pseudo Label is used in the semi-supervised learning, which combined the prior knowledge of signal to improve quality of pseudo labels of signal. By adding the method to semi-supervised learning, the model effect of yolov5 have been further improved, which verifies the effectiveness of the method.

4.3 Implementation Details

Our experiments were implemented based on pytorch 1.9.0 and run on NVIDIA Tesla T4. The training process is divided into two stages. At the epoch from 0 to 99, it is supervised learning. At the epoch from 100 to 199, it is semi-supervised learning. The batch size of labeled dataset and unlabeled dataset is both 16. Adam is used as optimizer, learning rate is $1e-3$ and weight_decay is $5e-4$. The lr_scheduler is ReduceLROnPlateau, which factor is 0.9 and patience is 10.

Weak data augmentation mainly includes normalization and random perspective. Strong data augmentation is based on weak data augmentation plus HSV augmentation, GaussianBlur and GaussianNoise.

Class-wise non-maximum suppression (NMS) is used to post-process the output of the model to retain better prediction results. The Iou and Score threshold value of NMS are both 0.5.

Because we need to detect the signal of the four-color image, we need to train a signal detection model for each channel. The models trained by different channels of data, independently.

4.4 Result and Discussion

F1 score is applied as the evaluation metric of the test set. The formula is as follows.

$$Precision = \frac{True\ Positive}{True\ Positive + False\ Positive} \tag{8}$$

$$recall = \frac{True\ Positive}{True\ Positive + False\ Negative} \tag{9}$$

$$F1 = 2 \times \frac{Precision \times Recall}{Precision + Recall} \qquad (10)$$

The experimental result is shown as Table 1. Table 1 shows the experimental results of supervised learning and semi-supervised learning on four-color image.

Table 1. Different methods comparison of results based on different data and different channels. MA represent mean teacher, DAPL represent Domain-Adaptive Pseudo Label.

Metohd	Channel	dataset	F1 score
yolov5s	Aqua	112(8%)	0.942
yolov5s	Aqua	1329(100%)	**0.9537**
yolov5s + MA	Aqua	112(8%)+1217	0.9423
yolov5s + MA +DAPL	Aqua	112(8%)+1217	**0.9435**
yolov5s	Gold	112(8%)	0.9625
yolov5s	Gold	1329(100%)	**0.9729**
yolov5s + MA	Gold	112(8%)+1217	0.9633
yolov5s + MA +DAPL	Gold	112(8%)+1217	**0.9666**
yolov5s	Green	112(8%)	0.9538
yolov5s	Green	1329(100%)	**0.9672**
yolov5s + MA	Green	112(8%)+1217	0.9568
yolov5s + MA +DAPL	Green	112(8%)+1217	**0.9593**
yolov5s	Red	112(8%)	0.9612
yolov5s	Red	1329(100%)	**0.9717**
yolov5s + MA	Red	112(8%)+1217	0.964
yolov5s + MA +DAPL	Red	112(8%)+1217	**0.9697**

4.5 Ablation Study

In previous studies, high-quality pseudo-labels is generated by using high threshold value [15–17, 21]. We also tried the method in this study. The results are shown in Table 2 (Fig. 3).

Figure 4 shows the validation set metrics of the five training methods at each epoch. We can see that the effect of our proposed semi-supervised learning is better and more stable. In addition, it can be noticed that if use high threshold to filter the pseudo labels in semi-learning, the effect of model will be lower and lower.

We use the Domain-Adaptive Pseudo Label to filter the false positive sample of signal's the pseudo labels, which improves the quality of the pseudo labels. As shown in Fig. 4.

Table 2. Different semi-supervised learning method comparison of results.

Metohd	Channel	dataset	F1 score
yolov5s+MA(thresh=0.5)	Aqua	112(8%)+1217	0.9423
yolov5s+MA(thresh=0.7)	Aqua	112(8%)+1217	0.934
yolov5s+MA(thresh=0.5)+DAPL	Aqua	112(8%)+1217	**0.9435**
yolov5s+MA(thresh=0.5)	Gold	112(8%)+1217	0.9633
yolov5s+MA(thresh=0.7)	Gold	112(8%)+1217	0.9656
yolov5s+MA(thresh=0.5)+DAPL	Gold	112(8%)+1217	**0.9666**
yolov5s+MA(thresh=0.5)	Green	112(8%)+1217	0.9568
yolov5s+MA(thresh=0.7)	Green	112(8%)+1217	0.9539
yolov5s+MA(thresh=0.5)+DAPL	Green	112(8%)+1217	**0.9593**
yolov5s+MA(thresh=0.5)	Red	112(8%)+1217	0.964
yolov5s+MA(thresh=0.7)	Red	112(8%)+1217	0.9586
yolov5s+MA(thresh=0.5)+DAPL	Red	112(8%)+1217	**0.9697**

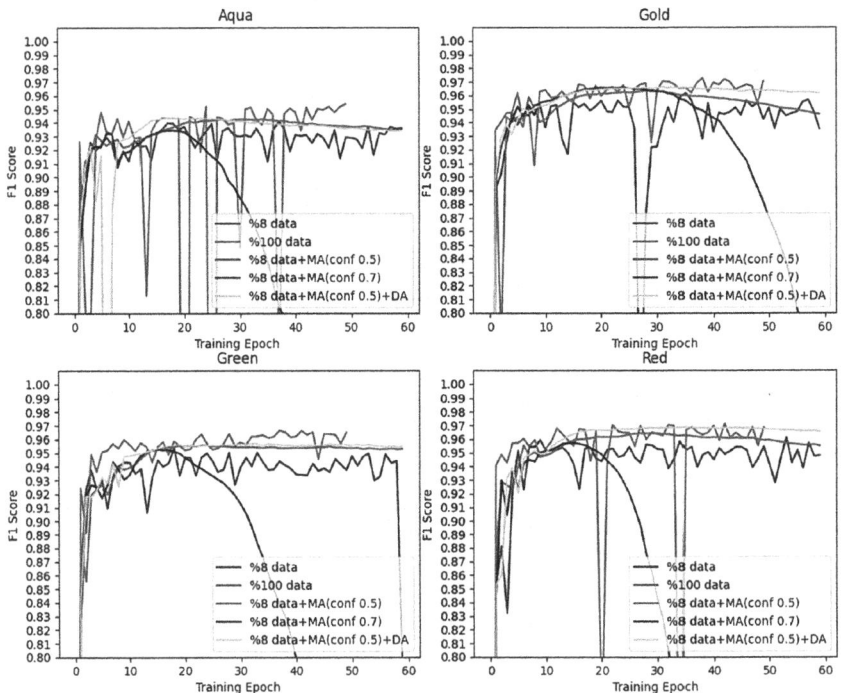

Fig. 3. Comparison of F1 score of different method in Training.

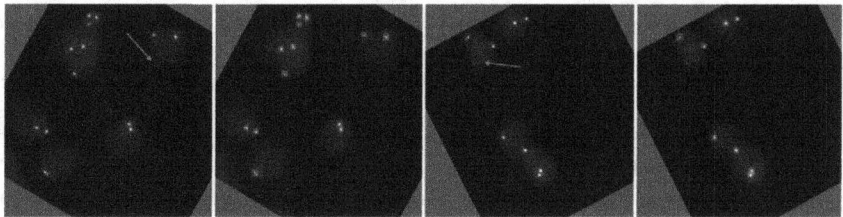

Fig. 4. This is comparison of Domain-Adaptive Pseudo Label. The red box represents the result without the method, and the green image represents the result after the method is applied.

5 Conclusions

In this paper, an end-to-end semi-supervised object detection algorithm in the field of signal of FISH-image is proposed. Unlabeled data could be used in the training of the model and improve the performance of the model on signal detection. Prior domain knowledge of signal determination is properly leveraged to reduce false positive detections for pseudo labels generated in the semi-supervised learning, which further improved the performance of the model. On the four-color image, The method can all achieve 0.15% 0.41% 0.55% 0.85% F1socre improvements against the supervised baseline when using only 8% of labeled data. Experimental results demonstrated that the proposed method is effective.

References

1. Poulet, G., Massias, J., Taly, V.J.A.c.: Liquid biopsy: general concepts, **63**(6), 449–455 (2019)
2. Qiu, X., et al.: Application of circulating genetically abnormal cells in the diagnosis of early-stage lung cancer, **148**(3), 685–695 (2022)
3. Liu, W.R., et al.: Detection of circulating genetically abnormal cells in peripheral blood for early diagnosis of non-small cell lung cancer,**11**(11), 3234–3242 (2020)
4. Feng, M., et al.: Detection of circulating genetically abnormal cells using 4-color fluorescence in situ hybridization for the early detection of lung cancer, **147**, 2397–2405 (2021)
5. Yang, H., et al.: Diagnostic value of circulating genetically abnormal cells to support computed tomography for benign and malignant pulmonary nodules, **22**(1), 382 (2022)
6. Ye, M., et al.: A classifier for improving early lung cancer diagnosis incorporating artificial intelligence and liquid biopsy **12**, 677 (2022)
7. Katz, R.L., et al.: Identification of circulating tumor cells using 4-color fluorescence in situ hybridization: validation of a noninvasive aid for ruling out lung cancer in patients with low-dose computed tomography–detected lung nodules, **128**(8), 553–562 (2020)
8. Ligthart, S.T., et al.: Unbiased and automated identification of a circulating tumour cell definition that associates with overall survival, **6**(11), e27419 (2011)
9. Lannin, T.B., Thege, F.I., Kirby, B.J.J.C.P.A.: Comparison and optimization of machine learning methods for automated classification of circulating tumor cells, **89**(10), 922–931 (2016)
10. Xu, C., et al.: An efficient fluorescence in situ hybridization (FISH)-based circulating genetically abnormal cells (CACs) identification method based on Multi-scale MobileNet-YOLO-V4, **12**(5), 2961 (2022)
11. Rasmus, A., et al.: Semi-supervised learning with ladder networks, **28** (2015)

12. Tarvainen, A., Valpola, H.: Mean teachers are better role models: weight-averaged consistency targets improve semi-supervised deep learning results, **30** (2017)
13. Xu, M.-C., et al.: Bayesian pseudo labels: expectation maximization for robust and efficient semi-supervised segmentation. In: Wang, L., Dou, Q., Fletcher, P.T., Speidel, S., Li, S. (eds.) MICCAI 2022. LNCS, vol. 13435, pp. 580–590. Springer, Cham (2022). https://doi.org/10.1007/978-3-031-16443-9_56
14. Wang, S., et al.: Annotation-efficient deep learning for automatic medical image segmentation, **12**(1), 5915 (2021)
15. Liu, Y.-C., et al.: Unbiased teacher for semi-supervised object detection (2021)
16. Xu, M., et al.: End-to-end semi-supervised object detection with soft teacher. In: Proceedings of the IEEE/CVF International Conference on Computer Vision (2021)
17. Zhou, Q., et al.: Instant-teaching: an end-to-end semi-supervised object detection framework. In: Proceedings of the IEEE/CVF Conference on Computer Vision and Pattern Recognition (2021)
18. Chen, B., et al.: Label matching semi-supervised object detection. In: Proceedings of the IEEE/CVF Conference on Computer Vision and Pattern Recognition (2022)
19. Li, H., et al.: Rethinking pseudo labels for semi-supervised object detection. In: Proceedings of the AAAI Conference on Artificial Intelligence (2022)
20. Liu, Y.-C., Ma, C.-Y., Kira, Z.: Unbiased teacher v2: semi-supervised object detection for anchor-free and anchor-based detectors. In: Proceedings of the IEEE/CVF Conference on Computer Vision and Pattern Recognition (2022)
21. Sohn, K., et al.: A simple semi-supervised learning framework for object detection (2020)

Advancing Delineation of Gross Tumor Volume Based on Magnetic Resonance Imaging by Performing Source-Free Domain Adaptation in Nasopharyngeal Carcinoma

Hongqiu Wang[1], Shichen Zhang[1], Xiangde Luo[2], Wenjun Liao[3], and Lei Zhu[1(✉)]

[1] Hong Kong University of Science and Technology (Guangzhou), Guangzhou, China
leizhu@ust.hk
[2] University of Electronic Science and Technology of China, Chengdu, China
[3] West China Hospital, Sichuan University, Chengdu, China

Abstract. Nasopharyngeal carcinoma (NPC) is a common and significant malignancy that primarily affects the head and neck region. Accurate delineation of Gross Tumor Volume (GTV) is crucial for effective radiotherapy in NPC. Although Magnetic Resonance Imaging (MRI) allows precise visualization of tumor characteristics, challenges arise due to the complex anatomy of the nasopharyngeal region and GTV localization. Recently, deep learning based methods have been extensively explored in automatically segmenting various types of tumors, and promising progress has been made. However, the substantial reliance on particular medical images with adequate supervised annotations, coupled with the restricted access to clinical data in hospitals, presents significant obstacles in employing computer-aided segmentation for radiotherapy. Therefore, we propose a novel source-free domain adaptation framework that transfers knowledge of tumor segmentation learned in the source domain to the unlabeled target dataset without the access to the source dataset and annotate the target domain, for the NPC. Specifically, We enhances model performance by jointly optimizing entropy minimization and pseudo-labeling based on source rehearsal. We validated our approach on 406 patients data collected from three hospital centers and achieved an effective accuracy improvements compared to directly employing model trained on the source domain.

Keywords: Nasopharyngeal Carcinoma · Gross Tumor Volume · Magnetic Resonance Imaging · Source-Free Domain Adaptation

1 Introduction

Nasopharyngeal Carcinoma (NPC) is a prevalent malignant tumor primarily observed in Southeast Asia [2,3]. NPC is frequently situated deep within the

---

H. Wang and S. Zhang—Contributed equally to this work.

© The Author(s), under exclusive license to Springer Nature Switzerland AG 2023
W. Qin et al. (Eds.): CMMCA 2023 (MICCAI Workshop), LNCS 14243, pp. 71–81, 2023.
https://doi.org/10.1007/978-3-031-45087-7_8

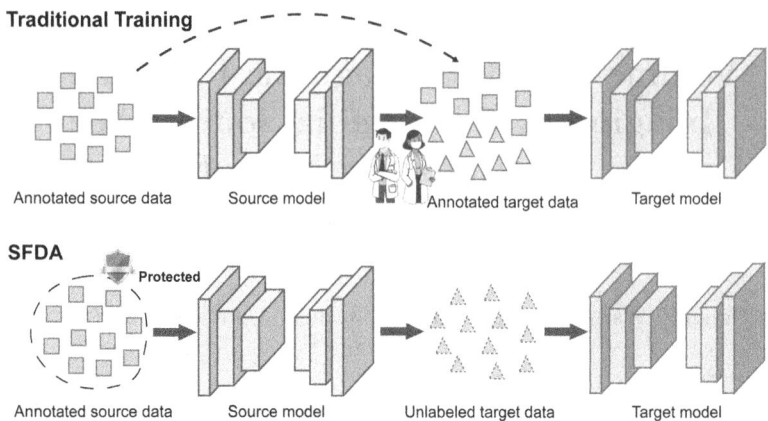

Fig. 1. Comparison of the pipeline of traditional training and our Source-Free Domain Adaptation training.

head and neck area, rendering surgical resection difficult due to its closeness to sensitive structures and tissues. Consequently, radiation therapy has evolved as a primary treatment modality for NPC [10,14]. Accurate delineation of Gross Tumor Volume (GTV) holds paramount importance in NPC radiotherapy. By leveraging Magnetic Resonance Imaging (MRI) technology, precise visualization of tumor location, dimensions, and invasive extent can be achieved, facilitating assessment of disease severity, personalized treatment planning, and disease progression monitoring [11,19]. The intricate anatomy of the nasopharyngeal region, encompassing vital structures like the carotid artery and lymph nodes, poses challenges to accurate GTV boundary delineation [13,22,25]. At present, most GTV delineation is carried out through manual means. However, manual delineation for NPC can be exhausting, prone to errors, and also susceptible to significant inter-observer differences [16]. Imprecise GTV segmentation has implications for increased recurrence risk, necessitating additional therapeutic interventions to gain control over disease progression [1]. Consequently, the significance of meticulous GTV delineation in the diagnosis and management of NPC is worthy of attention [27].

With the latest progressions, deep learning techniques have led to the development of successful auto-delineation models for medical tasks, particularly those utilizing convolutional neural networks (CNNs). The utilization of these models has resulted in highly promising segmentation outcomes for various cancers, including liver tumors [17], cervical cancer [21], NPC [15] and others [9]. Moreover, MRI is the preferred imaging modality for the diagnosis and treatment of nasopharyngeal carcinoma (NPC) due to its excellent soft tissue contrast [12]. Therefore, numerous segmentation protocols and experiments have been performed based on the MRI [18].

Despite advances in segmentation methods and data availability for GTV delineation research in NPC, several challenges still impede the clinical application of deep learning for GTV segmentation. First, GTV segmentation tasks typically necessitate a significant amount of well-annotated MRI training samples for training a deep learning model in fully supervised manner. Nonetheless, the process of manual annotation demands considerable effort and consumes a substantial amount of time. Second, the majority of deep models are specifically tailored to a particular training set and cannot be generalized across data from other source. However, in MRI-based GTV segmentation, different medical centers may employ equipment from various vendors, and the resolution or slice thickness of the imaging and the styles of the radiation oncologists' delineation outline may vary. Third, clinical settings frequently encompass hospitals and medical centers with distinct information systems and stringent data privacy requirements, hindering data sharing. However, most transfer learning and domain adaptation algorithms currently necessitate access to both source and target domain annotated data [24,26], as shown in Fig. 1, posing a challenge in practical implementation.

Considering the aforementioned challenges, this paper introduces a streamlined and efficient Source-Free Domain Adaptation (SFDA) framework for cross-domain segmentation of GTV based on MRI across various medical institutions. As illustrated in the second column in Fig. 1, the proposed SFDA approach effectively protects the privacy of the data from the source centre, while eliminating the need for manual annotation by radiation oncologists on the data from the target centre.

Main contributions of this study are summarized as follows:

- To the best of our knowledge, we take the first step to explore on an essential application, SFDA for GTV delineation based on MRI images for NPC.
- We propose a novel framework for domain adaptation that simultaneously optimizes the model in terms of entropy minimization and pseudo-label based on source rehearsal to improve performance.
- We elaborately collected original MRI images of patients with nasopharyngeal carcinoma from three different medical centers (406 patients) and their corresponding GTV mask annotations to conduct the experiment.
- Experimental results on collected MRI datasets show that our network clearly outperforms directly employing the original trained models. Even compared with other state-of-the-art method, our method still demonstrates effective and superior performance.

2 Methodology

2.1 Study Design and Participants

MRI datasets, accompanied by annotated labels, were procured from three eminent medical establishments, with a specific focus on patients diagnosed with nasopharyngeal carcinoma (NPC). The MRI images were obtained using 3.0-T scanners, where the median thickness for the entire cohort measured 1.10 mm (range, 1.00–1.25 mm), and the median in-plane voxel size was 1.36 mm (range,

Table 1. The volume and vendors of data collected from different medical centers.

Data source	Number of patients	Vendors
Sichuan Cancer Hospital (SCH)	52 cases	Siemens
Anhui Provincial Hospital (APH)	146 cases	GE, Siemens, Philips
Sichuan Provincial People's Hospital (SPH)	208 cases	Siemens

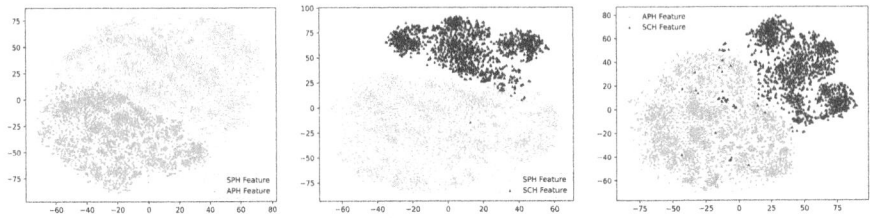

Fig. 2. Visualization (t-SNE [7]) of the multiple medical centers distribution distortion. The green dot and the blue star and purple triangle represent the latent representation of SPH and APH and SCH respectively. The distributions across different medical center domains vary significantly.

0.47–1.67 mm). Stringent selection criteria were imposed, which included histological confirmation of NPC and prior MRI evaluations of the nasopharynx and neck before initiating anticancer treatments. The assembled MRI sets comprised contrast-enhanced T1-weighted sequences, alongside unenhanced T1- and T2-weighted sequences, ensuring a thorough imaging spectrum.

A total of 406 patients' MRI images were diligently chosen, the specific data distribution and vendors shown in Table 1. To guarantee impartial assessment, each dataset was randomly divided into three distinct subsets (train:valid:test) utilizing a 7:1:2 ratio. In our setting, 70% of the data from each hospital centre is allocated to the training of the model and the tuning of the model parameters. The model with the best performance on the validation set is selected and its results on the test set are reported. Models trained in different centers will deliberately avoid using the labels of the training set from other datasets when transferring to other data centers, while preserving the privacy and confidentiality of the original patient data. As illustrated by the t-SNE [7] visualization in Fig. 2, the distributions of the different medical centre domains exhibit significant discrepancies with only a little overlap. Our objective was to surmount potential domain shift obstacles and generate precise GTV delineations for patients within the constructed test set.

2.2   Proposed Methodology

Figure 3 demonstrates the schematic illustration of our SFDA framework. The input for the whole framework include the source NPC patients' MRI images I^s: $\Omega_s \subset \mathcal{R}^2 \to \mathcal{R}$, the corresponding manual label Y^s for each pixel $i \in \Omega_s$,

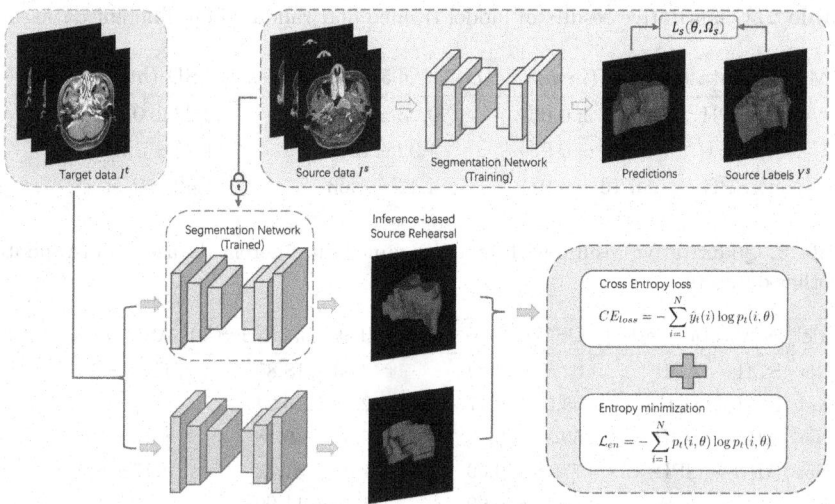

Fig. 3. The proposed framework consists of two training procedures: one for the source data (blue box) and the other for domain adaptation (green box). Initially, the model is trained on the source domain. Then, a fixed model with Inference-based Source Rehearsal is applied. Finally, the model is fine-tuned in the target domain using the loss function $Loss_{total}$ in the green box. (Color figure online)

$y_s(i) \in \{0, 1\}$, and the unlabeled target MRI images I^t. In the SFDA setting, the typical approach is firstly to train the segmentation network on source images I^s with corresponding ground truth labels Y^s in a fully supervised manner by minimizing the loss function with respect to network parameters θ as follows:

$$L_s(\theta, \Omega_s) = \frac{1}{|\Omega_s|} \sum_{i=1}^{S} \psi(y_s(i), p_s(i, \theta)), \tag{1}$$

where $p_s(i, \theta) \in [0, 1]$ represents the softmax output of the segmentation network at pixel i in the source image I^s. The loss function ψ we employed here, is a composite loss function defined as:

$$\psi(y_s(i), p_s(i, \theta)) = -\sum_{i=1}^{N} y_s(i) \log p_s(i, \theta) + 1 - \frac{2\sum_{i=1}^{N} y_s(i)\hat{y}_s(i)}{\sum_{i=1}^{N} y_s(i)^2 + \sum_{i=1}^{N} \hat{y}_s(i)^2}, \tag{2}$$

where $\hat{y}_s(i)$ represent the $i_t h$ element of the predicted labels, and N represents the total number of elements.

Once the model has been trained on the source domain, it can be transferred to the data domain of the target center I^t. Models that are trained on source domain data often produce very confident predictions for in-sample examples, but the uncertainty remains high for unseen data domains. Therefore, enforcing high confidence in the target domain can help to narrow the performance gap, which also implies entropy minimization. Accordingly, the first loss term in our

Table 2. Quantitative results of model trained and validated on different datasets

Model	Dataset	DSC (*mean ± SD*)	HD95 (*mean ± SD*)	ASD (*mean ± SD*)
U-Net	SCH	72.19 ± 0.06	9.25 ± 3.52	2.22 ± 0.86
U-Net	APH	86.79 ± 0.05	4.92 ± 3.35	1.13 ± 1.03
U-Net	SPH	80.16 ± 0.08	4.42 ± 1.63	1.42 ± 0.71

Table 3. Quantitative results with models trained on different datasets and validated on other datasets.

Model	Adaptation setting	DSC (*mean ± SD*)	HD95 (*mean ± SD*)	ASD (*mean ± SD*)
U-Net	SCH → APH	62.89 ± 0.22	43.03 ± 18.86	12.34 ± 7.05
U-Net	SCH → SPH	55.69 ± 0.17	42.89 ± 15.84	15.38 ± 7.86
U-Net	APH → SCH	59.12 ± 0.09	44.30 ± 19.18	8.37 ± 7.03
U-Net	APH → SPH	77.48 ± 0.09	17.92 ± 31.33	5.57 ± 8.05
U-Net	SPH → SCH	59.11 ± 0.09	31.35 ± 11.99	3.13 ± 1.73
U-Net	SPH → APH	78.25 ± 0.09	9.13 ± 8.49	2.68 ± 2.95

adaptation phase is designed to promote high confidence ($p_t(i, \theta) \in [0, 1]$) in the softmax prediction of the target domain samples. To achieve this, we minimize the entropy of each prediction for the target domain samples as follows:

$$\mathcal{L}_{en} = -\sum_{i=1}^{N} p_t(i, \theta) \log p_t(i, \theta) \tag{3}$$

However, it is worth noting that minimizing the entropy loss alone may not be sufficient to achieve optimal results. In fact, it has been shown in the literature on semi-supervised and unsupervised learning [5,8] that this approach can lead to performance degeneration, which may bias the prediction towards a single dominant class. Therefore, additional measures must be taken to ensure that the model is able to capture the true underlying distribution of the target domain data. Inspired by the rehearsal strategy in continuous learning [6,23], we plan to implement Inference-based Source Rehearsal on the target domain data by exploiting the prior knowledge of source domain segmentation, as shown in Fig. 3 to introduce additional computational evaluation to the network. This introduced Inference-based Source Rehearsal can be considered as a pseudo-label $\hat{y}_t(i)$ for the training of the target data domain from another perspective, and we adopt cross-entropy (CE) loss for the training of the network based on this pseudo-label, thus incorporating an additional constraint. To summarize, our loss function in the model adaptation phase consists of two components: the entropy minimization function $\mathcal{L}_{en}$ and the CE loss calculated based on the rehearsal pseudo-label, detail as:

$$Loss_{total} = \mathcal{L}_{en} - \sum_{i=1}^{N} \hat{y}_t(i) \log p_t(i, \theta), \tag{4}$$

where $\hat{y}_t(i)$ represents the pseudo-label from Inference-based Source Rehearsal.

Table 4. Quantitative results with models adapted on other datasets by utilizing SFDA methods. EM denotes entropy minimization, PL-CE represents the CE loss calculated with pseudo-label based on Inference-based Source Rehearsal.

Adaptation methods	Adaptation setting	Model	DSC (*mean* ± *SD*)	HD95 (*mean* ± *SD*)	ASD (*mean* ± *SD*)
–	SPH → SCH	U-Net	59.11 ± 0.09	31.35 ± 11.99	3.13 ± 1.73
–	SPH → APH	U-Net	78.25 ± 0.09	9.13 ± 8.49	2.68 ± 2.95
UncertainDA [4]	SPH → SCH	U-Net	60.43 ± 0.10	32.11 ± 11.96	2.66 ± 2.41
EM	SPH → SCH	U-Net	60.21 ± 0.08	31.06 ± 11.12	2.99 ± 2.28
EM+PL-CE (Ours)	SPH → SCH	U-Net	**61.09** ± 0.09	**30.87** ± 13.07	**2.57** ± 2.37
Improve	SPH → SCH	U-Net	↑ 1.98	↓ 0.48	↓ 0.56
UncertainDA [4]	SPH → APH	U-Net	80.09 ± 0.09	6.73 ± 6.95	1.79 ± 1.59
EM	SPH → APH	U-Net	78.13 ± 0.13	7.14 ± 7.32	1.81 ± 1.62
EM+PL-CE (Ours)	SPH → APH	U-Net	**81.91** ± 0.08	**6.66** ± 5.51	**1.78** ± 1.83
Improve	SPH → APH	U-Net	↑ 3.66	↓ 2.47	↓ 0.90

3 Experiments and Results

Evaluation Metrics. We adopted three commonly used metrics to evaluate the quality of the segmentation results produced by the deep learning model for GTV. These metrics are the Dice similarity coefficient (DSC), the 95% Hausdorff distance (HD95), and the average surface distance (ASD). The DSC is a pixel-wise metric that quantifies the degree of overlap between the network's predictions and the ground truth. On the other hand, the HD95 and ASD are distance-based metrics that specifically focus on measuring the distance between the predicted boundary and the ground truth boundary. In general, a better method should have a larger score on the DSC indicator and a smaller value on HD95 and ASD.

Implementation Details. All experiments were carried out using PyTorch and were trained on an NVIDIA GeForce RTX 3090 GPU with 24 GB of memory. To ensure consistency during training, all MRI images were resized to a uniform resolution of 256×256. The Segmentation networks are unified applying the classic U-net [20]. In addition, to increase the diversity of the training data and improve the robustness of the model, 50% of the images were randomly selected to be subjected to a rotation and flip operation, a random rotation operation, and an add noise operation, respectively. These random transform operations increase the diversity of the data and thus improve the generalisation ability of the model. All models were trained with 20000 iterations and a batch size of 32. The initial learning rate is 0.03 and after iteration the learning rate decays exponentially by 0.9. This allows the model to be more stable in the later stages of training.

Analysis of Experimental Results

Table 2 presents the results obtained from testing the models after training on their respective datasets, showing variable results due to different data volumes

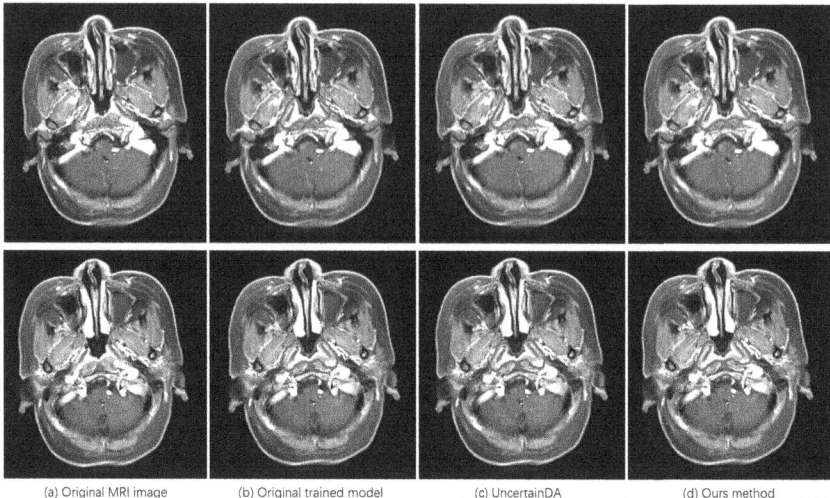

(a) Original MRI image   (b) Original trained model   (c) UncertainDA   (d) Ours method

Fig. 4. Visual comparisons of (b) directly employing originally trained model and (c) UncertainDA [4] and (d) Our method. The green contours represent the ground truth, while the red contours represent the network predictions. The contours of the delineation are significantly closer to ground truth after applying our method, compared with others.

and device vendors and patients conditions, with dice of 72.19%, 86.79% and 80.16% respectively. Table 3 demonstrates the results of directly applying the models trained on different data centers to other data domains. The results demonstrate a significant drop in performance across all models, indicating that the domain gap has a substantial impact on the model's performance. In particular, it can be found that the model performs poorly when transferring from smaller data centre to larger data centre, e.g. 62.89% and 55.69% for dice when SCH to APH and SCH. One possible explanation for this drop in performance is that small data centers may only provide a limited representation of the GTV features of NPC patients. As a result, the knowledge learned from small data centers may not be sufficient to support the model in handling more complex situations with larger data. With this in mind, we perform domain adaptation from large to small datasets, which results in better segmentation results in practice.

Table 4 presents a comparison of our proposed method with other methods, as well as an ablation experiment of our method. The results demonstrate that our method clearly outperforms the direct application of the model, with the exact improvement values listed in the "Improve" row. Furthermore, ablation experiments (EM v.s. EM+PL-CE) have proven the effectiveness of our proposed methods, demonstrating a consistent performance improvement. Our method also demonstrates superior performance when compared to other state-of-the-art method, the UncertainDA [4]. Figure 4 displays a comparison of the visualisation results of our segmentation.

4   Conclusion

In this paper, we investigated the application of SFDA to MRI-based GTV segmentation of NPC and collected MRI image data from a total of 406 patients at three different medical centers for the study. To improve the model's performance in handling data from unseen domains. We propose a novel framework for domain adaptation that optimizes the model in terms of both entropy minimization and pseudo-label based on source rehearsal to boost the accuracy of delineation. The experimental results demonstrate the effectiveness of our method. In the future, we plan to collect multimodal MRI medical images to develop a multimodal domain adaptation method and also consider exploring Clinical Target Volume (CTV) delineation.

References

1. Chen, S., et al.: Failure patterns of recurrence and metastasis after intensity-modulated radiotherapy in patients with nasopharyngeal carcinoma: results of a Multicentric clinical study. Front. Oncol. **11**, 5730 (2022)
2. Chen, Y.P., Chan, A.T., Le, Q.T., Blanchard, P., Sun, Y., Ma, J.: Nasopharyngeal carcinoma. The Lancet **394**(10192), 64–80 (2019)
3. Chua, M.L., Wee, J.T., Hui, E.P., Chan, A.T.: Nasopharyngeal carcinoma. The Lancet **387**(10022), 1012–1024 (2016)
4. Fleuret, F., et al.: Uncertainty reduction for model adaptation in semantic segmentation. In: Proceedings of the IEEE/CVF Conference on Computer Vision and Pattern Recognition, pp. 9613–9623 (2021)
5. Grandvalet, Y., Bengio, Y.: Semi-supervised learning by entropy minimization. In: Advances in Neural Information Processing Systems, vol. 17 (2004)
6. Hadsell, R., Rao, D., Rusu, A.A., Pascanu, R.: Embracing change: continual learning in deep neural networks. Trends Cogn. Sci. **24**(12), 1028–1040 (2020)
7. Hinton, G.E., Roweis, S.: Stochastic neighbor embedding. In: Advances in Neural Information Processing Systems, vol. 15 (2002)
8. Jabi, M., Pedersoli, M., Mitiche, A., Ayed, I.B.: Deep clustering: on the link between discriminative models and k-means. IEEE Trans. Pattern Anal. Mach. Intell. **43**(6), 1887–1896 (2019)
9. Jin, D., et al.: DeepTarget: gross tumor and clinical target volume segmentation in esophageal cancer radiotherapy. Med. Image Anal. **68**, 101909 (2021)
10. Kam, M.K., et al.: Treatment of nasopharyngeal carcinoma with intensity-modulated radiotherapy: the Hong Kong experience. Int. J. Radiat. Oncol. Biol. Phys. **60**(5), 1440–1450 (2004)
11. King, A., et al.: Magnetic resonance imaging for the detection of nasopharyngeal carcinoma. Am. J. Neuroradiol. **27**(6), 1288–1291 (2006)
12. King, A.D.: MR imaging of nasopharyngeal carcinoma. Magn. Reson. Imaging Clin. N. Am. **30**(1), 19–33 (2022)
13. Lee, A.W., et al.: Evolution of treatment for nasopharyngeal cancer-success and setback in the intensity-modulated radiotherapy era. Radiother. Oncol. **110**(3), 377–384 (2014)
14. Lee, N., et al.: Intensity-modulated radiotherapy in the treatment of nasopharyngeal carcinoma: an update of the UCSF experience. Int. J. Radiat. Oncol. Biol. Phys. **53**(1), 12–22 (2002)

15. Liao, W., et al.: Automatic delineation of gross tumor volume based on magnetic resonance imaging by performing a novel semisupervised learning framework in nasopharyngeal carcinoma. Int. J. Radiat. Oncol. Biol. Phys. **113**(4), 893–902 (2022)
16. Lin, L., et al.: Deep learning for automated contouring of primary tumor volumes by MRI for nasopharyngeal carcinoma. Radiology **291**(3), 677–686 (2019)
17. Liu, T., et al.: Spatial feature fusion convolutional network for liver and liver tumor segmentation from CT images. Med. Phys. **48**(1), 264–272 (2021)
18. Luo, X., et al.: Deep learning-based accurate delineation of primary gross tumor volume of nasopharyngeal carcinoma on heterogeneous magnetic resonance imaging: a large-scale and multi-center study. Radiother. Oncol. **180**, 109480 (2023)
19. Razek, A.A.K.A., King, A.: MRI and CT of nasopharyngeal carcinoma. Am. J. Roentgenol. **198**(1), 11–18 (2012)
20. Ronneberger, O., Fischer, P., Brox, T.: U-Net: convolutional networks for biomedical image segmentation. In: Navab, N., Hornegger, J., Wells, W., Frangi, A. (eds.) Medical Image Computing and Computer-Assisted Intervention – MICCAI 2015. MICCAI 2015. Lecture Notes in Computer Science, vol. 9351 pp. 234–241. Springer, Cham (2015). https://doi.org/10.1007/978-3-319-24574-4_28
21. Tian, M., et al.: Delineation of clinical target volume and organs at risk in cervical cancer radiotherapy by deep learning networks. Med. Phys. (2023)
22. Tian, Y.M., et al.: Long-term outcome and pattern of failure for patients with nasopharyngeal carcinoma treated with intensity-modulated radiotherapy. Head Neck **41**(5), 1246–1252 (2019)
23. Verwimp, E., De Lange, M., Tuytelaars, T.: Rehearsal revealed: the limits and merits of revisiting samples in continual learning. In: Proceedings of the IEEE/CVF International Conference on Computer Vision, pp. 9385–9394 (2021)
24. Wang, D., Shelhamer, E., Liu, S., Olshausen, B., Darrell, T.: Tent: fully test-time adaptation by entropy minimization. arXiv preprint arXiv:2006.10726 (2020)
25. Wang, T.J., Riaz, N., Cheng, S.K., Lu, J.J., Lee, N.Y.: Intensity-modulated radiation therapy for nasopharyngeal carcinoma: a review. J. Radiat. Oncol. **1**, 129–146 (2012)
26. Weiss, K., Khoshgoftaar, T.M., Wang, D.: A survey of transfer learning. J. Big data **3**(1), 1–40 (2016)
27. Yang, X., et al.: Analysis of clinical target volume delineation in local-regional failure of nasopharyngeal carcinoma after intensity-modulated radiotherapy. J. Cancer **11**(7), 1968 (2020)

BM-SMIL: A Breast Cancer Molecular Subtype Prediction Framework from H&E Slides with Self-supervised Pretraining and Multi-instance Learning

Zihao Shang[1,3], Hong Liu[1(✉)], Kuansong Wang[2], and Xiangdong Wang[1]

[1] Beijing Key Laboratory of Mobile Computing and Pervasive Device, Institute of Computing Technology, Chinese Academy of Sciences, Beijing 100190, China
`hliu@ict.ac.cn`

[2] Department of Pathology, Xiangya Hospital, Central South University, Changsha 410008, Hunan, People's Republic of China

[3] University of Chinese Academy of Sciences, Beijing 100086, China

Abstract. Breast cancer is the most commonly diagnosed cancer, and accurate molecular subtype prediction plays a crucial role in determining treatment strategies. While immunohistochemistry (IHC) is commonly used for molecular subtype diagnosis, it suffers from cost and labor limitations. The prediction of molecular subtypes using hematoxylin and eosin (H&E) stained slides has gained importance. However, the task is challenged by limited samples, weak annotations, and strong tumor heterogeneity. This paper proposes a scalable framework, BM-SMIL, for molecular subtype prediction of breast cancer based on self-supervised pretraining and multi-instance learning. Firstly, a self-supervised pretraining framework utilizing multi-scale knowledge distillation is introduced to obtain a representative patch encoder. Then, an attention-based instance selection strategy is employed to filter out noise instances. Finally, a Transformer integrated with subtype contrastive loss is proposed for effective aggregation and WSI-level prediction. Experimental results on the dataset from cooperative hospital demonstrate the effectiveness of our proposed framework. The BM-SMIL framework has the potential to enhance molecular subtype prediction performance and can be extended to other pathology image classification tasks.

Keywords: Molecular Subtype · H&E Slides · Self-supervised Pretraining · MIL

1 Introduction

Breast cancer has the highest global incidence rate among all cancers, bringing a significant health risk. According to molecular expressions of certain genes, breast cancer can be classified into four molecular subtypes including Luminal A, Luminal B, HER-2, and Basal-like [1]. In clinic, molecular subtype diagnosis usually comes from immunohistochemistry (IHC) [2] and diagnosed subtypes basically determine corresponding

© The Author(s), under exclusive license to Springer Nature Switzerland AG 2023
W. Qin et al. (Eds.): CMMCA 2023 (MICCAI Workshop), LNCS 14243, pp. 81–90, 2023.
https://doi.org/10.1007/978-3-031-45087-7_9

treatment strategies. However, for cost and labor savings, pathologists usually randomly select one paraffin block of a patient's tumor for IHC evaluation. Due to the heterogeneity of tumor tissue, this procedure may carry a misdiagnosis risk. The H&E-stained slides are easier and inexpensive to obtain, and an AI model that can predict molecular subtypes using H&E slides can assist pathologists in selecting proper paraffin blocks for IHC evaluation. Therefore, molecular subtype prediction based on H&E pathology slides has crucial clinical significance.

Pathologists can only diagnose molecular subtype from IHC slides, and molecular subtype prediction specifically from H&E slides is a challenging task with insufficient studies and limited performance. Rawat et al. [3] proposed deep tissue fingerprints to predict the expression status of ER, PR, and HER2 molecular markers by learning distinctive features from H&E images. Jaber et al. [4] introduced a molecular subtype classifier based on H&E slides and analyzed tumor heterogeneity within slides. Liu et al. [5] focused on the selection of discriminative patches, filtering out noisy patches through co-teaching [6] and LOF [7].

Whole Slide Images (WSIs) usually contain a huge number of pixels, causing difficult acquisition and annotation, which has led to increasing interest in leveraging self-supervised methods on unlabeled data. In the field of natural images, contrastive self-supervised learning [8, 9], distillation-based learning [10, 11], and generative learning [12, 13] have achieved remarkable performance in downstream tasks and have gradually been applied to pathology images. Li et al. [14] first utilized SimCLR contrastive learning for patch-level representation learning. Li et al. proposed SSLP [15], which defines negative pairs of spatial proximity as positive pairs. Wang et al. [16] continuously perform top-k sorting to discover similar patches as positive pairs. However, self-supervised learning in computational pathology has mainly adopted contrastive learning, lacking effective strategies specifically designed for pathology images.

Gigapixel pathology images need to be divided into many patches for processing, yet usually have only WSI-level labels. Multiple-instance learning (MIL) is usually utilized for this weakly supervised task, where each WSI is defined as a bag, and each patch within a WSI is considered an instance. Instance-level algorithms [17, 18] train an encoder by assigning patches bag labels, then select top patches for WSI-level aggregation. Embedding-level prediction algorithms [19, 20] map patches to feature vectors in an embedding space and aggregate WSI-level features using operators such as max-pooling. Ilse et al. [21] proposed attention-based MIL (ABMIL), where attention score of each instance represents its contribution to the bag embedding. Shao et al. [22] first applied Transformers to MIL in pathology slides and fused the morphological and 2D spatial information of patches. Due to tumor heterogeneity, many patches in H&E WSIs are unrelated to molecular pathology characteristics and are considered noise patches, which could hamper classification performance in aggregation.

To address the challenges of limited samples, weak annotations, and strong tumor heterogeneity, we propose a general and scalable framework, BM-SMIL, for breast cancer molecular subtype prediction based on self-supervised learning and multi-instance learning, which is also applicable to other pathology image classification task. The main contributions of this paper are as follows. (1) We propose a self-supervised pretraining framework based on multi-scale knowledge distillation to obtain a representative patch feature encoder. (2) We adopt an instance selection strategy based on attention mechanism to filter noise instances. (3) We present a multi-instance learning method based on Transformer and subtype discrimination to achieve effective WSI-level molecular subtype prediction. Experimental results verify the effectiveness of our proposed BM-SMIL framework on the dataset from the cooperative hospital.

2 Proposed Method

The proposed molecular subtype prediction framework, BM-SMIL, is depicted in Fig. 1. The framework encompasses two steps: feature encoding of patches and feature aggregation for WSI prediction. Firstly, a multi-scale knowledge distillation self-supervised paradigm is implemented to train a patch feature encoder on unlabeled patches cropped from WSIs. Considering many patches (instances) within a WSI (bag) contain no characteristics related to molecular subtype, an instance selection method based on attention mechanism is then adopted to filter patches by thresholding. Lastly, a Transformer-based multi-instance learning method that integrates subtype contrastive loss is utilized to fully explore the correlation among instances and emphasize subtype discrimination. During inference stage, the trained feature encoder is used to extract features of patches from WSIs. Then the features from each WSI are fed into a trained Transformer aggregator to obtain WSI-level molecular subtype prediction.

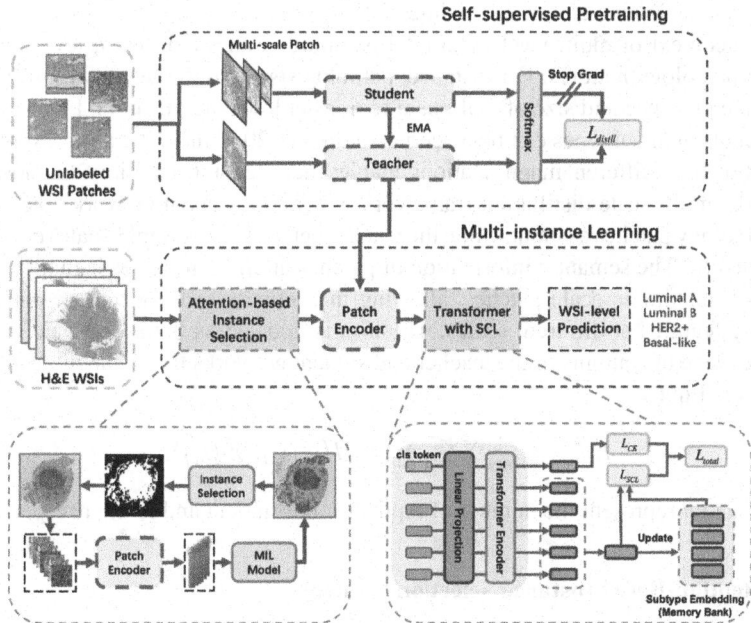

Fig. 1. The framework of proposed BM-SMIL

2.1 Self-supervised Pretraining Based on Multi-scale Distillation

We adopted a knowledge distillation-based framework for pretraining to obtain an effective patch encoder. The student and teacher networks have identical model structures but do not share weights. Let θ_s represent the parameters of the student S, and θ_t represent the parameters of the teacher T. For an input patch x, two augmented views x_1 and x_2 are obtained through random data augmentations, which are fed into student and teacher networks, respectively. The outputs of the student and teacher networks are probability distributions of K dimensions, denoted as $p^s(x_1)$ and $p^s(x_1)$, which are obtained by softmax with temperature, as shown in Eq. (1) and Eq. (2):

$$p^s(x_1) = softmax\left(\frac{S(x_1)}{\tau_s}\right), \tag{1}$$

$$p^T(x_2) = softmax\left(\frac{T(x_2)}{\tau_t}\right). \tag{2}$$

The cross-entropy loss is then calculated between the student and teacher distributions. By minimizing this loss, the student network is guided to produce similar output distributions as the teacher, thus learning augmentation-invariant representation. We swap the inputs of teacher and student to achieve robust representation learning.

To avoid collapse and smooth convergence [10], a momentum encoder is used as the teacher network, the parameters of which are updated by exponential moving average (EMA) instead of backpropagation. The update rule is $\theta_t = m\theta_t + (1 - m)\theta_S$, with coefficient m following a cosine schedule.

In the context of multi-level pyramidal pathology images, different levels contain different pathology features. For instance, pathologists can observe global information such as the presence and size of malignant regions at low magnification. Finer features such as molecular subtypes can be discerned at higher $20 \times$ magnification. Combining information from different magnifications enables more accurate auxiliary diagnosis. We proposed a multi-scale distillation framework, where the student network takes multi-scale pathology patches as input, while the teacher network takes single-scale (maximum scale) patches. The semantic information of patches at different scales is matched with that of the maximum-scale patches, allowing the network to learn representations of pathology features at different scales. The loss is updated as the average of pairwise losses between the outputs of the teacher and student networks for all the input patches, as shown in Eq. (3):

$$L_{distill} = \frac{1}{mn} \sum_{i=1}^{m} \sum_{j=1}^{n} H\left(p^s(x_i), p^T(x_j)\right), \tag{3}$$

where m and n represent the number of inputs for the student and teacher respectively.

2.2 Attention-Based Instance Selection Strategy

Many patches within the pathology tissue regions fail to indicate molecular-related characteristics, leading to a considerable number of noise patches that may hamper the performance of the model. Current methods in multiple instance learning, such as ABMIL [21], CLAM [23], and DSMIL [14], have introduced attention mechanism to learn the correlations among patches and their contributions to WSI-level prediction. We suppose that the learned attention weights can be utilized to filter out noise patches and select the most discriminative instances for bag-level aggregation.

We propose an attention-based instance selection strategy. In the first iteration, the attention scores and WSI predictions are obtained from the initial model and the attention scores for each patch are normalized to 0–100 and sorted in descending order. Then, a threshold is set for instance selection. For example, when the threshold is set to 20, patches with attention scores greater than 20 are selected, leading to approximately 20% of noise patches filtered out. Finally, the selected patches are used as new training set for the second iteration. Additionally, the selection is not performed for WSIs that were predicted incorrectly in the previous iteration to avoid erroneous filtering.

2.3 Multi-instance Learning Based on Transformer and Subtype Discrimination

TransMIL [22] was the first work to apply Transformer to MIL in pathology images, which assumed that all instances within a bag are related. We leverage the sequence of features extracted from all patches within a WSI as the input to the Transformer encoder. A class token is added to the sequence to aggregate the information from all patches, and its output is considered a bag-level feature, which is fed into an MLP for classification and WSI-level predictions.

In the context of breast cancer molecular subtype, the inter-subtype differences are not prominent while substantial intra-subtype variants exist in H&E slides. Additionally, our dataset suffers from class imbalance issue. Yu et al. [24] introduced a MIL head module to aggregate information from the outputs of other tokens (except class token), demonstrating that their information can benefit classification task. Inspired by this work, we generate new bag embeddings by pooling outputs of other tokens and obtain subtype embeddings by cumulatively combining bag embeddings. We employ a subtype contrastive loss to repel embeddings of different subtypes, encouraging the model to focus on capturing the discriminative characteristics of each subtype.

We introduce a memory bank to store subtype embeddings. When a new bag embedding is generated, it is used to update the corresponding subtype embedding in an EMA manner. If memory bank does not contain embedding for current subtype, the bag embedding is stored as subtype embedding; otherwise, triple loss [25] is calculated among subtype embeddings and current bag embedding. Using $d(e_1, e_2)$ to denote the distance between embeddings, the subtype contrastive loss (SCL) is defined in Eq. (4):

$$L_{SCL} = \sum_{i=1}^{3} \max(d(a, p) - d(a, n_i) + margin, 0), \quad (4)$$

where a (anchor) represents current bag embedding, p (positive) represents subtype embeddings of the same subtype of a, and n_i represents embeddings of other subtypes. Total loss is the weighted sum of L_{CE} from class token and L_{SCL}, as shown in Eq. (5):

$$L_{total} = L_{CE} + \lambda L_{SCL}. \quad (5)$$

3 Experiment and Results

Dataset: We utilize two breast cancer pathology image datasets. The molecular dataset is from the cooperative hospital, consisting of 912 breast cancer pathology slides with WSI-level molecular subtype annotations (364 Luminal A, 217 Luminal B, 182 HER-2, 149 Basal-like). The slides are stored in a pyramid structure, including four magnification levels: $5 \times$, $10 \times$, $20 \times$ and $40 \times$. The other dataset is Camelyon16 dataset from ICPR, which contains 399 breast cancer WSI slides with multiple magnifications and regional annotations of lymph node metastasis. We only used WSI-level labels in downstream molecular subtype prediction and ignored the labels in pretraining.

The patch extraction is performed using a sliding window strategy with a step size of 256, resulting in non-overlapping 256×256 patches. The Otsu [26] is used for tissue segmentation to remove non-tissue regions from each pathology slide. All WSIs from two datasets are split into patches at $20 \times$ magnification, and all the obtained patches are utilized for self-supervised pretraining. The molecular dataset is divided using 5-fold cross validation, with a training-validation ratio of 8:2. The statistics of the molecular dataset are shown in Table 1.

Table 1. Statistics of data partitioning and sample number of each subtype

Partition\Subtype	Luminal A	Luminal B	Her-2	Basal-like	Total
Train	291	173	145	120	729
Test	73	43	37	29	183
Total	364	217	182	149	912

Metrics: The precision (PR), sensitivity (SE), specificity (SP), accuracy (ACC), and area under curve (AUC) at WSI-level are used as evaluation metrics to compare the performance of different methods. The experimental results are the average value across five validation sets in cross validation.

Experimental Settings: Three experiments were conducted to verify the effectiveness of the proposed method. (1) The self-supervised pretraining paradigm based on multi-level knowledge distillation was compared with ResNet50 pretrained on ImageNet and DINO [10]. (2) The attention-based instance selection strategy was verified with different thresholds. (3) The Transformer aggregator with subtype contrastive loss of different coefficients was implemented in comparison to CLAM [23].

In self-supervised pretraining, both DINO and Multiscale (Ours) adopt ViT-S/16 as the feature extractor with AdamW [27] as optimizer. The initial learning rate is set to 0.0005 when the total batch size is 256, and it scales linearly with the batch size. The initial weight decay is set to 0.04. Both the learning rate and weight decay are adjusted using a cosine scheduler. We use four NVIDIA GeForce 2080Ti GPUs, where each bears a batch size of 32, resulting in a total batch size of 128. In DINO paradigm, teacher network takes 256×256 patches and student network takes 96×96 patches.

While in Multiscale paradigm, the input patches for student network are of 3 scales: 256 × 256, 128 × 128, and 64 × 64.

Experimental Results of Proposed Pretraining Method: In Table 2, ImageNet represents adopting resnet50 pretrained on ImageNet as patch encoder; SimCLR and DINO represent using patch encoder pretrained on our breast cancer dataset by SimCLR and DINO paradigm respectively. The patch encoder obtained through SimCLR pretraining shows significant improvements in all metrics compared to the ResNet50 pretrained on ImageNet, which demonstrates that pretraining on pathology images can learn morphological features relevant to pathology, bridging the domain gap between natural images and pathology images. In comparison to SimCLR, the DINO paradigm exhibits noticeable improvements, which indicates the advantage of negative-free distillation framework and its suitability for pathology images. Our proposed multiscale distillation framework outperforms (SE: 4.0%, SP: 1.3%, ACC: 3.4%, AUC: 1.7%) DINO in five metrics of both models, showing the representation capability of the encoder is further enhanced by learning features at multiple scales.

Table 2. Results of molecular subtype prediction by proposed pretraining method (20 ×, %)

Model	Pretraining	PR	SE	SP	ACC	AUC
ABMIL	ImageNet	32.23	32.97	78.00	41.76	61.20
	SimCLR	41.07	38.84	79.95	45.82	67.29
	DINO	55.04	54.13	85.09	57.02	76.93
	Ours	**56.16**	**65.33**	**85.76**	**58.35**	**80.96**
CLAM	ImageNet	40.70	40.77	81.01	46.81	72.64
	SimCLR	45.93	46.93	82.39	49.01	74.81
	DINO	58.62	57.34	85.92	59.12	83.26
	Ours	**61.95**	**61.34**	**87.21**	**62.53**	**84.91**

Experimental Results of Instance Selection Strategy: Table 3 shows the performance of molecular subtype prediction using CLAM with different instance selection thresholds. When the threshold value is small, increasing the threshold leads to the removal of more noise instances, resulting in performance improvements. However, with a larger threshold exceeding 30, the metrics suffer a gradual decline with the number of training samples decreasing. With a threshold value of 20, which filters out approximately 20% noise patches, the five metrics show an improvement of about 4%, 3%, 1.5%, 1%, and 4%, respectively, compared to no selection, which validates the effectiveness of the proposed instance selection strategy.

Experimental Results of Proposed MIL Method: We compared the performance of three MIL methods (CLAM, Trans and our proposed Transformer with SCL) at two magnifications (10×, 20×) in Table 4. At 20×, Trans exhibits a 1% increase in AUC compared to CLAM-SB, along with slight improvements in other metrics. While at

10 × resolution, Trans achieves respective improvements of 2%, 3%, 1%, 2%, and 2.4% in five metrics, suggesting that with a lower quantity and quality of features, Trans can more effectively mine related information, surpassing CLAM. Besides, the integration of our proposed subtype contrastive loss (SCL) can significantly improve the performance of Trans at both magnifications (SE: 4.5%, SP: 1.5%, ACC: 4.5%, AUC: 1% at 20 ×), showing our method successfully guides the model to focus on molecular subtype discrimination. Besides, we compared our results with junior pathologists (D1) and senior pathologists (D2). The metrics of molecular subtype prediction using our proposed framework (SE: 64.39%, SP: 88.42%, ACC: 66.26%) significantly surpassed D1 (SE: 39.00%, SP: 78.80%, ACC: 38.40%) and D2 (SE: 43.90%, SP: 80.5%, ACC: 42.40%), exhibiting prospects for clinical auxiliary diagnosis such as paraffin block selection.

Table 3. Comparison of molecular subtype prediction with attention instance selection (%)

Model	Threshold	PR	SE	SP	ACC	AUC
CLAM	0	47.15	48.30	51.37	47.15	75.68
	10	49.21	50.07	51.86	49.21	75.93
	20	**51.42**	**51.16**	**52.74**	**51.42**	**76.37**
	40	48.53	48.60	51.09	48.53	75.55
	60	48.19	48.19	49.89	48.1	74.95
	80	43.27	40.44	46.05	43.27	73.02

Table 4. Results of molecular subtype prediction by proposed Transformer with SCL (%)

Mag	MIL Model	PR	SE	SP	ACC	AUC
20×	CLAM	60.99	59.86	86.91	61.87	85.36
	Trans	61.07	59.74	87.01	61.98	86.28
	Trans + SCL(Ours)	**64.96**	**64.39**	**88.42**	**66.26**	**87.13**
10×	CLAM	56.81	55.20	85.82	58.79	82.05
	Trans	58.51	58.28	86.49	60.66	84.42
	Trans + SCL(Ours)	**61.77**	**61.07**	**87.30**	**63.19**	**84.88**

4 Conclusion

This paper proposed a BM-SMIL framework based on self-supervised pretraining and multi-instance learning for molecular subtype prediction. Multi-scale knowledge distillation pretraining paradigm was proposed to train an expressive patch encoder. Then, attention-based instance selection strategy was implemented to screen out noise patches unrelated to molecular subtype. Further, Transformer integrated with subtype contrastive loss was presented to explore correlation among patches and guide the model to focus on subtype discrimination. The experimental results on the cooperative hospital's dataset confirmed the effectiveness of our proposed BM-SMIL framework in breast cancer molecular subtype prediction. Besides, the framework can be easily extended to other pathology image classification tasks. We intend to further explore breast cancer molecular subtype prediction through more self-supervised and multi-instance modeling approaches in the future.

Acknowledgement. This work was supported by the National Natural Science Foundation of China (62276250).

References

1. Pusztai, L., Mazouni, C., Anderson, K., et al.: Molecular classification of breast cancer: limitations and potential. Oncologist **11**(8), 868–877 (2006)
2. Sengal, A.T., Haj-Mukhtar, N.S., Elhaj, A.M., et al.: Immunohistochemistry defined subtypes of breast cancer in 678 Sudanese and Eritrean women; hospitals based case series. BMC Cancer **17**(1), 1–9 (2017)
3. Rawat, R.R., Ortega, I., Roy, P., et al.: Deep learned tissue "fingerprints" classify breast cancers by ER/PR/Her2 status from H&E images. Sci. Rep. **10**(1), 1–13 (2020)
4. Jaber, M.I., Song, B., Taylor, C., et al.: A deep learning image-based intrinsic molecular subtype classifier of breast tumors reveals tumor heterogeneity that may affect survival. Breast Cancer Res. **22**(1), 1–10 (2020)
5. Liu, H., Xu, W.D., Shang, Z.H., et al.: Breast cancer molecular subtype prediction on pathological images with discriminative patch selection and multi-instance learning. Front. Oncol. **12**, 858453 (2022)
6. Han, B., Yao, Q., Yu, X., et al.: Co-teaching: robust training of deep neural networks with extremely noisy labels. In: Advances in Neural Information Processing Systems, vol. 31 (2018)
7. Breunig, M.M., Kriegel, H.P., Ng, R.T., et al.: LOF: identifying density-based local outliers. In: Proceedings of the 2000 ACM SIGMOD International Conference on Management of Data, pp. 93–104 (2000)
8. He, K., Fan, H., Wu, Y., et al.: Momentum contrast for unsupervised visual representation learning. In: Proceedings of the IEEE/CVF Conference on Computer Vision and Pattern Recognition, pp. 9729–9738 (2020)
9. Chen, T., Kornblith, S., Norouzi, M., et al.: A simple framework for contrastive learning of visual representations. In: Proceedings of the 37th International Conference on Machine Learning, vol. 119, pp. 1597–1607. JMLR.org, (2020)
10. Caron, M., Touvron, H., Misra, I., et al.: Emerging properties in self-supervised vision transformers. In: ICCV 2021 - International Conference on Computer Vision, p. 1 (2021)
11. Grill, J.B., Strub, F., Altché, F., et al.: Bootstrap your own latent-a new approach to self-supervised learning. In: Advances in Neural Information Processing Systems, vol. 33, pp. 21271–21284 (2020)
12. He, K., Chen, X., Xie, S., et al.: Masked autoencoders are scalable vision learners. In: Proceedings of the IEEE/CVF Conference on Computer Vision and Pattern Recognition, pp. 16000–16009 (2022)

13. Doersch, C., Gupta, A., Efros, A.A.: Unsupervised visual representation learning by context prediction. In: Proceedings of the IEEE International Conference on Computer Vision, pp. 1422–1430 (2015)
14. Li, B., Li, Y., Eliceiri, K.W.: Dual-stream multiple instance learning network for whole slide image classification with self-supervised contrastive learning. In: 2021 IEEE/CVF Conference on Computer Vision and Pattern Recognition (CVPR), pp. 14313–14323 (2021)
15. Li, J., Lin, T., Xu, Y.: SSLP: spatial guided self-supervised learning on pathological images. In: de Bruijne, M., et al. (eds.) MICCAI 2021. LNCS, vol. 12902, pp. 3–12. Springer, Cham (2021). https://doi.org/10.1007/978-3-030-87196-3_1
16. Wang, X., Yang, S., Zhang, J., et al.: Transformer-based unsupervised contrastive learning for histopathological image classification. Med. Image Anal. **81**, 102559 (2022)
17. Lerousseau, M., et al.: Weakly supervised multiple instance learning histopathological tumor segmentation. In: Martel, A.L., et al. (eds.) MICCAI 2020. LNCS, vol. 12265, pp. 470–479. Springer, Cham (2020). https://doi.org/10.1007/978-3-030-59722-1_45
18. Campanella, G., Hanna, M., Geneslaw, L., et al.: Clinical-grade computational pathology using weakly supervised deep learning on whole slide images. Nat. Med. **25**, 1 (2019)
19. Tomita, N., Abdollahi, B., Wei, J., et al.: Attention-based deep neural networks for detection of cancerous and precancerous esophagus tissue on histopathological slides. JAMA Netw. OpenNetw. Open **2**(11), e1914645 (2019)
20. Hashimoto, N., Fukushima, D., Koga, R., et al.: Multi-scale domain-adversarial multiple-instance CNN for cancer subtype classification with unannotated histopathological images. In: Proceedings of the IEEE/CVF Conference on Computer Vision and Pattern Recognition, pp. 3852–3861 (2020)
21. Ilse, M., Tomczak, J., Welling, M.: Attention-based deep multiple instance learning. In: Dy, J., Krause, A.: Proceedings of the 35th International Conference on Machine Learning, vol. 80, pp. 2127–2136. PMLR (2018)
22. Shao, Z., Bian, H., Chen, Y., et al.: TransMIL: transformer based correlated multiple instance learning for whole slide image classification. In: Advances in Neural Information Processing Systems (2022)
23. Lu, M.Y., Williamson, D.F., Chen, T.Y., et al.: Data-efficient and weakly supervised computational pathology on whole-slide images. Nat. Biomed. Eng. **5**(6), 555–570 (2021)
24. Yu, S., et al.: Mil-vt: Multiple instance learning enhanced vision transformer for fundus image classification. In: de Bruijne, M., et al. (eds.) MICCAI 2021. LNCS, vol. 12908, pp. 45–54. Springer, Cham (2021). https://doi.org/10.1007/978-3-030-87237-3_5
25. Schroff, F., Kalenichenko, D., Philbin, J.: FaceNet: a unified embedding for face recognition and clustering. In: 2015 IEEE Conference on Computer Vision and Pattern Recognition (CVPR), pp. 815–823 (2015)
26. Otsu, N.: A threshold selection method from gray-level histograms. IEEE Trans. Syst. Man Cybern.Cybern. **9**(1), 62–66 (1979)
27. Loshchilov, I., Hutter, F.: Decoupled weight decay regularization. In: International Conference on Learning Representations (2022)

PET-3DFlow: A Normalizing Flow Based Method for 3D PET Anomaly Detection

Zhe Xiong, Qiaoqiao Ding$^{(\boxtimes)}$, Yuzhong Zhao, and Xiaoqun Zhang$^{(\boxtimes)}$

Institute of Natural Sciences and School of Mathematical Sciences and MOE-LSC and Shanghai National Center for Applied Mathematics (SJTU Center), Shanghai Jiao Tong University, Shanghai 200240, China
{dingqiaoqiao,xqzhang}@sjtu.edu.cn

Abstract. Anomaly detection of Positron Emission Tomography (PET) are important tasks for clinical diagnosis and treatments. For 3D PET images, it is arduous for the annotations of lesions and the number of positive samples are generally very limited. Although there have been many work on deep learning based anomaly detection for medical images, most of them cannot be directly applied on 3D PET data. In this paper, from a set of normal PET data, we propose a tractable and efficient 3D normalizing flow based model, namely PET-3DFlow for anomaly detection and provide lesion localization for the reference of clinicians. The loss of In PET-3DFlow consists of the log-likelihood originated from the normalizing flow model and the reconstruction error of the autoencoder learned from the normal images. Experimental evaluation on 3D PET data showed that the proposed model outperformed the other approaches, which validated the effectiveness of our proposed PET anomaly detection method.

Keywords: PET · Normalizing Flow · Anomaly Detection

1 Introduction

As one of the powerful medical imaging techniques, Positron Emission Tomography (PET) allows to visualize metabolic and physiological processes in human body, which is commonly used for cancer diagnosis and treatments. On the one hand, PET image can provide much diagnostic information, which is able to detect small, low-density tumor deposits and micro-metastases. On the other hand, a fast anomaly screening from massive PET images is challenging as the resolution of PET images is often low and the large size of 3D images requires many effort from skilled clinicians. Thus there is a high demand for an efficient and robust anomaly detection methods.

Deep learning (DL) methods, especially convolutional neural networks (CNN) have been widely used in various medical images tasks. As for anomaly detection, there are two lines of DL based methods: reconstruction based and likelihood based methods. Reconstruction methods usually take normal images as inputs and utilize an auto-encoder to reconstruct an image as output, and the loss function is designed to be the difference between the reconstructed images and the

© The Author(s), under exclusive license to Springer Nature Switzerland AG 2023
W. Qin et al. (Eds.): CMMCA 2023 (MICCAI Workshop), LNCS 14243, pp. 91–100, 2023.
https://doi.org/10.1007/978-3-031-45087-7_10

original ones. The large difference is used as a criteria for detection of anomaly images. More complex representation tools, such as generative adversarial networks [12] (GAN) are further considered in the literature, for example AnoGAN [27]; f-AnoGAN [26] and GANomaly [1].

The second type of methods are based on the data likelihood calculated from normalizing flow (NF) structures [17]. The essential idea of NF is to utilize a series of invertible modules to transform the data from an unknown distribution to the standard Gaussian distribution. Several elegant structures have been carefully designed in the literature for the invertible modules, such as the affine coupling layers firstly introduced in NICE [9]; the multi-scale structures adopted in RealNVP [10] and 1×1 convolution blocks that used in Glow [16], which achieved an improved performance on some realistic datasets. For anomaly detection, several NF-based models have also be put forward and achieved impressive performances on a number of different datasets [2,7,8,14,25]. For example, DifferNet [25] computes the anomaly score of the encoded features using a one dimensional normalizing flow. However, these flow-based methods tend to output anomaly scores in terms of the likelihood of data but ignore the local structural information of images.

PET images anomaly detection has attracted the attention of researchers and many works have been proposed. However, there are many limitations of the current works. Firstly, it is time-consuming to label multiple lesions [13] and the labeled data is scarce for DL based lesion localization models. Secondly, many methods only consider the anomalies in a specific organ or region, for example [15] is devoted to lung lesion detection in FDG-PET/CT and a GAN based method for Alzheimer's disease by PET image was proposed in [4]. In some work [15,20–22], PET anomaly detection is combined with other modalities. In [20], PET in combination with MRI was put forward for detection of Alzheimer's Disease. In [22], an unsupervised anomaly detection and segmentation method using PET/CT imaging via transformers was proposed. In [21], Nakao et. al proposed a Bayesian Neural Network to calculate Z-score map with normal PET/CT images.

In this paper, we aim to propose an efficient anomaly detection and lesion localization method for 3D PET images. Motivated by a recent work using NF and the reconstruction error for x-Ray image anomaly detection [30], we propose an image representation and normalizing **Flow** based methods (PET-3DFlow) for the 3D PET anomaly detection. In the PET-3DFlow, the encoded features extracted from 3D images are transformed into a standard Gaussian distribution vector through a carefully designed NF blocks. In both training and inference process, both the likelihood of the data and the errors presents in the reconstructed image are taken into account for calculating the anomaly score. We note that the model is fully self-supervised and as a result, only the normal data are needed in the training process, which can relieve the difficulties of lesions delineation and the collections of large samples of anomaly samples in clinical practices.

2 Methodology

The idea of the proposed method takes advantage of both the self-supervised generative methods and the NF-based models. Figure 1 displays the overview of our PET-3DFlow structure, which consists of three components, i.e. a pretrained encoder, a 3D normalizing flow and a decoder, for the latter two are trainable. Firstly, the pretrained encoder takes a PET image patch as input and output a sequence of features, then the features are transformed to the standard Gaussian distribution of the same size through invertible NF blocks. Finally, the decoder reconstructs the Gaussian sample to a PET image patch. Compared to the encoder-decoder model, the normalizing flow is added to ensure that the normal images can be mapped to the high density area while the anomaly ones fall in the tail of Gaussian. The loss function and anomaly score both consist of the negative log-likelihood and the dissimilarity between the reconstructed image and the original one. In the following, we present the details of the proposed three blocks.

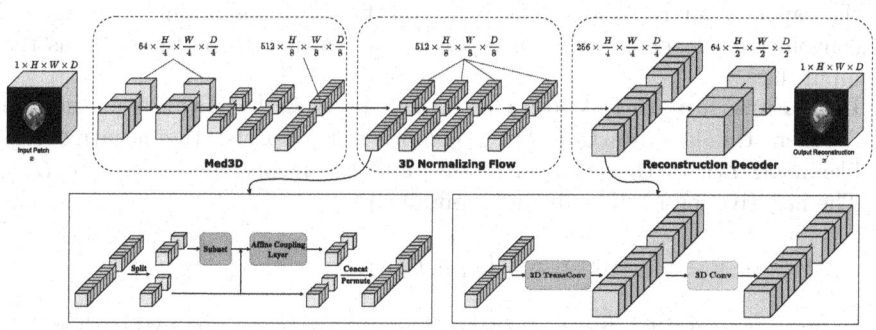

Fig. 1. Overview of our pipeline.

- **Pretrained Encoder:** For the stability of our model, we utilize the Med3D [6] as our encoder, which is a 3D-ResNet pretrained on a series of large-scale 3D medical datasets. More specifically, the encoder f_{med} maps the input PET patch $\vec{x} \in \mathcal{X}$ to the feature $\vec{z} \in \mathcal{Z}$. Each input patch $\vec{x} \in \mathbb{R}^{1 \times H \times W \times D}$ is transformed to a 512 channels feature $\vec{z} \in \mathbb{R}^{512 \times \frac{H}{8} \times \frac{W}{8} \times \frac{D}{8}}$, where H, W and D are the height, width and depth of the input image separately.

- **3D Normalizing Flow:** To calculate the likelihood of the feature $\vec{z}$, we apply an NF structure between the encoder and the decoder, which is an invertible transformation between the feature distribution and the standard Gaussian distribution. Suppose $\vec{z}$ is a feature through the pretrained encoder, then a flow $T : \mathcal{Z} \to \tilde{\mathcal{Z}}$ maps $\vec{z}$ to $\tilde{\vec{z}} = T(\vec{z}) \sim \mathcal{N}(\tilde{\vec{z}}|\mathbf{0}, \mathbf{I})$, which comes from a standard Gaussian distribution with the same dimension as $\vec{z}$. Besides, the invertible structure of NF is guaranteed by the composition of several bijective transformation blocks, each of which is mainly made up of a coupling layer and a channel permutation [10,16]. In the coupling layer, the input $\vec{z}$ is firstly split along the channels into two parts $(\vec{z}_1, \vec{z}_2)$ and then, the affine coupling structure transforms the $(\vec{z}_1, \vec{z}_2)$ into $(\vec{y}_1, \vec{y}_2)$ as follows, keeping the dimension invariant for both components:

$$\vec{y}_1 = \vec{z}_1,$$
$$\vec{y}_2 = \vec{z}_2 \odot \exp\left(\gamma * \tanh(\mathbf{s}_{\theta_1}(\vec{z}_1))\right) + \mathbf{t}_{\theta_2}(\vec{z}_1),$$

where γ is the affine clamp parameter, $\mathbf{s}_{\theta_1}(\cdot)$ and $\mathbf{t}_{\theta_2}(\cdot)$ are two subnets to be trained, whose structures can be different [10] or the same [16]. For channel permutation, the output $(\vec{y}_1, \vec{y}_2)$ are primarily concatenated and then disordered along the channels by an 1×1 invertible convolutional transform.

- **Reconstruction Decoder:** The decoder $g_{rec} : \tilde{\mathcal{Z}} \rightarrow \mathcal{X}$ is used to reconstruct patch $\vec{x}'$ from the Gaussian distributed data $\tilde{z}$. In training process, a similarity metric between the normal input patches and the corresponding reconstructed ones is minimized. Here, we adopt three upsampling blocks in decoder, where the first two blocks consist of a transposed convolutional layer for upsampling and a convolutional layer combined with a group normalization to improve the capacity for reconstruction, while the final layer is a single transposed convolutional layer to adjust the size of the features to be the same as the input data.

- **Loss Function and Anomaly Score:** To train both the flow and the decoder, the loss function L_{train} comprises two parts, the negative log-likelihood L_{nll} of the encoded feature and the reconstruction metric L_{rec}. The negative log-likelihood can be obtained by:

$$L_{\mathrm{nll}} = -\log(p(\vec{z})) = -\log(p(T(\vec{z}))) - \log\left|\det\left(\frac{\partial T(\vec{z})}{\partial \vec{z}}\right)\right|.$$

Besides, we consider the L_{rec} to be the mean square error (MSE) between the input data and the reconstructed ones:

$$L_{\mathrm{rec}} = \mathrm{MSE}(\vec{x}, \vec{x}') = \frac{1}{H \times W \times D} \sum_{i,j,k}^{H,W,D} (\vec{x}_{i,j,k} - \vec{x}'_{i,j,k})^2,$$

Then our loss function is formulated as the weighted sum of L_{nll} and L_{rec}:

$$L_{\mathrm{train}} = \alpha \times L_{\mathrm{nll}} + (1 - \alpha) \times L_{\mathrm{rec}}, \tag{1}$$

where $\alpha \in [0, 1]$ is a hypterparameter. For inference, the components of the anomaly score are similar to those in the loss function but different. Instead of MSE, we use the 3D Structural Similarity Index Measure (3D-SSIM) [29] as the similarity metric. With a well-trained model, the scores of the normal images are expected to be low while the ones for anomaly images are as high as possible. Therefore, for each input $\vec{x}$, we refer to the negative log-likelihood s_{nll} of the corresponding normally distributed feature $\tilde{z}$ and the negative 3D-SSIM s_{rec} and use the weighted sum of them as our anomaly score:

$$s_{\mathrm{infer}} = \beta \times s_{\mathrm{nll}} + (1 - \beta) \times s_{\mathrm{rec}}, \tag{2}$$

where $\beta \in [0, 1]$ controls the weight between s_{nll} and s_{rec}.

3   Experiments and Results

3.1   Dataset and Data Pre-processing

To evaluate the effectiveness of the proposed approach, we adopted the 2022 AutoPET Challenge [11] dataset, which consist of 1014 FDG-PET scans from 900 patients acquired by two large medical centers. There are 513 images without lesions, which will be used as the normal dataset for training, and the left 501 scans are anomaly data consisting of malignant melanoma, lung cancer, and lymphoma. Before training, each PET image volume is uniformly cropped into a patch size of $128 \times 224 \times 224$, where the central part of every slice with the size 224×224 is retained. Then, the images are scaled to the standardized uptake value [28] (SUV) range of $[0, 14.25]$ and further normalization to $[0, 1]$ [23].

3.2   Details of Implementation

In our model, the Med3D encodes the 3D image via five convolutional resnet-based layers, and then through the flow model with eight blocks, the features extracted by the encoder are transformed to normal distributed variables, which are finally restored to a reconstructed image via the decoder.

- **Encoder:** Restricted to the size of the input 3D image, we use the pretrained 3D-ResNet18 (one of the structures of the Med3D) whose settings are given in [6], which consists of 5 convolutional layers. In more detail, each image is with size $128 \times 224 \times 224$ and the size of the extracted feature is $16 \times 28 \times 28$ with 512 channels.
- **Flow:** The flow module contains 8 blocks which are built based on the FrEIA library [3]. Each block has the same structure, consisting of an affine coupling layer and a channel permutation transformation. In the coupling layer, to decrease the parameters of the whole flow, we use a simple subnet only composed of two 3D convolutional layers with ReLU activation function.
- **Decoder:** The decoder contains three upsampling blocks. The first two block consists of a 3D transposed convolutional with $2 \times 2 \times 2$ kernel and stride 2 and a 3D convolutional with $3 \times 3 \times 3$ kernel. And the last layer only contains a single $2 \times 2 \times 2$ kernel transposed convolution. The channel number changes as $512 \rightarrow 256 \rightarrow 64 \rightarrow 1$. The features size changes from $16 \times 28 \times 28$ to $128 \times 224 \times 224$.
- **Hyperparameters and Optimizer settings:** The whole network is trained for 500 epochs with a batch size of 5, using AdamW [19] optimizer with weight decay equal to 10^{-5} for network optimization. For the hyperparameters, we choose the weight of the loss $\alpha = 0.5$ and the weight of the anomaly score $\beta = 0.9$.

3.3   Results

We compare the proposed PET-3DFlow models with several deep learning methods, including two flow-based models, DifferNet [25] and FastFlow [2] and two reconstruction-based models, AutoEncoder [18] and GANomaly [1]. We adopted Area Under Curves (AUC) [5], F1-score (F1) [24], accuracy (ACC) to evaluate the effectiveness of the proposed PET-3DFlow method. Moreover, the number of trainable parameters in each model is also given.

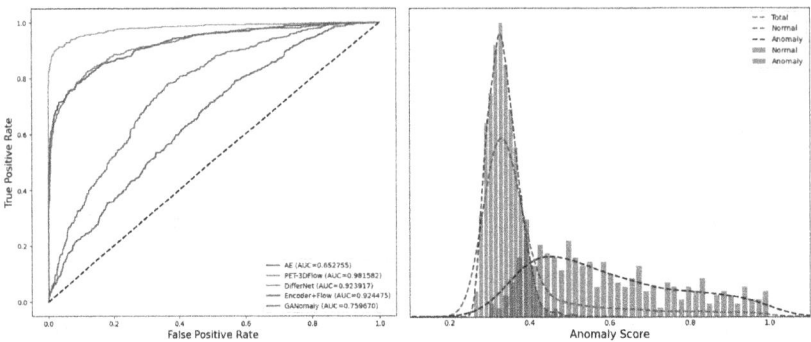

Fig. 2. On the **left** is the ROC curves and AUC values of different methods and on the **right** is the distributions and density curves of both normal and anomaly features through the flow.

The results are shown in Table 1 and the corresponding Receiver Operator Characteristic [31] (ROC) curve is also displayed in Fig. 2. For computational capacity, we draw the ROC curves of all the methods except FastFlow and only calculate the AUC value of the FastFlow model by taking small batches. The proposed method outperformed the four comparison methods by a noticeable margin in terms of AUC, F1 and ACC. Moreover, the proposed achieve higher AUC with less parameters in comparison with FastFlow.

Table 1. Quantitative Comparisons between several methods.

Method	AUC ↑	F1 ↑	ACC ↑	# of Parameters
GANomaly [1]	0.759	0.611	0.689	198.01 mil
DifferNet [25]	0.924	0.801	0.881	28.4 mil
FastFlow [2]	0.901	–	–	51.4 mil
AutoEncoder [18]	0.653	0.528	0.544	15.9 mil
Encoder + Flow	0.924	0.803	0.879	23.9 mil
Ours ($\alpha = 0.5$)	**0.982**	**0.929**	**0.958**	28.0 mil

To verify the proposed method, the distribution curves of the computed anomaly score for both normal and anomaly images are shown in Fig. 2. The horizontal and vertical axis represent the anomaly score and the probability density respectively. As shown in Fig. 2, the predicted anomaly score of anomaly data is larger than that of normal data. It is demonstrated that the proposed PET-3DFlow approach is effective and the anomaly score function is valid for distinguishing the anomaly samples from normal PET images.

The proposed model contains a decoder module and is able to reconstruct the image from the flow transferred feature. Figure 3 shows the reconstruction of normal image slices and Fig. 4 contains the results of anomaly ones. Each package of the three slices in the same line comes from the transverse plane, coronal plane and sagittal plane respectively. For the normal images, compared to the input images, the reconstructions can almost restore the critical features. For the anomaly images, the predicted lesion localization is obtained from the difference between the original images and the reconstructed ones. As we can see, compared to the ground truth, the major area can be determined even for the tiny lesions in this simple way.

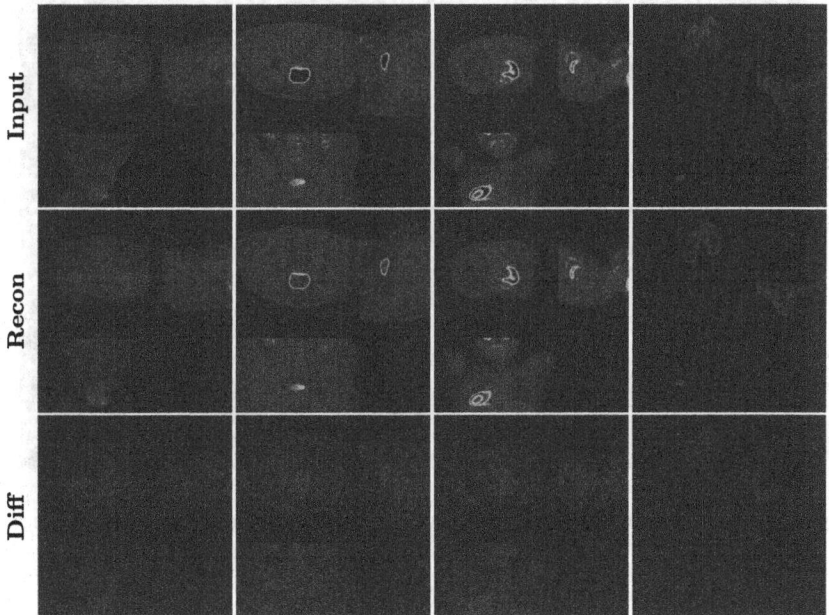

Fig. 3. The reconstructions of **normal** input data slices.

3.4   Ablation Study

The ablation study conducted focuses on how the following three parts impact the performance of image reconstruction: (1) pretrained encoder, (2) normalize flow, (3) decoder. We compare the performance of three cases: (1) A pretrained encoder + a trainable flow structure, (2) A pretrained encoder + a trainable decoder, which is exact from the AutoEncoder model, (3) Our model with the weighted parameter $\alpha = 0.5$ in the loss function. See last three lines of Table 1 for the results of different models.

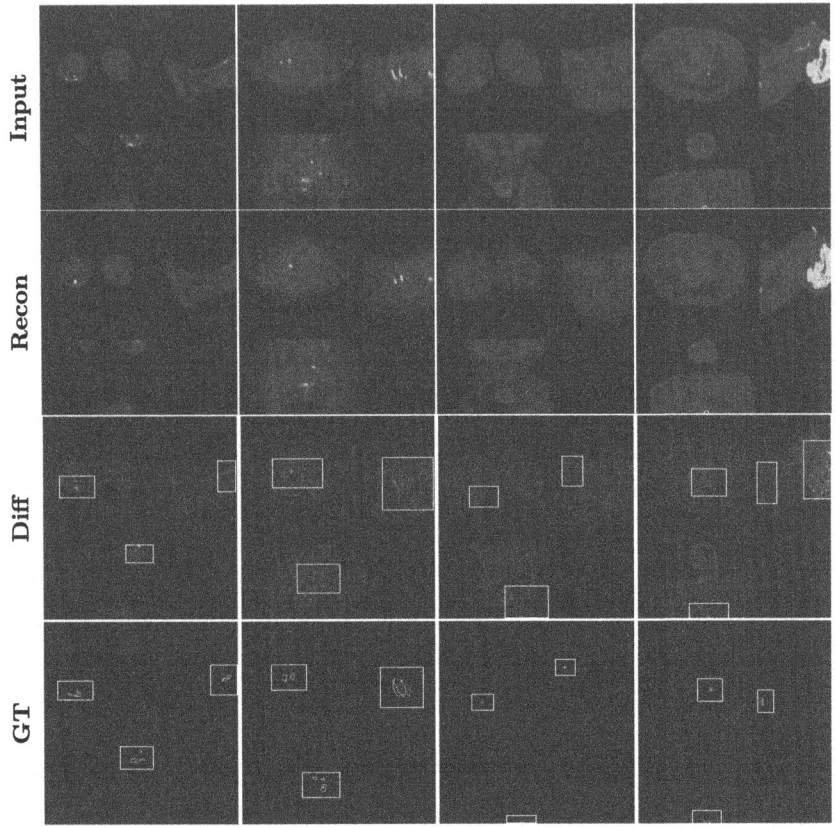

Fig. 4. Image reconstruction and lesion localization of **anomaly** input data slices.

4   Conclusion

In this paper, we proposed a 3D flow-based model for PET image anomaly detection. Aiming to take the advantage of reconstruction and flow-based methods, we designed the 3D normalizing flow with decode modules and utilized the data likelihood and the reconstructed error in the loss and the anomaly score. Experiments on the AutoPET dataset have shown that our method outperforms several widely used anomaly detection methods. Besides, the evaluation and ablation study demonstrate the rationality of our model.

Acknowledgment. The authors were support by Shanghai Municipal Science and Technology Major Project (2021SHZDZX0102) and NSFC (No. 12090024 and 12201402). We thank the Student Innovation Center at Shanghai Jiao Tong University for providing us the computing services.

References

1. Akcay, S., Atapour-Abarghouei, A., Breckon, T.P.: GANomaly: semi-supervised anomaly detection via adversarial training. In: Jawahar, C.V., Li, H., Mori, G., Schindler, K. (eds.) ACCV 2018. LNCS, vol. 11363, pp. 622–637. Springer, Cham (2019). https://doi.org/10.1007/978-3-030-20893-6_39
2. Aldinucci, M., Danelutto, M., Kilpatrick, P., Torquati, M.: Fastflow: high-level and efficient streaming on multicore. Programming Multi-core and Many-core Computing Systems, pp. 261–280 (2017)
3. Ardizzone, Let al.: Framework for easily invertible architectures (FrEIA). Source code (2018)
4. Baydargil, H.B., Park, J.S., Kang, D.Y.: Anomaly analysis of Alzheimer's disease in pet images using an unsupervised adversarial deep learning model. Appl. Sci. **11**(5), 2187 (2021)
5. Bradley, A.P.: The use of the area under the roc curve in the evaluation of machine learning algorithms. Pattern Recogn. **30**(7), 1145–1159 (1997)
6. Chen, S., Ma, K., Zheng, Y.: Med3D: transfer learning for 3D medical image analysis. arXiv preprint arXiv:1904.00625 (2019)
7. Cho, M., Kim, T., Kim, W.J., Cho, S., Lee, S.: Unsupervised video anomaly detection via normalizing flows with implicit latent features. Pattern Recogn. **129**, 108703 (2022)
8. Dai, E., Chen, J.: Graph-augmented normalizing flows for anomaly detection of multiple time series. arXiv preprint arXiv:2202.07857 (2022)
9. Dinh, L., Krueger, D., Bengio, Y.: Nice: non-linear independent components estimation. arXiv preprint arXiv:1410.8516 (2014)
10. Dinh, L., Sohl-Dickstein, J., Bengio, S.: Density estimation using real NVP. arXiv preprint arXiv:1605.08803 (2016)
11. Gatidis, S., et al.: A whole-body FDG-PET/CT dataset with manually annotated tumor lesions. Sci. Data **9**(1), 601 (2022)
12. Goodfellow, I., et al.: Generative adversarial networks. Commun. ACM **63**(11), 139–144 (2020)
13. Grossiord, E., Talbot, H., Passat, N., Meignan, M., Najman, L.: Automated 3D lymphoma lesion segmentation from PET/CT characteristics. In: 2017 IEEE 14th International Symposium on Biomedical Imaging (ISBI 2017), pp. 174–178. IEEE (2017)
14. Gudovskiy, D., Ishizaka, S., Kozuka, K.: CFLOW-AD: real-time unsupervised anomaly detection with localization via conditional normalizing flows. In: Proceedings of the IEEE/CVF Winter Conference on Applications of Computer Vision, pp. 98–107 (2022)
15. Kamesawa, R., et al.: Lung lesion detection in FDG-PET/CT with gaussian process regression. In: Medical Imaging 2017: Computer-Aided Diagnosis, vol. 10134, pp. 77–83. SPIE (2017)
16. Kingma, D.P., Dhariwal, P.: Glow: generative flow with invertible 1 ×1 convolutions. In: Advances in neural information processing systems, vol. 31 (2018)

17. Kobyzev, I., Prince, S.J., Brubaker, M.A.: Normalizing flows: an introduction and review of current methods. IEEE Trans. Pattern Anal. Mach. Intell. **43**(11), 3964–3979 (2020)
18. Kramer, M.A.: Nonlinear principal component analysis using autoassociative neural networks. AIChE J. **37**(2), 233–243 (1991)
19. Loshchilov, I., Hutter, F.: Decoupled weight decay regularization. arXiv preprint arXiv:1711.05101 (2017)
20. Lu, D., Popuri, K., Ding, G.W., Balachandar, R., Beg, M.F.: Multimodal and multiscale deep neural networks for the early diagnosis of Alzheimer's disease using structural MR and FDG-PET images. Sci. Rep. **8**(1), 5697 (2018)
21. Nakao, T., Hanaoka, S., Nomura, Y., Hayashi, N., Abe, O.: Anomaly detection in chest 18F-FDG PET/CT by bayesian deep learning. Jpn. J. Radiol. **40**(7), 730–739 (2022)
22. Patel, A., et al.: Cross attention transformers for multi-modal unsupervised whole-body pet anomaly detection. In: Mukhopadhyay, A., Oksuz, I., Engelhardt, S., Zhu, D., Yuan, Y. (eds.) Deep Generative Models. DGM4MICCAI 2022. Lecture Notes in Computer Science, vol. 13609, pp. 14–23. Springer, Cham (2022). https://doi.org/10.1007/978-3-031-18576-2_2
23. Peng, Y., Kim, J., Feng, D., Bi, L.: Automatic tumor segmentation via false positive reduction network for whole-body multi-modal PET/CT images. arXiv preprint arXiv:2209.07705 (2022)
24. Powers, D.M.: Evaluation: from precision, recall and F-measure to ROC, informedness, markedness and correlation. arXiv preprint arXiv:2010.16061 (2020)
25. Rudolph, M., Wandt, B., Rosenhahn, B.: Same same but differNet: semi-supervised defect detection with normalizing flows. In: Proceedings of the IEEE/CVF Winter Conference on Applications of Computer Vision, pp. 1907–1916 (2021)
26. Schlegl, T., Seeböck, P., Waldstein, S.M., Langs, G., Schmidt-Erfurth, U.: F-anogan: fast unsupervised anomaly detection with generative adversarial networks. Med. Image Anal. **54**, 30–44 (2019)
27. Schlegl, T., Seeböck, P., Waldstein, S.M., Schmidt-Erfurth, U., Langs, G.: Unsupervised anomaly detection with generative adversarial networks to guide marker discovery. In: Niethammer, M., et al. (eds.) IPMI 2017. LNCS, vol. 10265, pp. 146–157. Springer, Cham (2017). https://doi.org/10.1007/978-3-319-59050-9_12
28. Zasadny, K.R., Wahl, R.L.: Standardized uptake values of normal tissues at PET with 2-[fluorine-18]-fluoro-2-deoxy-d-glucose: variations with body weight and a method for correction. Radiology **189**(3), 847–850 (1993)
29. Zeng, K., Wang, Z.: 3D-SSIM for video quality assessment. In: 2012 19th IEEE International Conference on Image Processing, pp. 621–624. IEEE (2012)
30. Zhao, Y., Ding, Q., Zhang, X.: AE-FLOW: autoencoders with normalizing flows for medical images anomaly detection. In: The Eleventh International Conference on Learning Representations (2022)
31. Zweig, M.H., Campbell, G.: Receiver-operating characteristic (ROC) plots: a fundamental evaluation tool in clinical medicine. Clin. Chem. **39**(4), 561–577 (1993)

Fully Convolutional Transformer-Based GAN for Cross-Modality CT to PET Image Synthesis

Yuemei Li[1] (ID), Qiang Zheng[1] (ID), Yi Wang[1], Yongkang Zhou[2], Yang Zhang[2], Yipeng Song[4], and Wei Jiang[3,4,5,6](✉)

[1] School of Computer and Control Engineering, Yantai University, Yantai 264205, China
[2] Department of Radiation Oncology, Zhongshan Hospital, Shanghai 200032, China
[3] School of Precision Instrument and Opto-Electronics Engineering, Tianjin University, Tianjin 300072, China
[4] Department of Radiotherapy, Yantai Yuhuangding Hospital, Yantai 264000, China
[5] Academy of Medical Engineering and Translational Medicine, Department of Biomedical Engineering, School of Precision Instrument and Opto-Electronics Engineering, Tianjin University, Tianjin 300072, China
[6] Department of Radiotherapy, Yantai Yuhuangding Hospital Affiliated to Qingdao University, No. 20 Yuhuangding East Road, Yantai 264000, China
jiangwei21@qdu.edu.cn

Abstract. Positron emission tomography (PET) imaging is widely used for staging and monitoring the treatment of lung cancer, but the expensive cost of PET imaging equipment and the numerous contraindications for the examination present significant challenges to individuals and institutions seeking PET scans. Cross-modality image synthesis could alleviate this problem, but existing method still have deficiencies. Such as, pix2pix mode has stringent data requirements, while cycleGAN mode, although it can address this issue, does not produce a unique optimal solution. Additionally, models with convolutional neural network backbone still exhibit limitations when dealing with medical images containing contextual relationships between healthy and pathological tissues. In this paper, we propose a generative adversarial network (GAN) method based on a fully convolutional transformer and residual blocks called C2P-GAN for cross-modality synthesis of PET images from CT images. It composed of a generator and a discriminator that compete with each other, as well as a registration network that can eliminate noise interference. The generator integrates convolutional networks that excel in capturing local image features with the transformer that is sensitive to global contextual information. In the current dataset of 23 pairs of lung cancer patients collected, quantitative and qualitative experimental results demonstrate the superiority of the proposed method relative to competing methods and have great potential for clinical applications.

Keywords: Deep learning · GAN · CT · PET · Image synthesis

W. Qin et al. (Eds.): CMMCA 2023 (MICCAI Workshop), LNCS 14243, pp. 101–109, 2023.
https://doi.org/10.1007/978-3-031-45087-7_11

1 Introduction

In clinical settings, it is typically indispensable to acquire high-resolution images of both the structure and function of a body part concurrently in order to ensure an accurate assessment of disease morphology and metabolism [1]. Computed tomography (CT) and positron emission tomography (PET) are two distinct image modalities used in medical imaging. CT imaging primarily utilizes the absorption and scattering of X-rays to create high-resolution structural images that can reveal information about the shape, size, and position of various tissues and organs in the body [2]. The process of positron emission tomography (PET) imaging necessitates the injection of a radioactive isotope into the patient's body to serve as a tracer [3]. The detectors measure the energy released by the positrons to acquire functional information such as human metabolism [3]. Although modern PET technology has achieved a significant reduction in radiation levels, patients are still exposed to some radiation doses, and the application of radioactive isotopes can lead to contaminated radiation. Both the expensive cost of PET imaging equipment and the numerous contraindications for the examination present significant challenges for individuals and institutions seeking PET scans. Therefore, applying deep learning methods to synthesize virtual PET images from CT scans not only provides biologically sensitive images for patients who cannot undergo PET scans, but also allows for the acquisition of biological information images that are reproducible at various phases, thereby enhancing diagnostic efficiency while reducing radiation exposure to patients, which is highly promising in clinical practice.

Recently, Generative Adversarial Nets (GANs) [4] have been widely applied to cross-modality image synthesis tasks due to their unique adversarial training strategy. It was broadly divided into two modes. One refers to the supervised cGAN [5, 6] and Pix2Pix [7, 8] mode, which utilizes paired images from the source and target modality. However, it relies on paired and well pixel-wise aligned images, which may not always be realizable due to respiratory motion or anatomy change between the times when paired images are scanned. The other refers to the unsupervised Cycle-consistency GAN (CycleGAN) [9–11] mode, which is less stringent with training data and works well on unpaired or misaligned images. But its mode may produce multiple solutions [12, 13], signifying that the results may not be optimal and the training process may be sensitive. For instance, Avi et al. [14] proposed a novel method to generate virtual PET images using CT scans using fully convolutional network (FCN) [15] and conditional generative adversarial network (cGAN) to reduce false positives in lesion detection; Dong et al. [16] employed a 3D cycle-consistent generative adversarial networks (CycleGAN) framework to synthesize CT images from non-attenuation corrected (NAC) PET. In order to solve the above problems, Kong et al. proposed RegGAN [17] algorithm that integrates registration network, which treats the unpaired target images as noisy labels.

Via continuous improvement, existing methods have achieved high performance, but most of the synthetic models are based on a convolutional architecture that utilizes compact convolutional kernels to extract local image features, reducing the number of parameters in the model, but limiting expressiveness for contextual features owing to the limited receptive field. Especially for medical images with complex anatomical structures and containing contextual relationships between healthy and lesioned tissues, addressing this limitation can improve the performance of synthesis. At present, vision transformer (ViT) [18] is able to model long range dependencies within the image at a global level. So many researchers attempt to integrate it into their study to leverage their ability to create long range semantic context, but in turn, make the models bulky and computationally complex. Addressing this concern, Tragakis et al. proposed the fully convolutional transformer (FCT) [19] method, which significantly reduces the model of parameters.

In this paper, we propose a method called C2P-GAN based on fully convolutional transformer [19] and residual blocks for cross-modality synthesis of PET images from CT images. It blended convolutional structures that are good at capturing local features of images, transformers that are sensitive to global contextual information, GAN framework for adversarial learning, and registration network that can eliminate noise interference. Based on 23 pairs of lung cancer patient datasets that were collected, the experimental results demonstrate the superiority of the proposed method over competing methods and has great potential for clinical application.

2 Method

In order to achieve better translation effect from a given mode CT to a target PET image, we proposed a method based on full convolutional transformer [19] and RegGAN [17] framework. Figure 1 shows a flowchart of the entire framework. In this section we will introduce the model architecture and loss functions in detail.

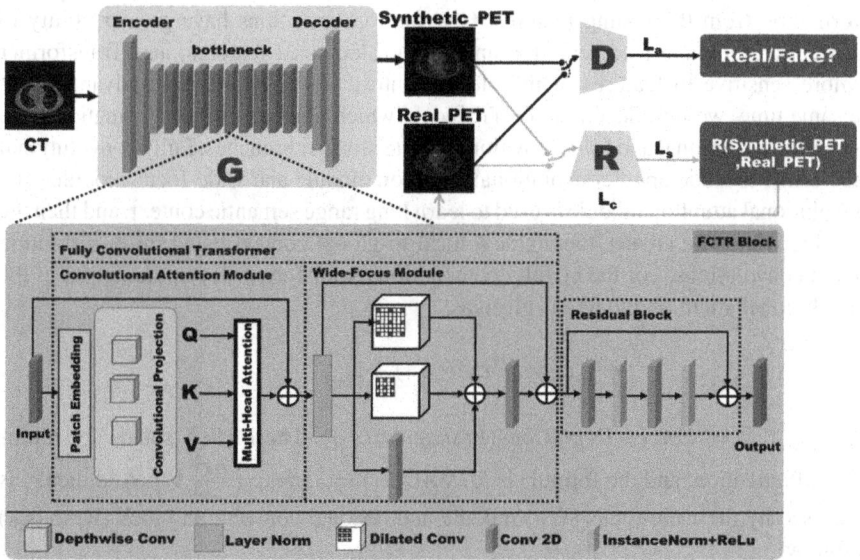

Fig. 1. The model diagram of Cross-Modality CT to PET Image Synthesis. The top row illustrates the overall framework of the model, while the bottom row depicts the specific structure of the generator.

Here we proposed a novel adversarial method for Cross-Modality CT to PET Image Synthesis named C2P-GAN, that can leverages a hybrid architecture of deep convolutional operators and transformer blocks to simultaneously learn local structural and global contextual features (Fig. 1). The generator subnetwork follows an encoder-central bottleneck-decoder architecture, and the subnetwork of discriminator and registration is composed of deep convolutional operators. The generator's bottleneck contains a stack of aggregated fully convolutional transformer and residual blocks. And the external skip connections are inserted around the two modules to create multiple paths of information flow through the block. These paths propagate multiple sets of features to the output so that it can aggregated the representation of lower-level input features along with their contextual, local, and hybrid local-contextual features. The registration network is trained to predict the deformable vector field. For the paired images used in our experiment, we assume that there are morphology mismatches or noise effects between the source domain and target domain images, which can be corrected by this network. The synthesized PET images, $G(x)$, are resampled using the deformable vector field, $R(G(x), y)$. The resampled images are then compared to the ground truth PET images to calculate the loss and correcting generated results.

2.1 Fully Convolutional Transformer-Based Generator

The first component of generator is a deep encoder network that contains a series of convolutional layers to capture a hierarchy of localized features of source images. Next, the generator takes advantage of the central bottleneck layer to extract task-specific information from the coding features. Convolution operations have greater ability to learn effective image representation and capture localized features, and Transformer is more sensitive to features of the global context. To maintain these advantages at the same time, we introduced the FCTR block, which aggregates the information from residual convolutional and fully convolutional transformer branches. Fully convolutional transformer is made up of convolutional attention module and wide-focus module. The convolutional attention module is used to learn long range semantic context, and then the wide-focus module creates hierarchical local-to-global context using multi-resolution dilated convolutions. For the i_{th} fully convolutional transformer layer, the output of the convolutional attention module is given as:

$$z_i' = MHSA(z_{i-1}) + z_{i-1}^{q/k/v}$$

where, $z_{i-1}^{q/k/v} = Flatten(DepthConv(Reshape(z_{i-1})))$. The MHSA stands for multihead self attention, and the formula is $MHSA(z_{i-1}) = Softmax\left(\frac{QK^T}{\sqrt{d}}V\right)$. And then z_i' is processed by the wide-focus (WF) module and residual convolution block (Resblock) as follow:

$$z_i = Resblock(WF(z_i) + z_i')$$

The last component of generator is a deep encoder based on transposed convolutional layers.

2.2 Loss Functions

The underlying network framework involves the minimax two-player game idea of GAN [4], where generator G and discriminator D competed with each other in the training process to achieve the desired ideal state. In this process, we train the generator G to generate the target image G(x) from the input image x, and train discriminator D to be able to distinguish between the real PET image y and the synthesized PET image G(x). The adversarial loss function is shown below, where G minimize this loss function and D maximize it.

$$\min_{G, D} \max L_a(G, D) = E_y\big[\log D(y)\big] + E_x\big[\log(1 - D(G(x)))\big]$$

In order to achieve better synthesis effect, we used a registration network R after the generator G as label noise model to correct the generated results G(x). The correction loss was as follow:

$$\min_{G, R} L_c(G, R) = E_{x,y}[\||y - G(x) \circ R(G(x), y)\||_1]$$

where, R(G(x), y) was the deformation field and ∘ represented the resample operation. Our registration network was based on the ResUNet [20]. The smoothness loss [21] was defined below to assess the smoothness of the deformation field and minimize the gradient of the deformation field.

$$\min_{R} L_s(R) = E_{x,y}[\||\nabla R(G(x), y)\||^2]$$

Finally, the total loss function of our entire network is as follows:

$$\min_{G, R} \max_{D} L_{Total}(G, R, D) = \lambda_1 L_a(G, D) + \lambda_2 L_c(G, R) + \lambda_3 L_s(R)$$

3 Experiment

3.1 Dataset

The scientific ethics committee approved this retrospective study and waived the requirement for informed patient consent. The data used in this work includes PET/CT scans (pairs of helical CT scans with their corresponding PET scans) from the local Hospital. The dataset contains 23 pairs of whole-body CT and PET, of which the training set included 18 PET/CT pairs and the testing was performed on 5 pairs. Among them, 11 cases are lung adenocarcinoma and 12 cases are lung squamous cell carcinoma. To obtain high-quality paired data, we initially converted the original Dicom format data acquired from the hospital to NIFTI format, subsequently employed the FSL toolbox (https://fsl.fmrib.ox.ac.uk/fsl/fslwiki/) to perform affine alignment of the PET images to the CT images, and finally converted the NIFTI format to PNG format and manually selected 2D slices of the lung region for specific studies.

3.2 Implementation Details

The deep learning models were trained by adopting Pytorch on NVIDIA GeForce RTX 3090 Ti GPU (1×24 GB). The optimizer used was Adam at a learning rate of $1e-4$ to test the developed methods. Each training process used for 80 epochs, and batch size of 1. The weights of different loss functions were $\lambda 1 = 1$, $\lambda 2 = 20$, and $\lambda 3 = 10$, respectively. Any of the feature maps were resized to 256×256 and normalized to $[-1,1]$. The error maps are calculated by calculating the absolute difference between the generated images with the ground truth images.

3.3 Comparison Methods and Evaluation Metrics

We demonstrated the proposed model against several state-of-the-art image synthesis methods. The baseline methods included supervised Pix2Pix [7], unsupervised Cycle-consistency generative adversarial network (CycleGAN) [9] and RegGAN [17]. To ensure fair comparison, we used the same training strategy and hyperparameters for all methods. The normalized mean absolute error (NMAE), peak-signal-to-noise-ratio (PSNR), and structural similarity index (SSIM) [22, 23] were used as metric to quantitatively evaluate the performance of our proposed method.

$$NMAE = \frac{1}{N} \sum_{i=1}^{N} \frac{\left| Real_{PET(i)} - Synthetic_{PET(i)} \right|}{2}$$

$$PSNR = 20log_{10} \frac{1}{\sqrt{MSE}}$$

$$SSIM = \frac{(2\mu_x\mu_y + c_1)(2\sigma_{xy} + c_2)}{(\mu_x^2 + \mu_y^2 + c_1)(\sigma_x^2 + \sigma_y^2 + c_2)}$$

In the above equation, the mean squared error $(MSE) = \frac{1}{N} \sum_{i=1}^{N} (Real_{PET(i)} - Synthetic_{PET(i)})^2$. The $\mu_x = \frac{1}{N} \sum_{i=1}^{N} Real_{PET(i)}$; $\mu_y = \frac{1}{N} \sum_{i=1}^{N} Synthetic_{PET(i)}$; $\sigma_x = (\frac{1}{N-1} \sum_{i=1}^{N} (Real_{PET(i)} - \mu_x)^2)^{\frac{1}{2}}$; $\sigma_y = (\frac{1}{N-1} \sum_{i=1}^{N} (Synthetic_{PET(i)} - \mu_y)^2)^{\frac{1}{2}}$; $c_1 = (K_1L)^2$; $c_2 = (K_2L)^2$; where is the dynamic range of the pixel values (255 for 8-bit grayscale images), and $K_1 << 1$ is a small constant. Here, we set $K_1 = 0.01$; $K_2 = 0.03$.

3.4 Results

We first qualitatively evaluate PET reconstruction results shown in Fig. 2, where C2P-GAN is the proposed network. From the visual quality evaluation, it is obvious to see the differences. C2P-GAN generates the structure closest to real PET image, and the lesion site generated is more accurate, which can better assist doctors in lung cancer diagnosis. The quantitative results for all methods under the current investigation are summarized Table 1. Compared with Pix2Pix, CycleGAN and RegGAN models, the proposed method significantly improve the reconstruction accuracy, with the normalized mean absolute error reduced by about 1.4%, 1.5% and 0.2%, the peak signal-to-noise ratio improved by 10dB, 3.5dB and 2.3dB, and the structural similarity index increased by 0.03, 0.03 and 0.005, respectively.

Real CT   Real PET   Pix2Pix   CycleGAN   RegGAN   C2P-GAN

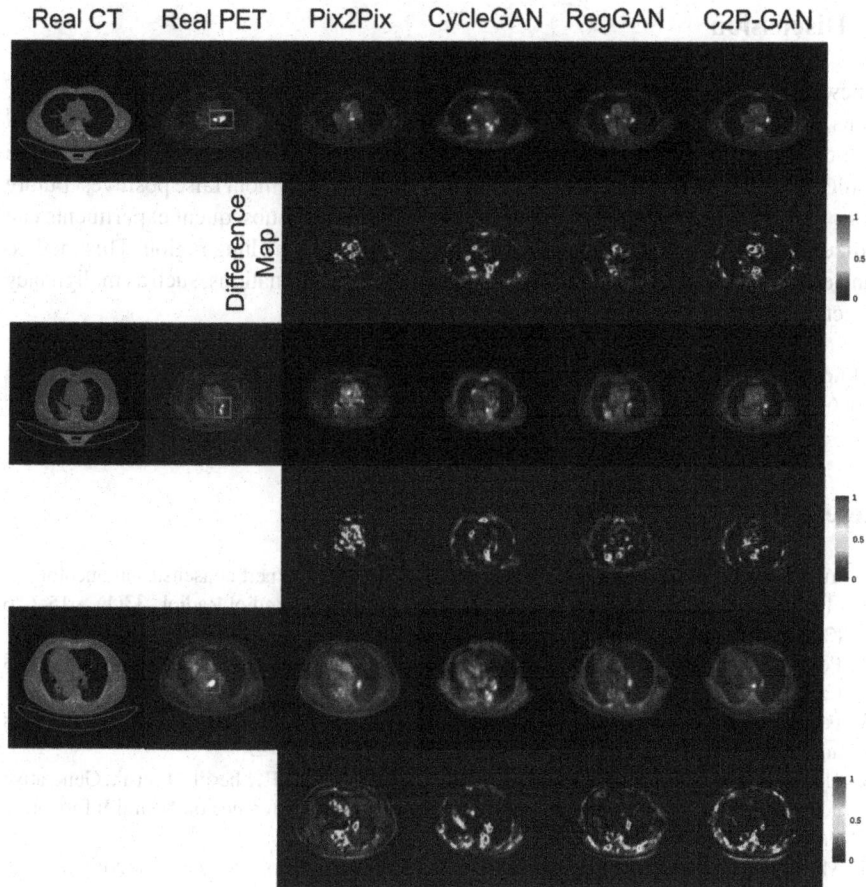

Fig. 2. The visualization results of different methods (Pix2Pix, CycleGAN, RegGAN and C2P-GAN). Each column represents the real CT image, the real PET image, the PET image synthesised by each method and their difference maps from the real PET image.

Table 1. The NMAE、PSNR and SSIM results of different methods.

	NMAE ↓	PSNR ↑	SSIM ↑
Pix2Pix	0.0870	38.89	0.8456
CycleGAN	0.0876	44.98	0.8489
RegGAN	0.0748	46.12	0.8716
C2P-GAN	**0.0720**	**48.47**	**0.8765**

4 Discussion

A new method has been proposed to automatically generate PET examinations using CT scans, achieving smaller NMAE, higher PSNR and SSIM compared to other advanced methods. In terms of visual effects, our artificially intelligent synthesized PET image results are expected to detect malignant tumors in real PET without false positives. Future work will entails acquiring larger datasets for training, and subsequent experiments can utilize the entire CT and PET, and should not be limited to the lung region. This method can be used for a variety of applications requiring PET examinations, such as malignancy detection and drug therapy evaluation.

Acknowledgements. This work was supported by National Natural Science Foundation of China (No. 61802330).

References

1. Yu, H., Gu, Y., Fan, W., Gao, Y., Wang, M., Zhu, X., et al.: Expert consensus on oncological [18F] FDG total-body PET/CT imaging (version 1). Eur. Radiol.Radiol. **33**(1), 615–626 (2023)
2. Pelc, N.J.: Recent and future directions in CT imaging. Ann. Biomed. Eng. **42**, 260–268 (2014)
3. Farwell, M.D., Pryma, D.A., Mankoff, D.A.: PET/CT imaging in cancer: current applications and future directions. Cancer **120**(22), 3433–3445 (2014)
4. Goodfellow Ian, J., Jean, P.-A., Mehdi, M., Bing, X., David, W.-F., Sherjil, O., et al.: Generative adversarial nets. In: Proceedings of the 27th International Conference on Neural Information Processing Systems, pp. 2672–80 (2014)
5. Mirza, M., Osindero, S.: Conditional generative adversarial nets. arXiv preprint arXiv:14111784 (2014)
6. Baydoun, A., Xu, K., Heo, J.U., Yang, H., Zhou, F., Bethell, L.A., et al.: Synthetic CT generation of the pelvis in patients with cervical cancer: a single input approach using generative adversarial network. IEEE Access **9**, 17208–17221 (2021)
7. Isola, P., Zhu, J.-Y., Zhou, T., Efros, A.A.: Image-to-image translation with conditional adversarial networks. In: Proceedings of the IEEE Conference on Computer Vision and Pattern Recognition, pp. 1125–1134 (2017)
8. Ranjan, A., Lalwani, D., Misra, R.: GAN for synthesizing CT from T2-weighted MRI data towards MR-guided radiation treatment. Magn. Reson. Mater. Phys. Biol. Med. **35**(3), 449–457 (2022)
9. Zhu, J.-Y., Park, T., Isola, P., Efros, A.A.: Unpaired image-to-image translation using cycle-consistent adversarial networks. In: Proceedings of the IEEE International Conference on Computer Vision, pp. 2223–2232 (2017)
10. Gu, X., Zhang, Y., Zeng, W., Zhong, S., Wang, H., Liang, D., et al.: Cross-modality image translation: CT image synthesis of MR brain images using multi generative network with perceptual supervision. Comput. Methods Programs Biomed.. Methods Programs Biomed. **237**, 107571 (2023)
11. Wang, J., Yan, B., Wu, X., Jiang, X., Zuo, Y., Yang, Y.: Development of an unsupervised cycle contrastive unpaired translation network for MRI-to-CT synthesis. J. Appl. Clin. Med. Phys. **23**(11), e13775 (2022)

12. Moriakov, N., Adler, J., Teuwen, J.: Kernel of cycleGAN as a principle homogeneous space. arXiv preprint arXiv:200109061 (2020)
13. Sim, B., Oh, G., Lim, S., Ye, J.C.: Optimal transport, cyclegan, and penalized ls for unsupervised learning in inverse problems (2019)
14. Ben-Cohen, A., Klang, E., Raskin, S.P., Soffer, S., Ben-Haim, S., Konen, E., et al.: Cross-modality synthesis from CT to PET using FCN and GAN networks for improved automated lesion detection. Eng. Appl. Artif. Intell.Artif. Intell. **78**, 186–194 (2019)
15. Long, J., Shelhamer, E., Darrell, T.: Fully convolutional networks for semantic segmentation. In: Proceedings of the IEEE Conference on Computer Vision and Pattern Recognition, pp. 3431–3440 (2015)
16. Dong, X., Wang, T., Lei, Y., Higgins, K., Liu, T., Curran, W.J., et al.: Synthetic CT generation from non-attenuation corrected PET images for whole-body PET imaging. Phys. Med. Biol. **64**(21), 215016 (2019)
17. Kong, L., Lian, C., Huang, D., Hu, Y., Zhou, Q.: Breaking the dilemma of medical image-to-image translation. Adv. Neural. Inf. Process. Syst. **34**, 1964–1978 (2021)
18. Dosovitskiy, A., Beyer, L., Kolesnikov, A., Weissenborn, D., Zhai, X., Unterthiner, T., et al.: An image is worth 16x16 words: Transformers for image recognition at scale. arXiv preprint arXiv:201011929 (2020)
19. Tragakis, A., Kaul, C., Murray-Smith, R., Husmeier, D.: The fully convolutional transformer for medical image segmentation. In: Proceedings of the IEEE/CVF Winter Conference on Applications of Computer Vision, pp. 3660–9 (2023)
20. Zhang, Z., Liu, Q., Wang, Y.: Road extraction by deep residual u-net. IEEE Geosci. Remote Sens. Lett.Geosci. Remote Sens. Lett. **15**(5), 749–753 (2018)
21. Balakrishnan, G., Zhao, A., Sabuncu, M.R., Guttag, J., Dalca, A.V.: Voxelmorph: a learning framework for deformable medical image registration. IEEE Trans. Med. Imaging **38**(8), 1788–1800 (2019)
22. Wang, Z., Bovik, A.C., Sheikh, H.R., Simoncelli, E.P.: Image quality assessment: from error visibility to structural similarity. IEEE Trans. Image Process. **13**(4), 600–612 (2004)
23. Avanaki, A.N.: Exact global histogram specification optimized for structural similarity. Opt. Rev. **16**(6), 613–621 (2009)

Contrast Learning Based Robust Framework for Weakly Supervised Medical Image Segmentation with Coarse Bounding Box Annotations

Ziqi Zhu[1,2], Jun Shi[1], Minfan Zhao[1], Zhaohui Wang[1], Liang Qiao[1], and Hong An[1,2(✉)]

[1] School of Computer Science and Technology, University of Science and Technology of China, Hefei, China
tally@mail.ustc.edu.cn,han@ustc.edu.cn
[2] School of Data Science, University of Science and Technology of China, Hefei, China

Abstract. The shortage of data due to high annotation costs has limited the development of supervised medical image segmentation methods that rely on tight pixel-level annotations. Recently, weakly supervised methods based on multiple instance learning have been proposed to reduce the annotation cost by using bounding box annotations and achieve competitive performance. However, most existing methods require accurate bounding box annotations to generate positive and negative sample bags, which is difficult to realize due to the inevitable errors associated with manually annotated bounding boxes. In this study, we propose a robust framework based on contrast learning for weakly supervised medical image segmentation. Specifically, our method involves a **F**ine-grained **S**emantic **R**epresentation **M**odule (FSRM), which is used to distinguish foreground and background pixels inside a coarse bounding box. Positive and negative sample bags are generated for multiple instance learning based on the obtained foreground results instead of bounding box constraints. Therefore, our proposed method can ensure the performance under coarse labeling by automatically extracting the boundaries of foreground and background. Our method achieves state-of-the-art results on two publicly available datasets, and extensive experiments validate the robustness of our method under noisy annotations. The source code will be available at https://github.com/tally/wsis-contrastlearning.

Keywords: Weakly supervised image segmentation · Contrast learning · Bounding box supervision

1 Introduction

In recent years, medical image segmentation has evolved with the development of deep learning, and a large number of methods have been proposed [1,2,19]. Most existing methods require massive precise pixel-level annotations to ensure the accuracy and robustness [21]. However, obtaining large-scale datasets that meet these requirements has been a major challenge, as medical image annotation relies on expert knowledge and data annotation is often considered labour-intensive and costly, with unavoidable human errors [24]. To address this problem, weakly supervised segmentation methods have been proposed to alleviate the need for pixel-level annotation by utilizing weak or noisy labels, such as image-level labels [8,13,16], bounding boxes [4,22,23], scribbles [11], and others [17].

In the recent study of weakly supervised approaches, the bounding-box-based methods stand out due to its ability to provide relatively accurate semantic and localization information with low annotation costs. One available approach is to use out-of-the-box methods such as CRF [14], GrabCut [20] to extract high quality pixel-level pseudo-labels from the bounding box by means of inter-pixel relationships. DeepCut [18] applies dense CRF [6] to iteratively pseudo labels. Box2Seg [7] introduces per-class attention maps that saliently guides the per-pixel cross entropy loss to focus on foreground pixels and refines the segmentation boundaries. While these methods have made great progress, they are limited for the blurred boundaries and low-contrast targets that are common in medical imaging [12].

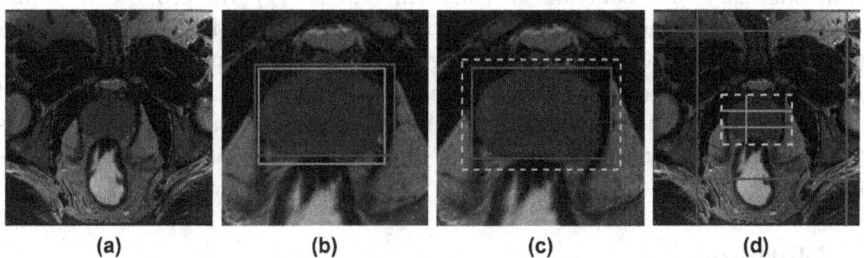

(a)   (b)   (c)   (d)

Fig. 1. (a) The prostate image with ground truth in the promise12 dataset (b) The green box is the tight bounding box generated from the ground truth, and the red box is the coarse bounding box . (c) The foreground proposal generated by our proposed FSRM based on the coarse bounding box, where the yellow dashed box represents the cropped area that extends outwards based on the coarse bounding box (d) The positive and negative sample bags generated based on the foreground proposal, where the red lines without foreground pixels are negative bags and the green lines with foreground pixels are positive bags. (b) and (c) have been enlarged for a better view. (Color figure online)

Multiple instance learning methods based on the bounding box tightness prior are also used to leverage bounding box annotations. Hsu *et al.* [3] generate positive and negative bags based on the sweeping lines of each bounding box, and train the network by optimizing positive bags and negative bags. Wang *et al.* [22] proposed a generalized multiple instance learning method to expand the number of samples. However, due to manual annotation errors and the difficulty of annotating small targets, the bounding box annotation may not be a tight bounding box as shown in Fig. 1(b). When the tightness constraint is not satisfied, sample bags around the boundary may be misclassified, which causes degradation of model accuracy. Wang *et al.* [23] attempts to solve the problem of loose bounding boxes, but still uses an alternative form of the bounding box tightening prior.

In this paper, we propose a contrast learning based robust framework for obtaining pixel-level segmentation results from coarse bounding box annotations. The pixels inside the bounding box are mixed with foreground regions corresponding to the target and background regions without the target pixels. The algorithm is based on the assumption that foreground and background features can be separated [25], and a fine-grained semantic representation module (FSRM) is designed to identify foreground and background regions. This module expands the distance between foreground and background features on the feature space by contrast learning methods, thus enabling the model to extract foreground regions from the coarse bounding box. We use the FSRM-extracted foreground regions to replace the bounding box regions as target candidates and generate sample bags from them for subsequent multiple instance learning. Our algorithm no longer relies on bounding box tightness prior, and thus works well even on coarse bounding box annotations.

In summary, our contributions are three-folds: (1) We propose a robust weakly supervised medical image segmentation framework for coarse bounding box annotation. (2) Our proposed fine-grained semantic representation module can be embedded into the U-shape segmentation network to extract foreground feature. (3) We are the first to replace manually annotated coarse bounding boxes with foreground-background boundaries extracted by contrast learning methods for multiple instance learning.

2 Methods

An overview of our proposed framework is shown in Fig. 2, consisting of two parts: fine-grained semantic representation module and multiple instance learning module with foreground proposal constraints. For simplicity and efficiency, we choose a residual version of unet [26] as our backbone, we name it as ResUnet.

2.1 Fine-Grained Semantic Representation Module (FSRM)

Given an input image $\mathbf{I} \in \mathbb{R}^{C \times H \times W}$ with m bounding boxes, in which C and $H \times W$ denote the channel number and spatial dimension of the input image respectively. The bounding box annotation $y_i = (c_i, b_i) \in \mathbf{Y}, \mathbf{Y} = \{y_1, y_2, ...y_m\}$ provides information about the latent spatial location of the foreground pixels of the objects it annotates, where c_i indicates the category label and b_i is a 4-dimensional vector representing the location of the bounding box.

Since the foreground pixels in the bounding box share the same target, there is similarity in the semantic information of the foreground pixels; correspondingly, the background is the surrounding non-target area, and there is similarity in the semantic information of the background pixels as well. In addition,

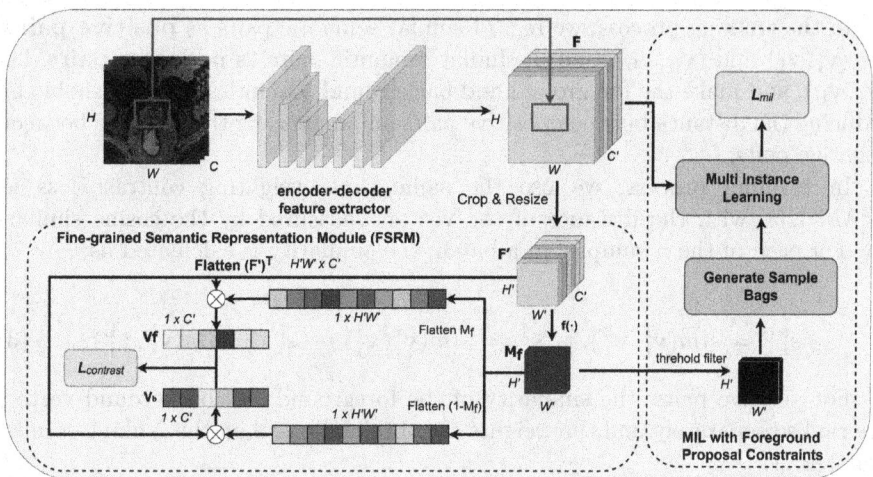

Fig. 2. Overview of the proposed method. The image input to our model will be fed into an encoder-decoder backbone network to extract semantic features, which will be cropped to produce a feature map of the region of interest(ROI) based on bounding box annotations. FSRM then generates foreground proposals from the cropped feature maps by contrast learning, and the MIL module generates sample bags for multiple instance learning training based on the foreground proposals. Finally the pixel-level output is supervised by multiple instance learning.

foreground and background pixels carry different semantic information. The backbone network extracts semantic information to generate the feature map $\mathbf{F} \in \mathbb{R}^{C' \times H \times W}$. The separation of foreground and background semantic features is achieved by narrowing the distance between similar features and expanding the distance between dissimilar features. C' denotes the channel number of the feature map.

As shown in Fig. 2, to explicitly extract the foreground region, a feature map $\mathbf{F}' \in \mathbb{R}^{C' \times H' \times W'}$ is obtained by cropping from the original feature map $\mathbf{F}$ according to the bounding box and using convolution $f(\cdot)$ to extract a foreground proposal map $\mathbf{M_f} \in \mathbb{R}^{1 \times H' \times W'}$. $H' \times W'$ denotes spatial dimension of the cropped feature map. Resizing is used to ensure that bounding boxes of different sizes can produce feature maps of the same size. The background proposal is considered to be the complementary map to $\mathbf{M_f}$. $\mathbf{M_f}$ and $\mathbf{M_b}$ can be expressed as:

$$\mathbf{M_f} = f(\mathbf{F}'), \qquad \mathbf{M_b} = 1 - \mathbf{M_f}. \tag{1}$$

For the sake of consistency between foreground candidates and feature maps, the product of the foreground proposal M_f and the transpose of the feature map $(F')^T$ is used as the representation vector v_f for the semantic similarity measure.

$$\mathbf{v_f} = \mathbf{M_f} \otimes (\mathbf{F}')^{\mathbf{T}}, \qquad \mathbf{v_b} = \mathbf{M_b} \otimes (\mathbf{F}')^{\mathbf{T}}. \tag{2}$$

In the training process, we regard similar semantic pairs as **positive pairs**, i.e. $(\mathbf{v_f}, \mathbf{v_f})$ and $(\mathbf{v_b}, \mathbf{v_b})$, and dissimilar semantic pairs as **negative pairs**, i.e. $(\mathbf{v_f}, \mathbf{v_b})$, and make the foreground and background semantics distinguishable by reducing the distance between positive pairs and increasing the distance between negative pairs.

In training process, we use the same rank weighting contrast loss as C^2AM [25], with the distance of the vectors measured by the cosine similarity. For each of the n samples in a batch, the similarity is calculated as:

$$s_{i,j}^{neg} = sim(\mathbf{v_i^f}, \mathbf{v_j^b}), \quad s_{i,j}^{f} = sim(\mathbf{v_i^f}, \mathbf{v_j^f}), \quad s_{i,j}^{b} = sim(\mathbf{v_i^b}, \mathbf{v_j^b}). \tag{3}$$

For positive pairs, the similarity of the foreground and background vectors are ranked separately and the weights are obtained based on the ranking results, denoted as:

$$w_{i,j}^{f} = exp(-\alpha \cdot rank(s_{i,j}^{f})), \quad w_{i,j}^{b} = exp(-\alpha \cdot rank(s_{i,j}^{b})). \tag{4}$$

α is the hyperparameter and loss can be calculated as follows:

$$\mathcal{L}_{pos}^{f} = -\frac{2}{n(n-1)} \sum_{1 \le i < j \le n} (w_{i,j}^{f} \cdot log(s_{i,j}^{f})) \tag{5}$$

$$\mathcal{L}_{pos}^{b} = -\frac{2}{n(n-1)} \sum_{1 \le i < j \le n} (w_{i,j}^{b} \cdot log(s_{i,j}^{b})) \tag{6}$$

$$\mathcal{L}_{neg} = -\frac{1}{n^2} \sum_{i=1}^{n} \sum_{j=1}^{n} log(1 - s_{i,j}^{neg}) \tag{7}$$

The final contrast loss function is a summation of the three contrast losses, written as:

$$\mathcal{L}_{contrast} = \mathcal{L}_{pos}^{f} + \mathcal{L}_{pos}^{b} + \mathcal{L}_{neg} \tag{8}$$

Note that directly using the feature map of the region corresponding to the bounding box for FSRM may not provide sufficient context, so we first extend the bounding box outward by β pixels during the cropping process before using it as input to FSRM as Fig. 1(c) shows. Another advantage of expanding the boundaries is that the expanded region can be used as a reference for the background region, and control of the training process can be achieved by monitoring whether the expanded boundary part is correctly classified as background.

2.2   MIL with Foreground Proposal Constraints

The bounding box tightness prior fails when dealing with coarse bounding boxes, and generating sample bags for multiple instance learning directly through bounding boxes may produce misclassified sample bags, leading to incorrect supervisory signals during training and affecting the accuracy of the model.

We devise a cascade structure for foreground proposal extraction with the generation of sample bags for multiple instance learning, using foreground proposals instead of bounding boxes as a prior.

As shown in Fig. 2, the foreground proposal map $\mathbf{M_f}$ in FSRM will be resized to its original size and then binarised foreground pseudo masks will be generated based on a threshold t. Based on the pseudo masks, sample bags are generated in a similar way to the bounding box tightness prior [22]: a crossing line containing at least one foreground pixel will be considered as a positive bag, otherwise a negative bag, as depicted in Fig. 1(d).

2.3   Total Loss Function

Following previous methods [4, 22], we use the same loss function $\mathcal{L}_{mil}$ as Wang et al. [22] for multiple instance learning. Besides, contrast loss function $\mathcal{L}_{contrast}$ is also involved in the total loss, denotes as:

$$\mathcal{L}_{total} = \mathcal{L}_{mil} + \mathcal{L}_{contrast} \tag{9}$$

3   Experiments

3.1   Datasets

We evaluate our model on two public datasets. The first one is the prostate MR image segmentation 2012 (PROMISE12) dataset [10] for prostate segmentation and the second one is the anatomical tracings of lesions after stroke (ATLAS) R2.0 dataset [9] for brain lesion segmentation.

Promise12. The PROMISE12 dataset is a commonly used publicly available dataset for prostate segmentation. It consists of the transversal T2-weighted MR images from 50 patients, including both benign and prostate cancer cases. Same as the study in [22], the dataset was divided into two non-overlapping subsets, one with 40 patients for training and the other with 10 patients for validation.

ATLAS R2.0. The ATLAS R2.0 dataset is a well-known open-source dataset for brain lesion segmentation. It consists of 655 T1-weighted MR images with manually-segmented lesion masks. These images were acquired from different cohorts and different scanners. The dataset was divided into two non-overlapping subsets, one with 500 images for training and the other with 155 images for validation.

3.2   Implementation Details

All experiments were implemented using PyTorch [15] in this study. We train the entire model for 50 epochs on each dataset in an end-to-end way using Adam [5] optimizer with parameter $(\beta_1, \beta_2) = (0.9, 0.99)$. Initial learning rate and batch size are set to 0.0001 and 16, respectively. Without special instructions, the hyper-parameter of rank weighting contrast loss was set to $\alpha = 0.25$ and the bounding box offset was set to $\beta = 8$. The threshold t used for binarizing the foreground proposal was set to 0.5.

3.3 Main Result

To prove the effectiveness of the proposed method, three state-of-the-art methods are used for comparison, as shown in Table 1. Dice coefficients(DC) are employed to assess the performance of the model. To evaluate the robustness of the model under different intensities of noise, we apply a perturbation of η pixel offset to the original tight bounding box generated from pixel-level annotations. When the noise parameter $\eta \geq 2$, our proposed method outperforms existing algorithms on two datasets and is less affected by changes in n, thus demonstrating the robustness and superiority of our method utilizing coarse bounding box annotation. As an upper bound for segmentation performance, the ResUNet-based fully supervised segmentation model achieves dice coefficients of 0.893 on the PROMISE12 dataset and 0.527 on the ATLAS R2.0 dataset.

Table 1. Comparison of Dice coefficients for different methods. η is the offset of the coarse bounding box from the tight bounding box and is used to indicate the noise intensity of the annotation.

Method	Promise12				Atlas R2.0			
	$\eta = 1$	$\eta = 2$	$\eta = 4$	$\eta = 8$	$\eta = 1$	$\eta = 2$	$\eta = 4$	$\eta = 8$
MIL [3]	0.863	0.861	0.838	0.811	0.432	0.401	0.383	0.370
Generalized MIL [22]	0.876	0.872	0.869	0.861	**0.493**	0.484	0.482	0.476
Polar Transformation [23]	**0.881**	0.878	0.875	0.870	0.491	0.485	0.483	0.479
Proposed	0.880	**0.879**	**0.876**	**0.873**	0.489	**0.490**	**0.487**	**0.485**

To evaluate the sensitivity of the proposed method to parameters, different parameters are used in experiments. Figure 3 shows the Dice values of our methods under different thresholds t (used to binarize the mask) and different bounding box offset β (used to crop the ROI) on PROMISE12 dataset.

Figure 4 shows the comparison of the visualization results of our method and the other three methods. It can be seen from the figure that our method can still provide sufficient details under large noise perturbations. In addition, the shape of the output of our method is closer to the ground truth.

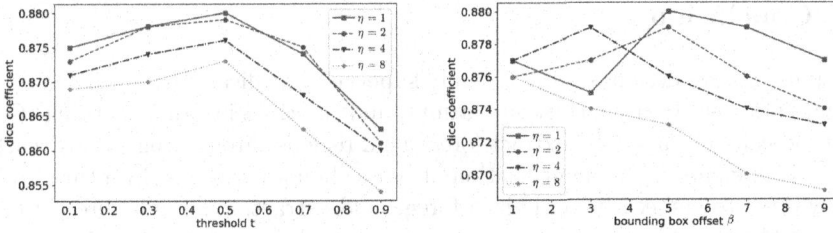

Fig. 3. Dice curves under different thresholds and different bounding box offset on PROMISE12 dataset

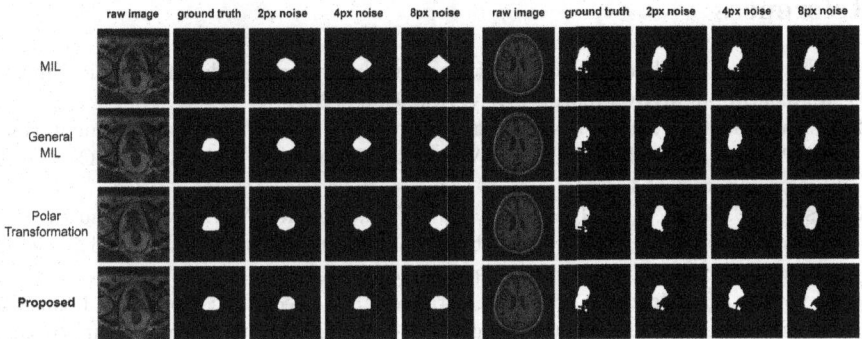

Fig. 4. Visual comparison between the proposed method and three state-of-the-art ones.

3.4 Ablation Study

To investigate the importance of each component in our proposed method, the dice coefficient is adopted. We evaluate the model on promise12 dataset for ablation studies. As shown in Table 2, all the proposed modules contribute to the final prediction results.

Table 2. Ablation study for our proposed method.

Method	Promise12			
	$\eta = 1$	$\eta = 2$	$\eta = 4$	$\eta = 8$
Base	0.876	0.872	0.869	0.861
Base + FSRM	0.875	0.874	0.871	0.867
Base + FSRM + foreground prior	**0.880**	**0.879**	**0.876**	**0.873**

4   Conclusion

In summary, we design a robust weakly supervised medical image segmentation framework based on contrastive learning and multiple instance learning. Our method can automatically extract foreground regions through contrastive learning, which enables reliable utilization of coarse bounding boxes. In future work, we will try to embed the optimized foreground extraction module directly into the backbone network to improve the quality and consider introducing coarse annotations from clinical practice to verify the performance of the algorithm.

References

1. Chen, J., et al.: TransUNet: transformers make strong encoders for medical image segmentation. arXiv preprint arXiv:2102.04306 (2021)
2. Hatamizadeh, A., et al.: UNETR: transformers for 3D medical image segmentation. In: Proceedings of the IEEE/CVF Winter Conference on Applications of Computer Vision, pp. 574–584 (2022)
3. Hsu, C.C., Hsu, K.J., Tsai, C.C., Lin, Y.Y., Chuang, Y.Y.: Weakly supervised instance segmentation using the bounding box tightness prior. In: Advances in Neural Information Processing Systems, vol. 32 (2019)
4. Kervadec, H., Dolz, J., Wang, S., Granger, E., Ayed, I.B.: Bounding boxes for weakly supervised segmentation: global constraints get close to full supervision. In: Medical Imaging with Deep Learning, pp. 365–381. PMLR (2020)
5. Kingma, D.P., Ba, J.: Adam: a method for stochastic optimization. arXiv preprint arXiv:1412.6980 (2014)
6. Krähenbühl, P., Koltun, V.: Efficient inference in fully connected CRFs with gaussian edge potentials. In: Advances in neural information processing systems, vol. 24 (2011)
7. Kulharia, V., Chandra, S., Agrawal, A., Torr, P., Tyagi, A.: Box2Seg: attention weighted loss and discriminative feature learning for weakly supervised segmentation. In: Vedaldi, A., Bischof, H., Brox, T., Frahm, J.-M. (eds.) ECCV 2020. LNCS, vol. 12372, pp. 290–308. Springer, Cham (2020). https://doi.org/10.1007/978-3-030-58583-9_18
8. Li, Z.W., Xuan, S.B., He, X.D., Wang, L.: Global weighted average pooling network with multilevel feature fusion for weakly supervised brain tumor segmentation. IET Image Proc. **17**(2), 418–427 (2023)
9. Liew, S.L., et al.: A large, curated, open-source stroke neuroimaging dataset to improve lesion segmentation algorithms. Sci. data **9**(1), 320 (2022)
10. Litjens, G., et al.: Evaluation of prostate segmentation algorithms for MRI: the promise12 challenge. Med. Image Anal. **18**(2), 359–373 (2014)
11. Liu, X., et al.: Weakly supervised segmentation of COVID19 infection with scribble annotation on CT images. Pattern Recogn. **122**, 108341 (2022)
12. Mahani, G.K., et al.: Bounding box based weakly supervised deep convolutional neural network for medical image segmentation using an uncertainty guided and spatially constrained loss. In: 2022 IEEE 19th International Symposium on Biomedical Imaging (ISBI), pp. 1–5. IEEE (2022)
13. Meng, Q., Liao, L., Satoh, S.: Weakly-supervised learning with complementary heatmap for retinal disease detection. IEEE Trans. Med. Imaging **41**(8), 2067–2078 (2022)

14. Papandreou, G., Chen, L.C., Murphy, K.P., Yuille, A.L.: Weakly-and semi-supervised learning of a deep convolutional network for semantic image segmentation. In: Proceedings of the IEEE International Conference on Computer Vision, pp. 1742–1750 (2015)
15. Paszke, A., et al.: PyTorch: an imperative style, high-performance deep learning library. In: Advances in Neural Information Processing Systems, vol. 32 (2019)
16. Patel, G., Dolz, J.: Weakly supervised segmentation with cross-modality equivariant constraints. Med. Image Anal. **77**, 102374 (2022)
17. Peng, J., Kervadec, H., Dolz, J., Ayed, I.B., Pedersoli, M., Desrosiers, C.: Discretely-constrained deep network for weakly supervised segmentation. Neural Netw. **130**, 297–308 (2020)
18. Rajchl, M., et al.: DeepCut: object segmentation from bounding box annotations using convolutional neural networks. IEEE Trans. Med. Imaging **36**(2), 674–683 (2016)
19. Ronneberger, O., Fischer, P., Brox, T.: U-Net: convolutional networks for biomedical image segmentation. In: Navab, N., Hornegger, J., Wells, W.M., Frangi, A.F. (eds.) MICCAI 2015. LNCS, vol. 9351, pp. 234–241. Springer, Cham (2015). https://doi.org/10.1007/978-3-319-24574-4_28
20. Rother, C., Kolmogorov, V., Blake, A.: "GrabCut" interactive foreground extraction using iterated graph cuts. ACM Trans. Graph. (TOG) **23**(3), 309–314 (2004)
21. Tajbakhsh, N., Jeyaseelan, L., Li, Q., Chiang, J.N., Wu, Z., Ding, X.: Embracing imperfect datasets: a review of deep learning solutions for medical image segmentation. Med. Image Anal. **63**, 101693 (2020)
22. Wang, J., Xia, B.: Bounding box tightness prior for weakly supervised image segmentation. In: de Bruijne, M., et al. (eds.) MICCAI 2021. LNCS, vol. 12902, pp. 526–536. Springer, Cham (2021). https://doi.org/10.1007/978-3-030-87196-3_49
23. Wang, J., Xia, B.: Polar transformation based multiple instance learning assisting weakly supervised image segmentation with loose bounding box annotations. arXiv preprint arXiv:2203.06000 (2022)
24. Wei, J., Hu, Y., Li, G., Cui, S., Kevin Zhou, S., Li, Z.: BoxPolyp: boost generalized polyp segmentation using extra coarse bounding box annotations. In: Wang, L., Dou, Q., Fletcher, P.T., Speidel, S., Li, S. (eds.) Medical Image Computing and Computer Assisted Intervention – MICCAI 2022. MICCAI 2022. Lecture Notes in Computer Science, vol. 13433, pp. 67–77. Springer, Cham (2022). https://doi.org/10.1007/978-3-031-16437-8_7
25. Xie, J., Xiang, J., Chen, J., Hou, X., Zhao, X., Shen, L.: C2AM: contrastive learning of class-agnostic activation map for weakly supervised object localization and semantic segmentation. In: Proceedings of the IEEE/CVF Conference on Computer Vision and Pattern Recognition, pp. 989–998 (2022)
26. Zhang, Z., Liu, Q., Wang, Y.: Road extraction by deep residual U-Net. IEEE Geosci. Remote Sens. Lett. **15**(5), 749–753 (2018)

MPSurv: End-to-End Multi-model Pseudo-Label Model for Brain Tumor Survival Prediction with Population Information Integration

Qingsong Wang[1], Xin Lin[1], Ruiquan Ge[1(⊠)], Ahmed Elazab[2], Xiangyang Hu[1], Jionghao Cheng[1], Yuqing Peng[3], Xiang Wan[4], and Changmiao Wang[4(⊠)]

[1] School of Computer Science and Technology, Hangzhou Dianzi University, Hangzhou 310018, China
gespring@hdu.edu.cn
[2] School of Biomedical Engineering, Shenzhen University, Shenzhen 518060, China
[3] Shenzhen Institutes of Advanced Technology, Chinese Academy of Sciences, Shenzhen 518055, China
[4] Shenzhen Research Institute of Big Data, Shenzhen 518172, China
cmwangalbert@gmail.com

Abstract. Predicting brain tumor survival can aid physicians in better assessing the efficacy of treatments and adjusting treatment plans in clinical practices to enhance patient survival. Recently, deep learning techniques have attracted massive attention in predicting brain tumor survival. However, the majority of existing methods necessitate at least two or more independent networks for knowledge sharing later in the model and overlook the significance of population information. In this paper, we propose an end-to-end multi-model brain tumor survival prediction (MPSurv) model that incorporates patient population information. Moreover, given the presence of censored data, we propose to address this issue by generating pseudo-labels, which in turn augments the original data and improves the utilization of the dataset. We have collected and supplemented survival labels based on the BraTS 2021 dataset for the training and validation of segmentation and prediction tasks. Experimental results demonstrate that our model enhances the accuracy of brain tumor survival prediction and exhibits superior generalizability. The source code is available at: https://github.com/APTX574/MPSurv.

Keywords: Survival Analysis · Image Segmentation · Brain tumor · Deep learning

Supplementary Information The online version contains supplementary material available at https://doi.org/10.1007/978-3-031-45087-7_13.

W. Qin et al. (Eds.): CMMCA 2023 (MICCAI Workshop), LNCS 14243, pp. 120–130, 2023.
https://doi.org/10.1007/978-3-031-45087-7_13

1   Introduction

Gliomas are malignant tumors originating from glial cells in the brain and represent one of the most prevalent intracranial malignancies. The World Health Organization classifies gliomas into four grades (I-IV), based on histological and cellular characteristics [14]. Grades I and II fall under the category of low-grade gliomas (LGGs), while Grades III and IV are classified as high-grade gliomas (HGGs). By predicting the survival time of patients, it can effectively help doctors to design adequate treatments and prolong the survival of patients. Therefore, survival prediction is an integral part of effective treatment and surgical planning.

With advancements in the field of deep learning, the extraction of key features from extensive clinical data for patient survival time prediction has become feasible. Compared to traditional survival analysis methods, deep learning models can predict patient survival time with higher accuracy. In the context of tumor survival prediction, Ali et al. [2] presented a series of 2D and 3D models for segmenting gliomas from MRI of the brain and predicting the overall survival (OS) time of patients. By integrating recent self-attention mechanisms, Islam et al. [12] proposed a new 3D attention U-Net model for survival prediction. Feng et al. [8] employed six different parameters of 3D U-Net for integration, selecting the average value for the final segmentation result.

From the perspective of data sets, there has been a notable uptick in the utilization of multimodal data by various methods in recent years. For example, Cui et al. [7] have proposed a method to mitigate the issue of mode loss, employing deep learning networks to effectively predict the survival rate of brain cancer using incomplete data derived from radiology, pathology, genomics, and demographics. Similarly, Nie et al. [16] harnessed the power of deep learning to distill multiple features from population information. Hermoza et al. [10] used medical images and patient age data as input variables to estimate OS time. However, it has been observed that in many instances, only age is considered as a key population variable, which often leads to the neglect of other important characteristics embedded within population information.

Another challenge with datasets in survival analysis is related to the processing of censored data. Censored data encapsulate samples representing instances where an event did not transpire, either due to the study concluding prior to the event's occurrence or the patient departing before the study's conclusion. Current methodologies for managing censored data generally rely on the Cox proportional hazards model [6]. However, this model primarily ranks patients based on their risk level rather than predicting survival time, thereby constraining its utility. Certain methodologies [1,8,19] directly predict survival time, but they do not account for censored data. Hermoza et al. [11] considered the potential discrepancy between censorship time and concealed survival time and estimating pseudo-labels to semi-supervise the prediction of survival time. Our work builds upon these insights and further extends them.

The task of predicting brain tumor survival is complex and challenging due to the limit of brain tumor datasets. Given the limited dataset, missing data patterns, and lack of population information, we propose a novel predictive model for brain tumor survival. This model incorporates population information factors, addresses the issue of missing modality, and employs a pseudo-labeling method to process censored data. These approaches enhance the utilization rate of the dataset, improve the accuracy of survival predictions, and increase the model's generalizability. Our contributions can be summarized as follows:

1) We propose a novel end-to-end model MPSurv for predicting brain tumor survival, which can improve the accuracy of brain tumor survival prediction.

2) Our model integrates multiple patient-relevant population information to provide a more comprehensive prediction outcome.

3) To overcome the issue of inadequate data utilization in the brain tumor dataset, we employ a semi-supervised learning technique to generate pseudo-labels for survival time, thereby improving the data's utilization rate.

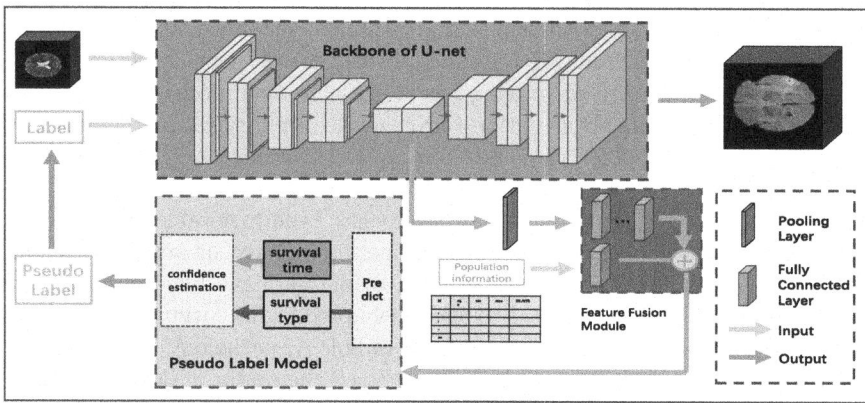

Fig. 1. The overall framework of MPSurv. Utilizing U-Net as the overarching framework for model training, we rely on survival tags and MRI as inputs into the U-Net. The Feature Fusion module is employed to merge demographic data with the features procured following the upsampling process on U-Net. Subsequently, the pseudo label module is employed to forecast both the survival time and survival type, followed by an evaluation of its corresponding confidence. Samples exhibiting high confidence are earmarked for input in subsequent training phases.

2   Methodology

We introduce MPSurv, an end-to-end model for brain tumor survival prediction, as depicted in Fig. 1. To enhance efficiency and convenience, we employ an end-to-end architecture throughout the model (Sect. 2.1). Our model incorporates population information for survival prediction and uses a semi-supervised pseudo-label module to generate pseudo-labels. After conducting a confidence evaluation, we expand the dataset (Sect. 2.2). Lastly, we provide a detailed discussion on the proposed loss function term and its implications (Sect. 2.3).

2.1 Overall Architecture

To facilitate the explanation of our methodology, we define the dataset as $D = \{(x_i, y_i, z_i, e_i)\}_{i=1}^{|D|}$, where $x_i \in X$ denotes a medical image with $X \subset \mathbb{R}^{128,128,128}$, $y_i \in \mathbb{N}$ represents the observation time in days, z_i signifies the population information vector including age, sex, and race, and $e_i \in \{1,0\}$ indicates whether the data is censored or not. When $e_i = 0$, it designates uncensored data, with y_i corresponding to a survival time t_i, which signifies the individual's time of death. Conversely, when $e_i = 1$, it signifies censored data. In this case, although t_i is unknown, it is understood that $t_i > y_i$.

2.2 Pseudo Label

The pseudo-label module, as depicted in Fig. 1, employs pseudo labels to semi-supervise our survival time regressor. To calculate confidence, most methods either compare the results of the two models, or use the probability of pseudo-labels as an indication of confidence. However, considering that pseudo-labeling is more commonly used in classification tasks rather than regression tasks, we introduce a novel method of confidence calculation based on two concepts. Our model is capable of outputting both the result of the survival prediction classification and the duration of survival, and relies on these two data to calculate the confidence level. The confidence level is determined by calculating the correlation between these two outcomes. We select high-confidence samples through confidence assessments. The determination of the time range is based on the predicted $\tilde{t}_i$. Subsequently, the relative confidence $\tilde{p}_i{'}$ of the model for each sample's prediction type is calculated, in accordance with varying time ranges. Ultimately, the final confidence level, denoted as $Confidence$, is computed as the average of the absolute value differences between the original survival type probability $\tilde{p}_i$ and $\tilde{p}_i{'}$. These confidence levels, $Confidence$, can be used to evaluate the degree of confidence in the prediction results. Based on the segmented definition of the survival time of the Brats2019 [5], the piecewise function used to calculate $\tilde{p}_i{'}$ is as follows:

$$\tilde{p}_i{'} = \begin{cases} \left(1 - \dfrac{\tilde{t}_i}{600}\right), & 0 < \tilde{t}_i \leq 300 \\[2mm] \left(\dfrac{\tilde{t}_i}{150} - 1.5\right), & 300 < \tilde{t}_i \leq 375 \\[2mm] -1 \cdot \left(\dfrac{\tilde{t}_i}{150} - 3.5\right), & 375 < \tilde{t}_i \leq 450 \\[2mm] \left(0.05 + \dfrac{\tilde{t}_i}{1000}\right), & 450 < \tilde{t}_i \leq 1300 \end{cases} \tag{1}$$

$$Confidence = \frac{\left| \tilde{p}_i - \tilde{p}_i{'} \right|}{len(\tilde{p}_i)}. \tag{2}$$

Lower confidence scores suggest predictions that align more closely with the ground truth, thereby indicating a higher confidence level. Samples with high confidence are adopted as input for the subsequent epoch training. The value of the pseudo-label is recalculated at the commencement of each epoch. Importantly, it should be noted that prior to the initiation of any training, all data lacks a pseudo label.

2.3 Proposed Loss Function

Given that the network simultaneously performs two tasks, brain tumor segmentation and survival prediction, the amalgamation of these three losses is crafted into the ultimate objective function. The training of our model aims to minimize this loss function:

$$\mathcal{L}_{MPSurv} = \alpha \cdot \mathcal{L}_{mse} + \beta \cdot \mathcal{L}_{ed} + \gamma \cdot \mathcal{L}_{type}, \tag{3}$$

where $\mathcal{L}_{mse}$ represents the mean squared error of the survival prediction, $\mathcal{L}_{ed}$ denotes the mean squared error of the segmentation, and $\mathcal{L}_{type}$ is the cross-entropy loss of the survival type. The weights are adjusted dynamically with each epoch. The segmentation loss $\mathcal{L}_{ed}$ quantifies the similarity between the predicted outcome and the actual label by calculating the Dice loss.

$$\mathcal{L}_{ed} = \frac{2\sum_i^{128} \tilde{p}_i p_i + smooth}{\sum_i^n \tilde{p}_i^2 + \sum_i^N p_i^2 + smooth}, \tag{4}$$

where p_i is the ground truth and $\tilde{p}_i$ represents the model prediction. The term *smooth* is a smoothing element employed to prevent situations where the denominator equals zero. The computation of the mean squared error $\mathcal{L}_{mse}$ encompasses two loss functions: $\mathcal{L}_{m\_true}$ and $\mathcal{L}_{m\_pseudo}$, which calculate the loss of real samples and pseudo-samples if pseudo-labels exist, respectively. The final loss is the weighted sum of both the real sample loss and the pseudo-sample loss:

$$\mathcal{L}_{mse} = \mathcal{L}_{m\_true} + \delta \cdot \mathcal{L}_{m\_pseudo}, \tag{5}$$

where the weight $\delta = 0.5$, and when calculating $\mathcal{L}_{m\_true}$, for a sample of censor data, if the predicted survival time is greater than that of censor data, the loss for this part is not calculated. In a similar fashion to the computation of $\mathcal{L}_{mse}$, the loss of both the true sample and the pseudo-sample is assessed, independently. Subsequently, their weighted sum is calculated to derive our $\mathcal{L}_{type}$. In this scenario, we employ a cross-entropy loss calculation method with a weight.

$$\mathcal{L}_{type} = \mathcal{L}_{t\_true} + \eta \cdot \mathcal{L}_{t\_pseudo}, \tag{6}$$

where the weight $\eta = 0.5$, $\mathcal{L}_{t\_pseudo}$ is the loss of pseudo-sample and $\mathcal{L}_{t\_true}$ is the loss of real samples.

3   Experiments and Results

3.1   Datasets

In our experimental setup, we amalgamated a large-scale dataset, drawing from the TCGA, TCIA, and the Multimodal Brain Tumor Segmentation Challenge

(BraTS) datasets [3,4,15]. Our dataset encompasses preoperative MRI scans of both HGGs and LGGs, totaling 1254 cases. Via data mapping of BraTS 2021 and BraTS 2020, we derived the survival information of 236 patients. The BraTS 2021 dataset, which incorporated subjects from TCIA, also provided a name mapping file that supplemented the survival information of 105 patients by matching subject IDs. We partitioned these statistics into censored and uncensored data based on patient survival and the presence of survival time. The involved population information included age, gender, ethnicity and type of tumor resection, and tumor resection type included Subtotal Resection (SR) and gross total resection (GTR). Upon observing the distribution of patient survival time, we noted that there were few data entries with a survival time exceeding 1300 d. Consequently, we set the survival time surpassing 1300 d as the survival limit. Patients who were still alive at the end of the trial were considered samples with an upper limit of survival time, and censored data were treated as samples with a lower limit of mortality time.

3.2 Comparisons

Survival time was categorized into three distinct segments: (1) short-term survivors (i.e., $\leq$ 10 months), (2) mid-term survivors (i.e., between 10 and 15 months), and (3) long-term survivors (i.e., $\geq$ 15 months). For comparison, we utilized two models for brain tumor survival analysis: 3D U-Net [20] and MFEN [18]. The latter, MFEN, is a feature extraction model, from which we selected the highest-performing combination for comparison. It should be noted that only 29 subjects in the BraTS 2019 and 2020 Challenge validation cohort offered GTR status. Therefore, we utilized a five-fold cross-validation method to perform comparisons on the 2019 training set. To ensure a fair comparison of experimental results, our model was subjected to training from scratch. The evaluation metrics we used included *Accuracy* and *MSE* related to survival prediction performance, and *Dice* to evaluate segmentation performance, and we will calculate the *Dice* scores of the enhanced tumor (ET), tumor core (TC) and whole tumor (WT) regions, respectively. All our experiments were executed using two Nvidia RTX 3090Ti GPUs, with our model being rigorously trained from scratch over the course of 800 epochs. The parameters were optimized using the Adam optimizer algorithm [13], with an established learning rate of 0.00005 and a batch size of 6.

From Table 1, it is evident that our MPSurv model demonstrates competitive performance when compared to other models, particularly in terms of *Accuracy*. However, there was no significant enhancement in the *Dice* indicator for *ET*, *TC*, and *WT*, showcasing that the inclusion of pseudo-label modules and demographic information provides our model with an advantage in terms of survival prediction accuracy, but not as much in brain tumor segmentation compared to other models.

Table 1. Five-fold cross-validation results are compared with the two best performing models on the 2019 training set. The best results are highlighted in **bold**.

Methods	$Accurary(\uparrow)$	$MSE(\downarrow)$	Dice		
			$ET(\uparrow)$	$TC(\uparrow)$	$WT(\uparrow)$
3D U-Net [20]	0.448	100000	0.737	0.807	0.894
MFEN [18]	0.493	–	**0.815**	**0.902**	0.828
MPSurv(ours)	**0.581**	**59017**	0.774	0.874	**0.926**

Table 2. Ablation experiments. It focuses on the presence or absence of pseudo-labeling modules, and the inclusion or exclusion of combined population information. The best results are highlighted in **bold**.

Methods	$Accurary(\uparrow)$	$MSE(\downarrow)$	Dice		
			$ET(\uparrow)$	$TC(\uparrow)$	$WT(\uparrow)$
Baseline [17]	0.449	164673	0.758	0.864	0.882
Baseline + population information	0.538	161318	0.835	0.874	0.925
Baseline + pseudo label	0.462	**142946**	0.826	0.870	0.901
MPSurv(ours)	**0.569**	148773	**0.842**	**0.882**	**0.926**

3.3   Ablation Study

To evaluate the efficacy and significance of the pseudo-labeling module within MPSurv, as well as the combined training using population information, we independently trained three models. The baseline model was trained without incorporating pseudo-label modules or population information. Comparatively, the other two models were trained with the exclusive use of either population information or pseudo-label modules. Our distinct model, however, utilized the pseudo-label module and incorporated population information during the training phase. All models were trained on datasets that we personally curated and were subsequently evaluated through five cross-validations. To assess the impact of segmentation, we computed the *Dice* values of the three segmentation sections (ET, TC, WT). Regression indicators MSE and *Accuracy* were employed to appraise prognostic performance. The performance of the three models is compared in Table 2. Evidently, the model that was trained incorporating both the pseudo-labeling module and population information produced superior results, thereby demonstrating enhanced accuracy.

As shown in Table 2, compared with the model without population information added, the model that only includes population information can improve performance by nearly 20%. Compared with models that do not include pseudo label modules, models that only include pseudo label modules may not contribute significantly to the accuracy of survival prediction, but their performance on MSE is more prominent. At the same time, our model also achieved the best results on *Accuracy* and all *Dice*. The research results indicate that group information not only helps predict survival rates, but also plays a crucial role in brain tumor segmentation.

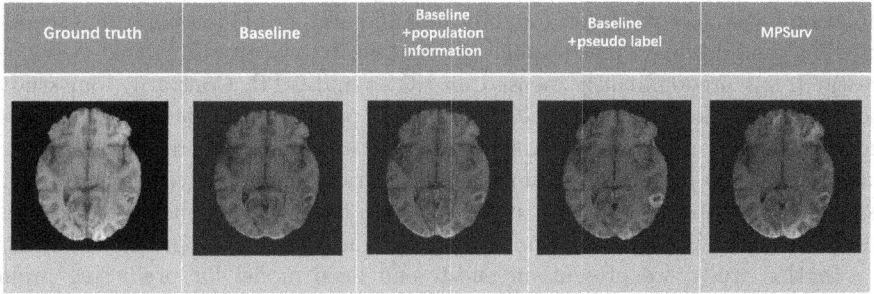

Fig. 2. Visualization of survival prediction process for brain tumors. The highlighted part indicates the activation area of the network for the prediction results.

3.4   Prediction Process Analysis

To gain a deeper understanding of the task's challenges and assess the prediction process of the network, we selected certain images from the dataset for analysis [9]. Fig. 2 visualizes the survival prediction process of four distinct models, where the highlighted regions represent the areas that the model primarily concentrates on during the prediction process. We established our baseline by directly conducting supervised training on actual data, where we labeled brain tumor regions and posterior cranial positions, as illustrated in the second column of images. The third column displays a visual plot trained after the addition of demographic information to the baseline, revealing a stronger response in the posterior brain region compared to the baseline. As seen in the fourth column, the incorporation of a pseudo-label module to the baseline resulted in a model that focuses more on the brain tumor and its surrounding area. The fifth column represents our model, which incorporates demographic information and pseudo-labeling methods during training, leading to stronger focus on the brain tumor regions and intracranial posterior regions. The improved performance of our model in survival prediction can perhaps be attributed to this attention shift. We theorize that the inclusion of demographic information during training can shift the model's focus to other regions, such as the posterior intracranial region, due to significant variance in this area resulting from differences in age, sex, race, and other demographic factors. Furthermore, the pseudo-labeling technique can enhance the model's understanding of the brain tumor region. This suggests that the addition of demographic information and pseudo-label modules potentially aids in brain tumor segmentation and survival prediction.

4   Discussion and Conclusion

In the comparative experiment section, our model demonstrated strong performance during cross-validation on the BraTS 2019 dataset. Furthermore, the ablation study accentuated the significance and efficacy of incorporating pseudo-labeling modules and demographic information. It's worth noting that previous research has predominantly focused on HGGs and GTR. Contrarily, our study took into consideration both LGGs and HGGs present in the dataset, while preserving different resection types, specifically SR and GTR. As a result, MPSurv is able to estimate patient survival time under various resection types by adjusting a single parameter to alter the tumor resection type. This further demonstrates that our model possesses superior generalization compared to previous models.

In this study, we present an end-to-end deep model for predicting brain tumor survival that incorporates patient population information. This method enhances data utilization via pseudo-labeling technology, thereby addressing the issue of pattern loss in brain tumor datasets to a certain extent. Experimental results indicate that our model outperforms other end-to-end models in terms of accuracy in predicting brain tumor survival. Our findings, corroborated by multiple ablation experiments, confirm that integrating population information can indeed enhance the model's accuracy and generalizability. Nonetheless, certain aspects of our approach could benefit from further refinements, such as the inclusion of multimodal data from genomics and pathological imaging. We aim to explore these issues in our future research.

Data Acknowledgements This research study was conducted retrospectively using human subject data made available in open access by [3,4,15]. Ethical approval was not required as confirmed by the license attached with the open access data.

Acknowledgements. This work was supported by the Zhejiang Provincial Natural Science Foundation of China (No. LY21F020017), National Natural Science Foundation of China (No.U20A20386, U22A2033), Chinese Key-Area Research and Development Program of Guangdong Province (2020B0101350001), GuangDong Basic and Applied Basic Research Foundation (No. 2022A1515110570), Innovation teams of youth innovation in science and technology of high education institutions of Shandong province (No. 2021KJ088), the Shenzhen Science and Technology Program (JCYJ20220818103001002), and the Guangdong Provincial Key Laboratory of Big Data Computing, The Chinese University of Hong Kong, Shenzhen.

References

1. Agravat, R.R., Raval, M.S.: Brain tumor segmentation and survival prediction. In: Crimi, A., Bakas, S. (eds.) BrainLes 2019. LNCS, vol. 11992, pp. 338–348. Springer, Cham (2020). https://doi.org/10.1007/978-3-030-46640-4_32

2. Ali, M.J., Akram, M.T., Saleem, H., Raza, B., Shahid, A.R.: Glioma segmentation using ensemble of 2D/3D U-Nets and survival prediction using multiple features fusion. In: Crimi, A., Bakas, S. (eds.) BrainLes 2020. LNCS, vol. 12659, pp. 189–199. Springer, Cham (2021). https://doi.org/10.1007/978-3-030-72087-2_17

3. Baid, U., et al.: The RSNA-ASNR-MICCAI brats 2021 benchmark on brain tumor segmentation and radiogenomic classification. arXiv preprint arXiv:2107.02314 (2021)

4. Bakas, S., et al.: Advancing the cancer genome atlas glioma MRI collections with expert segmentation labels and radiomic features. Sci. data 4(1), 1–13 (2017)

5. Bakas, S., et al.: Identifying the best machine learning algorithms for brain tumor segmentation, progression assessment, and overall survival prediction in the brats challenge. arXiv preprint arXiv:1811.02629 (2018)

6. Cox, D.R.: Regression models and life-tables. J. Roy. Stat. Soc.: Ser. B (Methodol.) 34(2), 187–202 (1972)

7. Cui, C., et al.: Survival prediction of brain cancer with incomplete radiology, pathology, genomic, and demographic data. In: Wang, L., Dou, Q., Fletcher, P.T., Speidel, S., Li, S. (eds.) Medical Image Computing and Computer Assisted Intervention – MICCAI 2022. MICCAI 2022. Lecture Notes in Computer Science, vol. 13435, pp. 626–635. Springer, Cham (2022). https://doi.org/10.1007/978-3-031-16443-9_60

8. Feng, X., Dou, Q., Tustison, N., Meyer, C.: Brain tumor segmentation with uncertainty estimation and overall survival prediction. In: Crimi, A., Bakas, S. (eds.) BrainLes 2019. LNCS, vol. 11992, pp. 304–314. Springer, Cham (2020). https://doi.org/10.1007/978-3-030-46640-4_29

9. Fernandez, F.G.: TorchCAM: class activation explorer (2020). https://github.com/frgfm/torch-cam

10. Hermoza, R., Maicas, G., Nascimento, J.C., Carneiro, G.: Post-HOC overall survival time prediction from brain MRI. In: 2021 IEEE 18th International Symposium on Biomedical Imaging (ISBI), pp. 1476–1480. IEEE (2021)

11. Hermoza, R., Maicas, G., Nascimento, J.C., Carneiro, G.: Censor-aware semi-supervised learning for survival time prediction from medical images. In: Wang, L., Dou, Q., Fletcher, P.T., Speidel, S., Li, S. (eds.) Medical Image Computing and Computer Assisted Intervention – MICCAI 2022. MICCAI 2022. Lecture Notes in Computer Science, vol. 13437, pp. 213–222. Springer, Cham (2022). https://doi.org/10.1007/978-3-031-16449-1_21

12. Islam, M., Vibashan, V.S., Jose, V.J.M., Wijethilake, N., Utkarsh, U., Ren, H.: Brain tumor segmentation and survival prediction using 3D attention UNet. In: Crimi, A., Bakas, S. (eds.) BrainLes 2019. LNCS, vol. 11992, pp. 262–272. Springer, Cham (2020). https://doi.org/10.1007/978-3-030-46640-4_25

13. Kingma, D.P., Ba, J.: Adam: a method for stochastic optimization. arXiv preprint arXiv:1412.6980 (2014)

14. Louis, D.N., et al.: The 2021 who classification of tumors of the central nervous system: a summary. Neuro Oncol. 23(8), 1231–1251 (2021)

15. Menze, B.H., et al.: The multimodal brain tumor image segmentation benchmark (brats). IEEE Trans. Med. Imaging 34(10), 1993–2024 (2014)

16. Nie, D., Zhang, H., Adeli, E., Liu, L., Shen, D.: 3D deep learning for multi-modal imaging-guided survival time prediction of brain tumor patients. In: Ourselin, S., Joskowicz, L., Sabuncu, M.R., Unal, G., Wells, W. (eds.) MICCAI 2016. LNCS, vol. 9901, pp. 212–220. Springer, Cham (2016). https://doi.org/10.1007/978-3-319-46723-8_25

17. Ronneberger, O., Fischer, P., Brox, T.: U-Net: convolutional networks for biomedical image segmentation. In: Navab, N., Hornegger, J., Wells, W.M., Frangi, A.F. (eds.) MICCAI 2015. LNCS, vol. 9351, pp. 234–241. Springer, Cham (2015). https://doi.org/10.1007/978-3-319-24574-4_28

18. Shi, W., Pang, E., Wu, Q., Lin, F.: Brain tumor segmentation using dense channels 2D U-Net and multiple feature extraction network. In: Crimi, A., Bakas, S. (eds.) BrainLes 2019. LNCS, vol. 11992, pp. 273–283. Springer, Cham (2020). https://doi.org/10.1007/978-3-030-46640-4_26

19. Tang, Z., et al.: Deep learning of imaging phenotype and genotype for predicting overall survival time of glioblastoma patients. IEEE Trans. Med. Imaging **39**(6), 2100–2109 (2020)

20. Wang, F., Jiang, R., Zheng, L., Meng, C., Biswal, B.: 3D U-Net based brain tumor segmentation and survival days prediction. In: Crimi, A., Bakas, S. (eds.) BrainLes 2019. LNCS, vol. 11992, pp. 131–141. Springer, Cham (2020). https://doi.org/10.1007/978-3-030-46640-4_13

Shape-Aware Diffusion Model for Tumor Segmentation on Gd-EOB-DTPA MRI Images of Hepatocellular Carcinoma

Ruodai Wu[1], Yue Peng[2], Bing Xiong[2], Wenjian Qin[2(✉)], and Songxiong Wu[1]

[1] Department of Radiology, Shenzhen University General Hospital, Shenzhen University Clinical Medical Academy, Shenzhen, China

[2] Shenzhen Institute of Advanced Technology, Chinese Academy of Sciences, Shenzhen, China
wj.qin@siat.ac.cn

Abstract. Gd-EOB-DTPA MRI provides high-contrast imagesthat offer clear visualization of liver anatomy and the vascular system, making it the preferred method for early screening of hepatocellular carcinoma (HCC). However, the complex morphology and wide variations of liver and tumors in MRI images may not be fully captured by relying solely on pixel-level information. Therefore, combining shape-aware information becomes critical, as it provides additional constraints to better distinguish liver and tumor regions, enabling more accurate segmentation. In this paper, we present a novel approach that incorporates shape-aware information into the diffusion model. Firstly, the diffusion-based feature learning was used to represent complex details of tumor tissue microstructure for overcome the imbalance of tumor target distribution. Then, the shape-aware information is introduced into diffusion model for effectively adapting to the variable characteristics of liver and tumor geometries, boundary shapes to achieve more accurate segmentation of HCC on Gd-EOB-DTPA MRI images. We conducted validation experiments on Gd-EOB-DTPA MRI images from 25 HCC patients, and the results demonstrated Dice and IoU coefficients of 0.974 and 0.956, respectively.

Keywords: Gd-EOB-DTPA MRI · Shape-aware information · HCC segmentation

1 Introduction

Primary liver cancer, predominantly hepatocellular carcinoma (HCC), presents a significant global health challenge, accounting for 75–85% of cases [1]. Gd-EOB-DTPA-enhanced MRI scans have emerged as the preferred method for early detection [2], preoperative evaluation, and postoperative follow-up of HCC due to their exceptional sensitivity and specificity in detecting liver lesions [3]. However, accurate segmentation of HCC in MRI images remains challenging. Existing segmentation methods encounter

---

R. Wu and Y. Peng—These authors contributed equally to this work.

© The Author(s), under exclusive license to Springer Nature Switzerland AG 2023
W. Qin et al. (Eds.): CMMCA 2023 (MICCAI Workshop), LNCS 14243, pp. 131–139, 2023.
https://doi.org/10.1007/978-3-031-45087-7_14

issues such as limited resolution, low signal-to-noise ratio [4], and morphological variations, resulting in suboptimal sensitivity and imprecise boundaries [5]. Deep learning-based approaches, particularly convolutional neural networks (CNNs) [6], have shown promise but are sensitive to resolution and contrast variations [7]. Furthermore, the scarcity of annotated data and class imbalances impact segmentation performance [8]. We trained the LiTS challenge dataset [9] using DeepLabV3p [10] and U2Net [11] for CT images segmentation. However, when the above-mentioned segmentation models are applied to Gd-EOB-DTPA MRI images, the Dice scores drops significantly. This highlights the necessity of exploring alternative approaches, such as the adoption of diffusion models, to address the challenges on Gd-EOB-DTPA MRI images of HCC.

2 Related Work

Medical image segmentation is crucial for diagnosing and treating various conditions, including HCC [12], by dividing images into meaningful regions. However, limited labeled data and class imbalance significantly affect segmentation performance. To address the challenge of segmenting small structures [13], researchers have developed specialized architectures. These architectures, such as hierarchical representations [14], contextual information [15], and attention mechanisms [16]. Some popular models in this area include U-Net [17], as well as improved versions of U-Net and attention-based models [18–21]. Despite significant progress in medical image segmentation, accurately segmenting liver, and tumor regions in MRI images of HCC remains challenging due to low contrast and blurred boundaries. Limited availability of Gd-EOB-DTPA-enhanced MRI images can lead to imbalanced datasets, negatively impacting segmentation model performance (Fig. 1). To tackle these challenges, researchers propose diffusion models, which enhance robustness to noisy and blurred images by controlling diffusion coefficients for smoothing and noise removal. The diffusion model analyzes different image features using multiple scale spaces, enabling accurate segmentation of HCC lesions of varying sizes and shapes [22]. Building upon this, the present study utilizes a combination of the diffusion model and deep learning to enhance the accuracy and efficiency of MRI image segmentation in HCC patients.

We summarize the contributions of this paper as follows:

- To ensure accurate representation of the intricate details pertaining to tumor tissue microstructure in Gd-EOBDTPA MRI, the diffusion-based feature learning was used to overcome the imbalance of tumor target distribution.
- To improve the model's ability to learn boundaries, we introduced shape-aware information into the diffusion model, enabling it to better capture the variable shape characteristics of tumors.
- The reliability and accuracy of our dataset was ensured by utilizing Gd-EOB-DTPA-enhanced MRI images obtained from 25 patients diagnosed with HCC, carefully annotated by three radiologists specializing in diagnostic abdominal imaging. This helps to advance the development of tumor segmentation techniques for HCC.

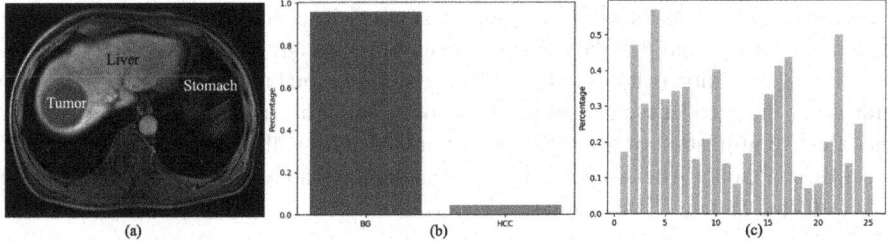

Fig. 1. Gd-EOB-DTPA-enhanced MRI images of 25 patients with HCC showing (a) poorly defined borders of the liver and stomach in the MRI images of patients with HCC; (b) the percentage of background versus tumor; (c) Percentage of slices with tumors vs. slices without tumors.

3 Methods

While Gd-EOB-DTPA MRI provides high-contrast images, relying solely on pixel-level information may not capture the intricate details and shape characteristics of liver and tumor regions. To address this, we present a novel approach that combines diffusion model feature learning and shape-aware information integration. In Sect. 3.1, we describe how diffusion model feature learning captures complex tumor microstructure, overcoming the imbalance in tumor target distribution. This enhances the representation of tumor regions for improved segmentation. In Sect. 3.2, we introduce the integration of shape-aware information into the diffusion model. By considering the variable characteristics of liver and tumor geometries, including boundary shapes, our approach adapts to the specific shape variations in Gd-EOB-DTPA MRI images, leading to more accurate HCC segmentation.

3.1 Diffusion Model Feature Learning

By leveraging the diffusion-based feature learning technique, we aim to capture the intricate details and subtle variations in tumor tissue microstructure, thereby addressing the imbalance in tumor target distribution. This enables us to obtain a more comprehensive and informative representation of the tumor regions, enhancing the subsequent segmentation process. Our model is built upon Medsegdiff-v2 [23], which utilizes a diffusion model to generate high-quality samples from complex data distributions through an iterative denoising process [24]. The inverse process is calculated, and the loss function is formulated as follows:

$$p_\theta(x_{t-1}|x_t) = \mathcal{N}(x_{t-1}; \mu_\theta(x_t, t), \sigma_t^2 I) \tag{1}$$

$$\mathcal{L}_{total}^t = \mathcal{L}_{noise}^t + (t \equiv 0(mod\ \alpha))(\mathcal{L}_{dice} + \beta\mathcal{L}_{ce}) \tag{2}$$

At step t of x_t can be sampled directly from the initial sample x_0. Each x_t fits a multivariate Gaussian distribution. The noise mask x_t is inputted to UNet through conditional integration. The diffusion model is then initialized using a coarse, static reference to reduce the variance in diffusion. Where α and β are denoted as hyperparameters,

$t \equiv 0 \pmod{\alpha}$ controls the number of supervisions of the conditional model through the hyperparameter α, and β is the hyperparameter of the weighted cross-entropy loss.

The segmentation features obtained from the conditional model are seamlessly integrated into the encoder features of the diffusion model. This integration process ensures the effective utilization of the segmentation information within the broader context of the diffusion model. The last conditional segmentation feature f_c^{-1} is integrated into the first diffusion feature f_d^0 denoted as:

$$f_{anc} = Max\left(f_c^{-1} * k_{Gauss}, f_c^{-1}\right) \tag{3}$$

$$f_d'^0 = Sigmoid\left(f_{anc} * k_{Conv_{1\times1}}\right) \cdot f_d^0 + f_d^0 \tag{4}$$

In the aforementioned equation, * denotes the kernel operation of the sliding window and · denotes the operation of the general elements. Sigmoid activation function serves to add the anchor features to each channel of f_d^0 and integrate them into the diffusion model.

Let us consider c^0 as the deepest embedded feature in the conditional UNet and e as the deepest embedded feature in the diffusion UNet. To facilitate further analysis, we transfer c^0 and e to Fourier space, denoted as $F(c^0)$ and $F(e)$, respectively. Subsequently, we combine the two feature maps through linear projection. Next, by considering e as the query and c^0 as the key, the formula is calculated as follows:

$$\mathcal{M} = asin(\omega(F(c^0)\mathcal{W}^q)\left(F(e)\mathcal{W}^k\right)^{\mathrm{T}}) \tag{5}$$

$$f = F^{-1}(M)\left(c^0\omega^v\right) \tag{6}$$

Where $\mathcal{W}^q$ and $\mathcal{W}^k$ represent the query weights and key weights, respectively. These weights can be learned in Fourier space. The affine mapping is then converted back to Euclidean space using the Fast Fourier Inverse Transform (IFFT). Additionally, ω^v is used to represent the learnable value weights.

3.2   Binary Mask Decoder for Shape-Aware Information Extraction

By integrating shape-aware constraints into the diffusion model, we aim to adapt the segmentation process to the specific geometries and shape characteristics of the liver and tumor regions in Gd-EOB-DTPA MRI images. This facilitates a more precise delineation of the HCC regions by incorporating prior knowledge of shape and structure. Drawing inspiration from PANet [25], we generate attention maps related to regions of interest (ROIs) by integrating decoders guided by shape perception information into the conditional network. The feature compression fusion is formulated as follows:

$$Z_5 = W_{c5}^T X_5 \oplus X_4 \tag{7}$$

$$Z_4 = (W_{c4}^T(W_4^T Z_5)) \oplus X_3 \tag{8}$$

$$Y = \sigma(W_{out}^T(W_3^T Z_4)) \tag{9}$$

We consider X_5, X_4 and X_3 as fused feature. By performing elementwise addition, we obtain Z_5 and Z_4, where $Z_5 \in R^{C_4 \times H_4 \times W_4}$ and so on. $\oplus$ indicates feature connection. $W_3 \in R^{C_3 \times C_3}$ Indicates the number of fused volumes to be fused X_4 and X_3. $W_{out} \in R^{C_3 \times 1}$ indicates the output convolution. σ denotes Sigmoid activation.

The formula for calculating the binary loss, denoted as l, between the computed binary ground truth of the background G_b, and the computed binary ground truth of the generated attention map, y_b, by the attention-guided decoder, Y, is expressed as follows:

$$G_b = \sum_{i=1}^{C} G_i \tag{10}$$

$$l = \mathcal{L}_b(y_b, Y) \tag{11}$$

where $\mathcal{L}_b$ is used to supervise the attention and guide the parameter update of the decoder (Fig. 2).

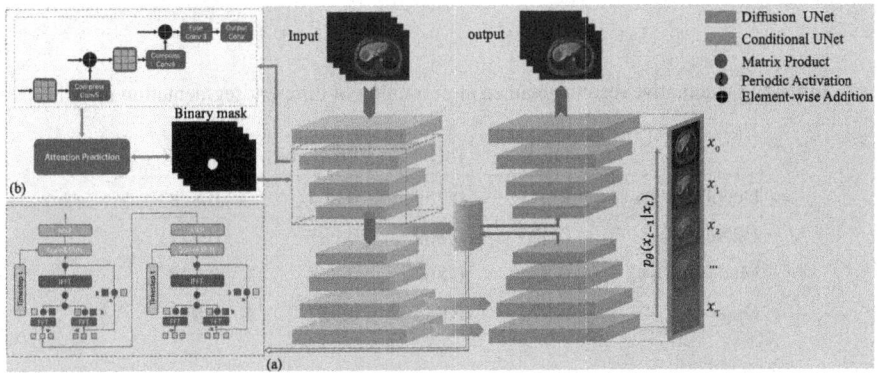

Fig. 2. Illustration of the network structure.

4 Experiments

4.1 Datasets and Experimental Setting

Our dataset consists of Gd-EOB-DTPA-enhanced MRI images of 25 HCC patients obtained from the clinic, with manual annotations of tumor anatomical structures by experts. All experiments were conducted using the PyTorch platform, with training and testing performed on 2 NVIDIA A100 GPUs. The resolution of all images was uniformly adjusted to 256×256 pixels, and a batch size of 16 was used. The initial learning rate was set to 1×10^{-4}. Our study was conducted in accordance with ethical guidelines, and the use of the dataset was approved by the appropriate institutional review board. All patient information was anonymized and handled in compliance with data protection regulations to ensure privacy and confidentiality.

4.2 Experiments and Results

The integration of shape-aware information in our model has yielded significant improvements in the segmentation results, as demonstrated by notable increases in both the Dice coefficient (Dice) and Intersection over Union (IoU). Our baseline is derived from Medsegdiff-v2 [23], achieved Dice and IoU scores of 0.885 and 0.867, respectively. In contrast, with the addition of shape information, the performance was greatly enhanced, yielding a Dice coefficient of 0.974 and an improved IoU of 0.956. These findings provide compelling evidence for the effectiveness of incorporating shape-aware information, as it enables better discrimination of liver and tumor regions, resulting in more accurate and precise segmentation outcomes (Tables 1 and 2).

Table 1. Quantitative demonstration of ablation experiments.

	Shape-aware	Dice	IoU
Baseline	–	0.885	0.867
Ours	√	**0.974**	**0.956**

Table 2. Quantitative results obtained after training of different segmentation models

	Dice	IoU	Precision	Recall
DeepLabV3p	0.841	0.759	0.854	0.868
U2Net	0.925	0.869	0.937	0.911
Medsegdiff-v2	0.885	0.867	0.868	0.998
Ours	**0.974**	**0.956**	**0.957**	**0.999**

Comparing the quantitative results obtained by training our model on Gd-EOB-DTPA-enhanced MRI images of 25 HCC patients with other existing models, our approach consistently demonstrated superior performance. Specifically, when evaluating metrics such as the Dice and IoU, our model exhibited significant improvements. These results underscore the effectiveness and superiority of our approach in accurately delineating HCC tumors in Gd-EOB-DTPA-enhanced MRI images, ultimately contributing to enhanced diagnostic capabilities and facilitating treatment planning in clinical practice. Furthermore, the segmentation results depicted in Fig. 3 vividly showcase our model's proficiency in accurately identifying small or ill-defined structures that may be overlooked by conventional segmentation methods. This further emphasizes the effectiveness and superiority of our approach in precisely segmenting HCC tumors in Gd-EOB-DTPA-enhanced MRI images. As a result, our approach holds great potential in enhancing diagnostic capabilities and facilitating more precise treatment planning in clinical practice.

Based on the above discussion and findings, our research demonstrates the rationality and effectiveness of incorporating shape-aware information and diffusion model feature learning in enhancing the accuracy of HCC segmentation. The promising results obtained from our experiments highlight the potential clinical impact of our approach in improving the detection and characterization of HCC tumors, ultimately benefiting patients and healthcare professionals in their decision-making processes.

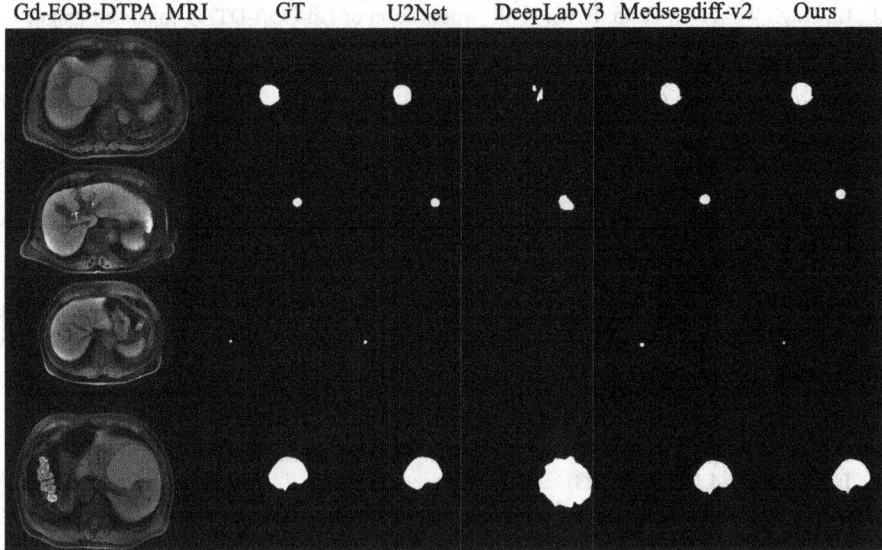

Gd-EOB-DTPA MRI   GT   U2Net   DeepLabV3   Medsegdiff-v2   Ours

Fig. 3. Results of HCC segmentation by each model

5   Conclusion

This paper presents a novel approach for accurately segmenting HCC tumors in Gd-EOB-DTPA MRI images by incorporating shape-aware information into a diffusion model. The proposed method effectively adapts to the complex morphology and wide variations observed in the liver and tumors, which greatly helps to improve segmentation performance compared to existing models. However, a limitation of this study is the relatively small sample size, and future research will focus on increasing the number of samples and conducting a multicenter clinical evaluation to verify the effectiveness of the proposed method on a larger scale.

Acknowledgement. The work is supported by "Shenzhen Municipal Scheme for Basic Research" (JCYJ20210324100208022).

References

1. Ronot, M., Chernyak, V., Burgoyne, A., et al.: Imaging to predict prognosis in HCC: current and future perspectives. Radiology **307**(3), e221429 (2023)
2. Zhang, H., Zhang, W., Jiang, L., et al.: Recent advances in systemic therapy for HCC. Biomarker Res. **10**, 1–21 (2022)
3. Li, X.Q., Wang, X., Zhao, D.W., et al.: Application of Gd-EOB-DTPA-enhanced magnetic resonance imaging (MRI) in hepatocellular carcinoma. World J. Surgical Oncology **18**(1), 1–8 (2020)
4. Ma, X., Zhang, M.J., Wang, J., et al.: Emerging biomaterials imaging antitumor immune response. Adv. Materials **34**(42), 2204034 (2022)
5. Yang, Z., Zhao, Y., Liao, M., et al.: Semi-automatic liver tumor segmentation with adaptive region growing and graph cuts. Biomed. Signal Process. Control **68**, 102670 (2021)
6. Tong, N., Gou, S., Yang, S., et al.: Shape constrained fully convolutional DenseNet with adversarial training for multiorgan segmentation on head and neck CT and low-field MR images. Med. Phys. **46**(6), 2669–2682 (2019)
7. Jiang, H., Diao, Z., Shi, T., et al.: A review of deep learning-based multiple-lesion recognition from medical images: classification, detection and segmentation. Comput Biol. Med., 106726 (2023)
8. Billot, B., Greve, D.N., Puonti, O., et al.:SynthSeg: segmentation of brain MRI scans of any contrast and resolution without retraining. Med. Image Anal. **86**,102789 (2023)
9. Bilic, P., Christ, P., Li, H.B., et al.: The liver tumor segmentation benchmark (lits). Med. Image Anal. **84**,102680 (2023)
10. Chen, L.-C., Zhu, Y., Papandreou, G., et al.: Encoder-decoder with atrous separable convolution for semantic image segmentation. ECCV, 801–818 (2018)
11. Qin, X., Zhang, Z., Huang, C., et al.: U2-Net: going deeper with nested U-structure for salient object detection. Pattern Recogn.Recogn. **106**, 107404 (2020)
12. Granata, V., Grassi, R., Fusco, R., et al.: Diagnostic evaluation and ablation treatments assessment in hepatocellular carcinoma. Infectious Agents Cancer **16**, 1–22 (2021)
13. Wang, Y., Fei, J., Wang, H., et al.: Balancing Logit Variation for Long-tailed Semantic Segmentation. IEEE/CVF, 19561–19573 (2023)
14. Chen, J., Xia, Y., Yao, J., et al.: Towards a single unified model for effective detection, segmentation, and diagnosis of eight major cancers using a large collection of ct scans. arXiv preprint arXiv:2301.12291 (2023)
15. Roy, M., Kong, J., Kashyap, S., et al.: Convolutional autoencoder based model HistoCAE for segmentation of viable tumor regions in liver whole-slide images. Sci Rep-Uk **11**(1), 139 (2021)
16. Jiang, H., Shi, T., Bai, Z., et al.: Ahcnet: An application of attention mechanism and hybrid connection for liver tumor segmentation in ct volumes. IEEE Access **7**, 24898–24909 (2019)
17. Ronneberger, O., Fischer, P., Brox, T.: U-net: convolutional networks for biomedical image segmentation. MICCAI 2015, Part III **18**, 234–241 (2015)
18. Li, D., Rahardja, S.: BSEResU-Net: An attention-based before-activation residual U-Net for retinal vessel segmentation. Comput. Meth. Prog. Bio. **205**, 106070 (2021)
19. Li, C., Tan, Y., Chen, W., et al.: ANU-Net: Attention-based nested U-Net to exploit full resolution features for medical image segmentation. Comput. Graph.. Graph. **90**, 11–20 (2020)
20. Wang, J., Zhang, X., Lv, P., et al.: EAR-U-Net: EfficientNet and attention-based residual U-Net for automatic liver segmentation in CT. arXiv preprint arXiv:2110.01014 (2021)
21. Liu, S., Liu, S., Zhang, S., et al.: SSAU-Net: A spectral–spatial attention-based U-Net for hyperspectral image fusion. IEEE T Geosci Remote **60**, 1–16 (2022)

22. Gupta, B., Lamba, S.S.: An efficient anisotropic diffusion model for image denoising with edge preservation. Comput. Math. Appl.. Math. Appl. **93**, 106–119 (2021)
23. Wu, J., Fu, R., Fang, H., et al.: Medsegdiff-v2: diffusion based medical image segmentation with transformer. arXiv preprint arXiv:2301.11798 (2023)
24. Yu, S., Sohn, K., Kim, S., et al.: Video probabilistic diffusion models in projected latent space. IEEE/CVF, 18456–18466 (2023)
25. Zhao, X., Zhang, P., Song, F., et al.: Prior attention network for multi-lesion segmentation in medical images. IEEE T Med. Imaging **41**(12), 3812–3823 (2022)

Style Enhanced Domain Adaptation Neural Network for Cross-Modality Cervical Tumor Segmentation

Boyun Zheng[1,2], Jiahui He[1,3], Jiuhe Zhu[1,2], Yaoqin Xie[1], Nazar Zaki[4], and Wenjian Qin[1(✉)]

[1] Shenzhen Institute of Advanced Technology, Chinese Academy of Sciences, Shenzhen, China
wj.qin@siat.ac.cn
[2] Shenzhen College of Advanced Technology, University of Chinese Academy of Sciences, Shenzhen, China
[3] School of Computer Science, Faculty of Science and Engineering, University of Nottingham Ningbo China, Ningbo, China
[4] Department of Computer Science and Software Engineering, College of Information Technology, United Arab Emirates University, Al Ain 15551, United Arab Emirates

Abstract. Cervical tumor segmentation is an essential step of cervical cancer diagnosis and treatment. Considering that multi-modality data contain more information and are widely available in clinical routine, multi-modality medical image analysis has emerged as a significant field of study. However, annotating tumors for each modality is expensive and time-consuming. Consequently, unsupervised domain adaptation (UDA) has attracted a lot of attention for its ability to achieve excellent performance on unlabeled cross-domain data. Most current UDA methods adapt image translation networks to achieve domain adaptation, however, the generation process may create visual inconsistency and incorrect generation styles due to the instability of generative adversarial networks. Therefore, we propose a novel and efficient method without image translation networks by introducing a style enhancement method into Domain Adversarial Neural Network (DANN)-based model to improve the generalization performance of the shared segmentation network. Experimental results show that our method achieves the best performance on the cross-modality cervical tumor segmentation task compared to current state-of-the-art UDA methods.

Keywords: Unsupervised domain adaptation · Cervical tumor segmentation · Shuffle Remap

1 Introduction

In clinical practice, Magnetic resonance (MR) imaging is a standard imaging technique for cervical cancer diagnosis and treatment [1]. MR imaging is useful

© The Author(s), under exclusive license to Springer Nature Switzerland AG 2023
W. Qin et al. (Eds.): CMMCA 2023 (MICCAI Workshop), LNCS 14243, pp. 140–149, 2023.
https://doi.org/10.1007/978-3-031-45087-7_15

for defining the extent of tumor involvement, including the depth of cervical stromal or parametrial invasion [2] and cervical tumor segmentation on MR images is a crucial step in these applications. However, manual segmentation by experienced physicians is laborious and observer-dependent. With the rapid development of deep learning techniques, automatic medical image segmentation has proven quite effective [3,4]. Simultaneously, driven by the potential of different modalities to mutually provide complementary information, there has been multiple research on multi-modality medical image analysis based on deep neural networks recently [5–9]. Within cervical magnetic resonance (MR) imaging, the utilization of different modalities such as T1 and T2 can effectively highlight distinct characteristics and enhance the overall imaging results [10]. However, annotating data for each modality is often labour-intensive and time-consuming, especially in the medical health field where expertise is required. In addition, there is often a distribution gap between different modalities, which will lead to a severe degradation of the model's performance if conducting cross-modality image segmentation without domain adaptation. For example, in Fig. 1, we train the neural network purely on T1 or T2 cervical cancer images and perform cross-modality tumor segmentation. It can be observed that the model trained on one modality image cannot be generalized well to another modality image due to the domain gap.

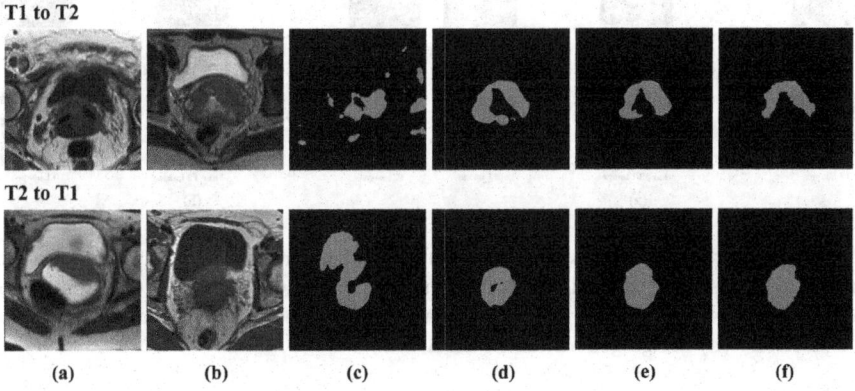

Fig. 1. Illustration of the degradation of model performance due to domain gap. The first and second rows indicate T1 to T2 adaptation and T2 to T1 adaptation respectively: a) example of training data b) example of test data c) segmentation results without adaptation d) segmentation results using our proposed method e) segmentation results with supervised information f) the ground truth

To address these problems, unsupervised domain adaptation for medical image segmentation has attracted widespread attention due to its advantage of not requiring annotated target data. Existing unsupervised domain adaptation methods for medical image segmentation typically reduce the domain gap from three perspectives: feature alignment, image alignment and feature+image alignment. Specifically, from the feature alignment perspective, most models adopt an architecture similar to the Domain Adversarial Neural Network (DANN) structure [11], using a separate network to extract domain-invariant features via adversarial learning. However, aligning feature distributions via an independent network is difficult, especially in the case when distribution discrepancy is large [12]. From the image alignment perspective, a common approach [13,14] is to transform source-domain images into semantically preserved target-domain images using an image-to-image translation network, such as the Cycle-Consistent GAN (CycleGAN) [15]. Considering that the advantages of image and feature alignment can be combined to reduce domain differences, recent studies have mostly adopted both feature and image alignment [12,16,17]. For example, [16] introduces synergistic fusion of alignments from both image and feature perspectives. [12] uses two symmetric translation subnetworks to achieve bidirectional alignment of feature distributions between source and target domains. However, due to the instability of GAN-based methods, as in Fig. 2, there may be visual inconsistency, incorrect generation style, and semantic information damage during image generation [12,18], which may affect subsequent learning.

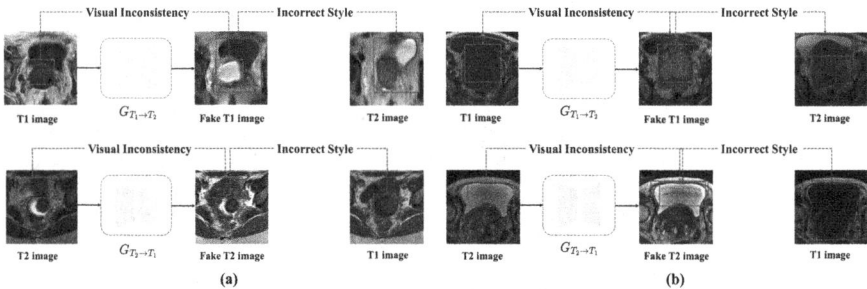

Fig. 2. Illustration of the visual inconsistency and incorrect style during image generation in CycleGAN[16] and SIFA[17]. The first row indicates T1 to T2 adaptation and the second row indicates T2 to T1 adaptation respectively: (a) image generation in CycleGAN (b) image generation in SIFA

In this paper, we propose a novel unsupervised domain adaptation method without translation networks for cross-modality cervical tumor segmentation. We introduce a style enhancement method named Shuffle Remap [19] to a DANN-based network to enhance the generalisation performance of the model by allowing the data distribution to become diverse while eliminating visual inconsistencies in the generation process. The main contributions are as follows:

- We propose a novel domain adaptation method for cross-modality cervical tumor segmentation without domain translation subnetworks and domain-specific encoders or decoders. By introducing Shuffle Remap into the DANN-based network, the performance is greatly improved without adding any additional computational resources.

- To the best of our knowledge, we are the first unsupervised domain adaptation study on cervical tumor segmentation.
- We validate the proposed method on bidirectional cross-modality adaptation between T2 and T1 for cervical tumor segmentation task and achieve the best performance comparing with other state-of-the-art methods.

2   Methodology

2.1   Preliminary

In the UDA setting, pixel-level annotations are available for the source domain S, but not for the target domain T. Our goal is to train a model on the source data $D^s = \{x_i^s, y_i^s\}_{i=1}^{N_s}$ and the unannotated target data $D^t = \{x_i^t\}_{i=1}^{N_t}$ that can achieve accurate segmentation on the target images. Figure 3 shows an overview of our proposed method. The entire framework is built on the basis of the Domain Adversarial Neural Network (DANN) [11] and consists of a segmentor and a discriminative network. To enhance the generalization performance of the segmentor, we introduce the Shuffle Remap method, which aims to diversify the distribution of source domain images. In the following, we will detail each component.

2.2   Shared Segmentor for Extracting Features

The source domain image x_i^s is fed to the style enhancement module named Shuffle Remap(see Sect. 2.4 for the specific form) to create a distribution different from $x_i^s : x_i^{s'} = \mathrm{SR}(x_i^s)$. We then feed $x_i^{s'}$ and x_i^t into a shared segmentor M_{seg}, where all normalization layers are set to instance normalization. The shared convolutional neural network for the source and target images can better extract domain invariant anatomical information from different domains and eliminate the interference of some domain-specific information, and also have a lower computational complexity. Using instance normalization rather than batch normalization can help prevent the gradual widening of domain discrepancies during the forward propagation of the source and target domain images in the weight-sharing network. The total segmentation loss is as follows:

$$\mathcal{L}_{\mathrm{seg}}\left(M_{\mathrm{seg}}\right) = \mathcal{L}_{\mathrm{CE+Dice}}\left(M_{\mathrm{seg}}\left(\mathbf{x}^s\right), \mathbf{y}^s\right) \tag{1}$$

where $\mathcal{L}_{\mathrm{CE+Dice}}$ is the sum of the soft Dice and pixel-wise cross-entropy losses.

2.3   Feature Alignment in Semantic Prediction Space

Due to the lack of label information guiding the target domain and the distribution differences between the target domain and the source domain, the target domain segmentation map p^t will contain errors that create some visual appearance that is different from the source domain image segmentation map p^s.

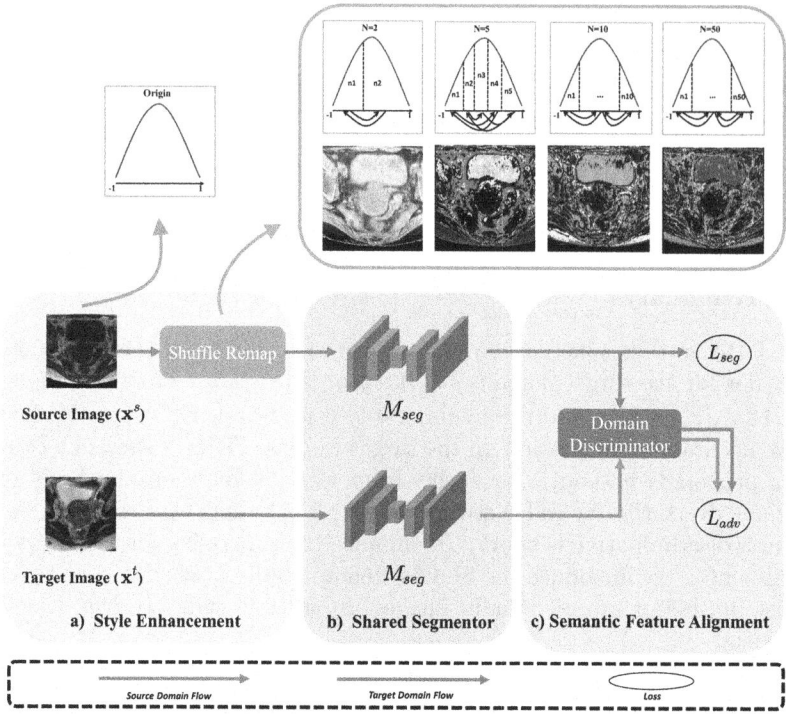

Fig. 3. A overview of our method. The shared segmentor M_{seg} is trained with Shuffle Remap [19] as style enhancement in the source domain. The domain discriminator differentiates source domain segmentation maps from target domain segmentation maps. The blue and green arrows indicate the data flows for the source and target images respectively. This figure is best viewed in color. (Color figure online)

Therefore, we introduce adversarial learning by adding a domain discriminator D at the end of the network, the segmentor M_{seg} and the discriminator D are trained in an adversarial manner. The Discriminator tries to distinguish source domain segmentation maps from target domain segmentation maps, while the segmentor tries to fool the discriminator, which reduces the visual appearance difference between the source and target output maps and aids the shared segmentor extracting domain-invariant information for both the source and target domains. The segmentor and the discriminator are optimized by the following adversarial loss:

$$\mathcal{L}_{\text{adv}}\left(M_{\text{seg}}, D\right) = E_{x^s \in D^s}\left[\log\left(D\left(M_{\text{seg}}\left(x^s\right)\right)\right)\right] + E_{x^t \in D^t}\left[\log\left(1 - D\left(M_{\text{seg}}\left(x^t\right)\right)\right)\right] \quad (2)$$

Here, D is required to maximize $\mathcal{L}_{\text{adv}}$ so that it can distinguish between source and target domain maps, while the segmentation network M_{seg} attempts to minimize $\mathcal{L}_{adv}$ to make the target domain maps similar to the source domain maps.

In summary, the whole objective of our proposed network is formulated as follows:

$$\mathcal{L} = \lambda_{\text{seg}} \, \mathcal{L}_{\text{seg}} + \lambda_{adv} \mathcal{L}_{\text{adv}} \tag{3}$$

where λ_{seg}, λ_{adv} are hyper-parameters to balance the weight of each module. The corresponding values in our experiment are set to 1.0 and 0.1, respectively.

2.4 Style Enhancement Method: Shuffle Remap

Shuffle Remap [19] is a simple yet effective method of style enhancement. The distribution of the original image X is first normalised to $[-1,1]$, then some random control points are generated between $[-1,1]$ with endpoints P_0 and P_N fixed at -1 and 1 respectively. These control points randomly divide the image distribution into N parts. Each part is assigned an index number n in ascending order, after which the segments are randomly remapped. For example, the equation shows the remapping of a given pixel from range $(P_i; P_i + 1)$ to range $(P_j; P_j + 1)$:

$$x' = \frac{x - p_i}{p_{i+1} - p_i} * (p_{j+1} - p_j) + p_j \tag{4}$$

Shuffle Remap allows the distribution of the source domain images to be diverse, thus allowing the segmentor to resist performance degradation from distribution differences and to improve its generalization.

3 Experiment and Results

3.1 Dataset

In our experiments, we performed a bidirectional cross-modality cervical tumor segmentation task on the TCGA-CESC dataset [20]. We performed bidirectional adaptation of MRI imaging in 35 cases with T1 and T2, and the field of view of their images are complete. The tumor labeling was performed and reviewed by two experienced physicians. Our goal was to segment the entire tumor in an unpaired manner.

All experiments are applied on five-fold cross-validation. Two evaluation metrics are used, including the Dice similarity coefficient (Dice) and the average surface distance (ASD). Higher Dice value and lower ASD values indicate better performance. We performed reorientation on all cases and resample volume spacing to $0.5 \times 0.5 \times 5 \, \text{mm}^3$, and then use a 3D bounding box with a fixed axial plane size of 320×320 to crop a data volume, which centers on the cervical area. The image intensity is normalized to range $[-1, 1]$. We employed data augmentation with rotation and affine transformations to reduce over-fitting.

3.2   Implementation Details

We employ U-Net [3] as segmentation backbone with replacing all BN layers to IN layers. As to the discriminator, we use PatchGAN [21], the channel number for each layer is [64, 128, 256, 512, 1], respectively. The random range of N in Shuffle Remap is [2, 50]. We implement our model with the PyTorch framework on a Tesla V100 with 32 GB memory. The model is trained for 100 epochs and the batch size is set to 8. We use the Adam optimizer to train all modules and the learning rate is set to 1×10^{-4} for the segmentation network(M_{seg}) and discriminators (D). The discriminators (D) are optimized every 20 iterations as is common in GAN network training.

3.3   Results and Discussions

Table 1 show the adaptation results of the different methods on the TCGA-CESC dataset [20]. Note that the results for Adda [22], CycleGAN [15], CyCADA [23] and SIFA [16] were obtained by ourselves according to the released code. The results of "supervised training" can be considered as an upper bound of unsupervised domain adaption methods, "No adaptation" is the result of applying the segmentor trained on the source domain directly to the target domain without domain adaptation and can be considered as a lower bound of unsupervised domain adaption methods. Compared to 'supervised training', we can observe a severe performance degradation of 'unsupervised adaptation' due to the domain gap. We select some recently proposed SOTA methods for comparison. Adda [22] adapts feature alignment to achieve domain adaptation. CycleGAN [15] transforms the target domain image into an image with source domain style through the image-to-image translation module. CyCADA [23] and SIFA [16] achieve alignment on both the feature and image domains. According to Tables I, methods that combine feature and image alignment perform better than methods that only use feature or image alignment. Compared with the existing SOTA method, our proposed method achieves higher Dice and lower ASD for cervical tumor segmentation. Ablation study shows that Shuffle Remap enhances the domain adaptation performance of the model by increasing the generalization ability of the shared encoder. Quantitative results show that for cross-modality cervical tumor segmentation, Shuffle Remap can partially replace the image translation module in medical image segmentation tasks, solving the issues that could arise with the image translation module. Some representative examples of segmentation results are shown in Fig. 4. Although there are still some instances of incorrect segmentation compared to the ground truth, our method is more accurate than other methods.

Table 1. Comparison results on TCGA-CESC.

Method	T1 to T2		T2 to T1	
	Dice(%)↑	ASD(mm)↓	Dice(%)↑	ASD(mm)↓
Supervised training	66.7	5.16	68.1	3.87
No adaptation	34.4	15.55	50.2	7.87
Adda [22]	34.5	14.17	51.8	7.42
CycleGAN [15]	51.2	8.04	56.8	6.50
CyCADA [23]	51.5	7.93	57.0	6.42
SIFA [16]	55.1	6.53	57.8	6.27
Ours w/o Shuffle Remap [19]	40.8	11.89	56.3	6.57
Ours	**56.4**	**6.21**	**65.1**	**3.91**

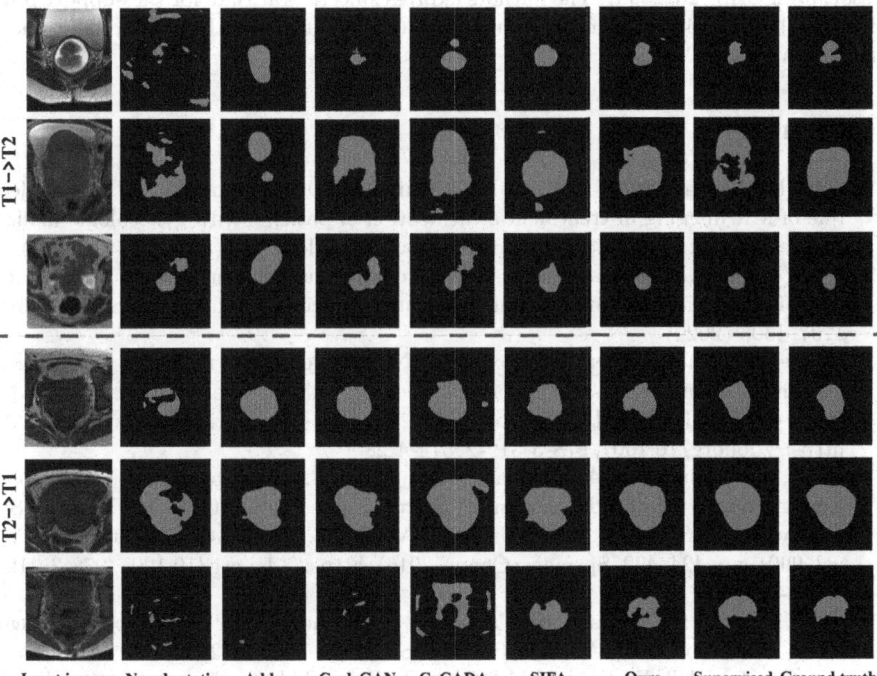

Fig. 4. Qualitative segmentation results of different unsupervised domain adaptation methods. The first three rows are the T2-weighted MR images in the "T1 to T2" task, and the last three rows are the T1-weighted MR images in the "T2 to T1" task. The tumor is indicated in green color. Each row corresponds to one example. (Color figure online)

4   Conclusion

In this paper, we proposed a novel and effective unsupervised domain adaptation method without image-translation networks for cross-modality cervical tumor segmentation. Shuffle Remap [19] not only improves the generalization ability of the segmentation network and achieves good adaptation between T1-T2 MR images, but also avoids the visual inconsistency and other problems that may occur in the generative network. The experimental results on TCGA-CESC [20] show the superiority of our approach compared to other SOTA methods on the cross-modality cervical tumor segmentation task.

Acknowledgements. This work was supported by the Shenzhen Science and Technology Program of China grant JCYJ20200109115420720, and the National Natural Science Foundation of China (No. U20A20373); and the Youth Innovation Promotion Association CAS (2022365); The authors express sincere gratitude for the support provided by the United Arab Emirates University (UAEU) through the joint collaboration grant number G00003558.

References

1. Sala, E., Rockall, A.G., Freeman, S.J., Mitchell, D.G., Reinhold, C.: The added role of MR imaging in treatment stratification of patients with gynecologic malignancies: what the radiologist needs to know. Radiology **266**(3), 717–740 (2013)
2. Lin, Y.C., et al.: Deep learning for fully automated tumor segmentation and extraction of magnetic resonance radiomics features in cervical cancer. Eur. Radiol. **30**, 1297–1305 (2020)
3. Ronneberger, O., Fischer, P., Brox, T.: U-Net: convolutional networks for biomedical image segmentation. In: Navab, N., Hornegger, J., Wells, W.M., Frangi, A.F. (eds.) MICCAI 2015. LNCS, vol. 9351, pp. 234–241. Springer, Cham (2015). https://doi.org/10.1007/978-3-319-24574-4_28
4. Çiçek, Ö., Abdulkadir, A., Lienkamp, S.S., Brox, T., Ronneberger, O.: 3D U-Net: learning dense volumetric segmentation from sparse annotation. In: Ourselin, S., Joskowicz, L., Sabuncu, M.R., Unal, G., Wells, W. (eds.) MICCAI 2016. LNCS, vol. 9901, pp. 424–432. Springer, Cham (2016). https://doi.org/10.1007/978-3-319-46723-8_49
5. Chen, T., et al.: A corresponding region fusion framework for multi-modal cervical lesion detection. IEEE/ACM Trans. Comput. Biol. Bioinf. (2022)
6. Ouyang, J., Adeli, E., Pohl, K.M., Zhao, Q., Zaharchuk, G.: Representation disentanglement for multi-modal brain MRI analysis. In: Feragen, A., Sommer, S., Schnabel, J., Nielsen, M. (eds.) IPMI 2021. LNCS, vol. 12729, pp. 321–333. Springer, Cham (2021). https://doi.org/10.1007/978-3-030-78191-0_25
7. Kaur, M., Singh, D.: Multi-modality medical image fusion technique using multiobjective differential evolution based deep neural networks. J. Ambient. Intell. Humaniz. Comput. **12**, 2483–2493 (2021)
8. Korot, E., et al.: Code-free deep learning for multi-modality medical image classification. Nat. Mach. Intell. **3**(4), 288–298 (2021)
9. Wang, K., Zheng, M., Wei, H., Qi, G., Li, Y.: Multi-modality medical image fusion using convolutional neural network and contrast pyramid. Sensors **20**(8), 2169 (2020)

10. Akita, A., et al.: Comparison of T2-weighted and contrast-enhanced T1-weighted MR imaging at 15 t for assessing the local extent of cervical carcinoma. Eur. Radiol. **21**, 1850–1857 (2011)

11. Ganin, Y., Lempitsky, V.: Unsupervised domain adaptation by backpropagation. In: International Conference on Machine Learning, pp. 1180–1189. PMLR (2015)

12. Han, X., et al.: Deep symmetric adaptation network for cross-modality medical image segmentation. IEEE Trans. Med. Imaging **41**(1), 121–132 (2021)

13. Gholami, A.: A novel domain adaptation framework for medical image segmentation. In: Crimi, A., Bakas, S., Kuijf, H., Keyvan, F., Reyes, M., van Walsum, T. (eds.) BrainLes 2018. LNCS, vol. 11384, pp. 289–298. Springer, Cham (2019). https://doi.org/10.1007/978-3-030-11726-9_26

14. Zhang, T., et al.: Noise adaptation generative adversarial network for medical image analysis. IEEE Trans. Med. Imaging **39**(4), 1149–1159 (2019)

15. Zhu, J.Y., Park, T., Isola, P., Efros, A.A.: Unpaired image-to-image translation using cycle-consistent adversarial networks. In: Proceedings of the IEEE International Conference on Computer Vision, pp. 2223–2232 (2017)

16. Chen, C., Dou, Q., Chen, H., Qin, J., Heng, P.A.: Unsupervised bidirectional cross-modality adaptation via deeply synergistic image and feature alignment for medical image segmentation. IEEE Trans. Med. Imaging **39**(7), 2494–2505 (2020)

17. Yan, W., et al.: The domain shift problem of medical image segmentation and vendor-adaptation by Unet-GAN. In: Shen, D., et al. (eds.) MICCAI 2019. LNCS, vol. 11765, pp. 623–631. Springer, Cham (2019). https://doi.org/10.1007/978-3-030-32245-8_69

18. Cheng, Y., Wei, F., Bao, J., Chen, D., Zhang, W.: ADPL: adaptive dual path learning for domain adaptation of semantic segmentation. IEEE Trans. Pattern Anal. Mach. Intell. **45**, 9339–9356 (2023)

19. Kong, L., et al.: Indescribable multi-modal spatial evaluator. In: Proceedings of the IEEE/CVF Conference on Computer Vision and Pattern Recognition, pp. 9853–9862 (2023)

20. Clark, K., et al.: The cancer imaging archive (TCIA): maintaining and operating a public information repository. J. Digit. Imaging **26**, 1045–1057 (2013)

21. Isola, P., Zhu, J.Y., Zhou, T., Efros, A.A.: Image-to-image translation with conditional adversarial networks. In: Proceedings of the IEEE Conference on Computer Vision and Pattern Recognition, pp. 1125–1134 (2017)

22. Tzeng, E., Hoffman, J., Saenko, K., Darrell, T.: Adversarial discriminative domain adaptation. In: Proceedings of the IEEE Conference on Computer Vision and Pattern Recognition, pp. 7167–7176 (2017)

23. Hoffman, J., et al.: CyCADA: cycle-consistent adversarial domain adaptation. In: International Conference on Machine Learning, pp. 1989–1998. PMLR (2018)

Automated Segmentation of Nasopharyngeal Carcinoma Based on Dual-Sequence Magnetic Resonance Imaging Using Self-supervised Learning

Zongyou Cai[1], Yufeng Ye[3,4], Zhangnan Zhong[1], Haiwei Lin[1], Ziyue Xu[5],
Bin Huang[1], Wei Deng[3,4], Qiting Wu[1], Kaixin Lei[1], Jiegeng Lyu[1],
Hanwei Chen[2(✉)], and Bingsheng Huang[1(✉)]

[1] Medical AI Lab, School of Biomedical Engineering, Medical School,
Shenzhen University, Shenzhen, China
huangb@szu.edu.cn

[2] Panyu Health Management Center (Panyu Rehabilitation Hospital), Guangzhou,
China
doctezwei@sina.com

[3] Department of Radiology, Panyu Central Hospital, Guangzhou, China

[4] Medical Imaging Institute of Panyu, Guangzhou, China

[5] NVIDIA Corporation, Bethesda, MD, USA

Abstract. Radiation therapy stands as a principal treatment for nasopharyngeal carcinoma (NPC). The contouring of tumor regions for radiotherapy planning is traditionally done manually by oncologists, a process that is time-consuming and subject to individual subjectivity. Although fully automated deep-learning models could offer a solution, their segmentation performance is often hindered by the lack of abundant annotated data. We retrospectively analyzed the image data of 116 NPC patients, with lesions from 44 patients labeled and those from the remaining 72 left unlabeled. We proposed a fully automated method leveraging self-supervised learning to overcome the issue of scarce data annotations, aiming to achieve precise segmentation of NPC lesions from dual-sequence magnetic resonance images. The mean Dice Similarity Coefficient in a ten-fold cross-validation was 0.75, comparable to results using 4100 annotated cases for training, while only utilizing 44 annotated cases in our study. Examination of the results demonstrated that our method

Z. Cai, Y. Ye, Z. Zhong and H. Lin—Contributed equally to this work.

This work is supported by the Science and Technology Plan Project of Panyu District, Guangzhou (No. 2021-Z04-01); Science and Technology Project of Guangzhou Health Commission (No. 20211A011114); Shenzhen-Hong Kong Institute of Brain Science-Shenzhen Fundamental Research Institutions (No.2021SHIBS0003); and Guangdong Basic and Applied Basic Research Foundation (2020A1515010571).

Supplementary Information The online version contains supplementary material available at https://doi.org/10.1007/978-3-031-45087-7_16.

W. Qin et al. (Eds.): CMMCA 2023 (MICCAI Workshop), LNCS 14243, pp. 150–159, 2023.
https://doi.org/10.1007/978-3-031-45087-7_16

requires minimal modification, less than 20% for the Dice score primarily, to fulfill clinical application requirements. We proposed a fully automatic segmentation method for NPC, showcasing both accuracy and stability. This approach, constructed with a minimal amount of labeled data and enhanced with unlabeled data, can significantly contribute to the automated segmentation of tumor lesions, easing the annotation burden on oncologists, diminishing subjectivity, and increasing the reliability of lesion delineation.

Keywords: Nasopharyngeal carcinoma · deep learning ·
self-supervised learning · automatic segmentation

1   Introduction

Nasopharyngeal carcinoma (NPC) is a significant global cancer, particularly prevalent in Southern China, with an incidence rate of 0.2 per 1,000 in endemic areas. Its sensitivity to radiation makes radiation therapy the standard treatment [16]. MRI is preferred over CT for assessing NPC due to its superior soft tissue clarity. Manual delineation of lesions by oncologists is a standard but time-consuming, labor-intensive, and subjective practice. Hence, automatic segmentation methods, which are both faster and more objective, are urgently needed in clinical practice, despite challenges like blurred boundaries [24] and lack of adequately labeled data.

Deep learning has become the primary solution for NPC segmentation tasks due to its robust feature extraction and ease of use compared to traditional machine-learning methods. These methods for NPC lesion segmentation include semi-automatic [10,11,25] and fully automatic [3,6,9,12,14,26]methods. For instance, Lin et al. [10] trained a 3D CNN for NPC lesion segmentation using 3D patches from ROIs, but specific atlas variability limited generalizability. Consequently, fully automatic methods have gained prominence. Ke et al. [6] enhanced performance with an end-to-end multi-task method based on 4100 cases. Tang et al. [21] enhanced performance by using attention modules and fine-tuning network features, and Tao et al. [22] minimized background interference with the Q-learning method to achieve a state-of-the-art model on three multi-sequences.

Due to difficulties in obtaining pixel-level annotated images, researchers are exploring solutions using scarce labeled data, such as synthetic augmentation [4, 15,27], model optimization [7,8], and training paradigm [1,2,18–20,23,28]. The first two are hard to generalize due to unpredictable quality and overfitting risks, and meta-learning's specificity restricts it to certain tasks. Thus, self-supervised learning, efficiently using unlabeled data, becomes preferable for NPC lesion segmentation. Models Genesis (MG) [28] has shown robustness across datasets, but potential improvements in merging multiparametric data remain unexplored.

In this study, we present the Unlabeled-based Optimization Models (UOM), a fully automatic NPC lesion segmentation model utilizing self-supervised learning and an H-shaped reconstruction proxy task. Trained and tested on 44 labeled and

72 unlabeled sets of dual-sequence MRI, the model achieved accuracy comparable to a state-of-the-art model trained with 4100 annotated cases. Moreover, our method significantly lessened the manual delineation workload for oncologists, as confirmed by two experienced practitioners who checked and adjusted the automatic segmentation results.

2   Materials and Methods

2.1   Dataset and Preprocessing

We collected image data from 116 NPC patients at Panyu Central Hospital in Guangzhou. Of these patients, 44 had labeled lesions, while 72 were unlabeled. The unlabeled data from 50 patients was augmented and combined with 36 labeled cases for pre-training, resulting in 86 instances, with the remaining 22 patients' data for evaluation. The study's retrospective nature waived the need for patient consent. T1-weighted (T1W) and T2-weighted (T2W) images were acquired using a 1.5T Siemens Avanto magnetic resonance scanner with resolutions of $0.93 \times 0.93 \times 4\,\mathrm{mm}^3$ and $0.48 \times 0.48 \times 4\,\mathrm{mm}^3$, respectively. The scans ranged from the angle of the mandible to the suprasellar cistern for 25-slice images or from the upper thoracic fossa to the suprasellar cistern for 45-slice images. The NPC lesions' gold standard was manually delineated by an oncologist and verified by another, both with over a decade of experience in NPC radiotherapy planning. Both T1W and T2W images were registered and interpolated to a 256×256 uniform resolution in X and Y directions (excluding the Z direction), using rigid-body transformation and Mattes mutual information [13]. The T2W image, on which the lesion mask was delineated, was used as the reference, and the T1W image as the floating image.

2.2   Deep Learning Network and Proxy Task

UOM. The UOM structure (Fig. 1) we created consists of two components: the pre-training module and the segmentation module, executed using the HR and dual-way network. We initially perform the proxy task and pre-train the unlabeled data to establish a model, which is then used for nasopharyngeal carcinoma segmentation.

Dual-Way Network. We employed a 2D network structure for lesion segmentation using dual-sequence MRI to efficiently manage extensive slice thickness and computational resources. As demonstrated by Ye et al. [26], the integration of dual-sequence MRI could yield a more insightful representation. Therefore, we developed a dual-path segmentation network, drawing from the principles of a 2D U-net [17]. The T1W and T2W images were independently introduced into the network via two separate paths (Fig. 2). The resulting feature maps were concatenated, forming the input for the next encode block. Due to the small batch size, the batch normalization (BN) layer was replaced with a group

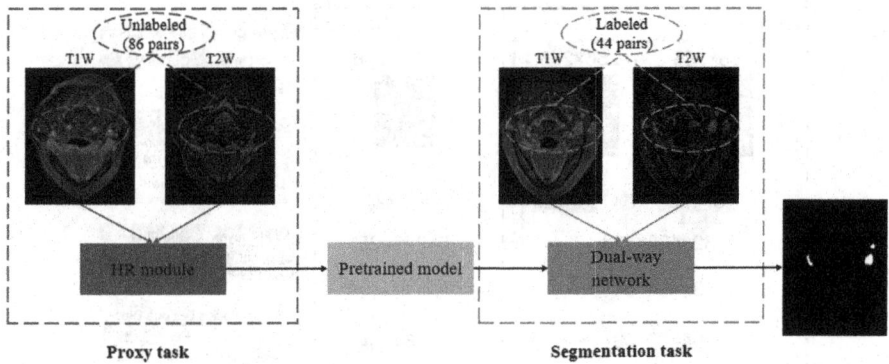

Fig. 1. Flowchart of the UOM. The left diagram illustrates the proxy task, using 86 pairs of unlabeled dual-sequence images in the HR module for pre-training, resulting in the pre-training model. The right diagram depicts the segmentation task, utilizing 44 labeled dual-sequence pairs for cross-validation, performing nasopharyngeal carcinoma segmentation with the pre-trained model.

normalization (GN) layer. Additionally, to preserve more feature information, pooling layers were substituted with convolution layers with a stride of 2 and kernel size of 3×3, and deconvolution layers replaced upsampling layers, while leaky rectified linear units (LeakyReLU) were used instead of standard rectified linear units (ReLU).

Proxy Task. Our network model encountered two major challenges when processing dual-sequence images. First, the large disparities in gray intensities across various MR imaging sequences could easily affect processing. Despite normalizing the images, the network-trained using sparse labeled data-still struggled to integrate the features effectively. Second, due to the limited medical data and significant morphological differences in NPC lesions, the network parameters were prone to getting trapped in local optimums if optimized from random initialization.

Echoing the study by MG [28], we introduced a novel proxy task to tackle the dual-sequence MRI images' information integration challenge and the lack of annotated data. Utilizing a dual-path network, we devised a reconstruction task for these images, subjecting them to multiple transformations, and named this task H-shaped Reconstruction (HR) (see Fig. 3) due to its symmetrical structure. Furthermore, building on contrastive learning principles, each image within the input pair underwent distinct transformations. While these transformations may alter parts of the images, the overall anatomical structure should remain consistent, allowing the extraction of more discriminative features. This task can also bypass registration issues between different sequences, as slight registration deviations can be considered additional transformations, but control is needed to not exceed the network's reconstruction capability. Further details on image

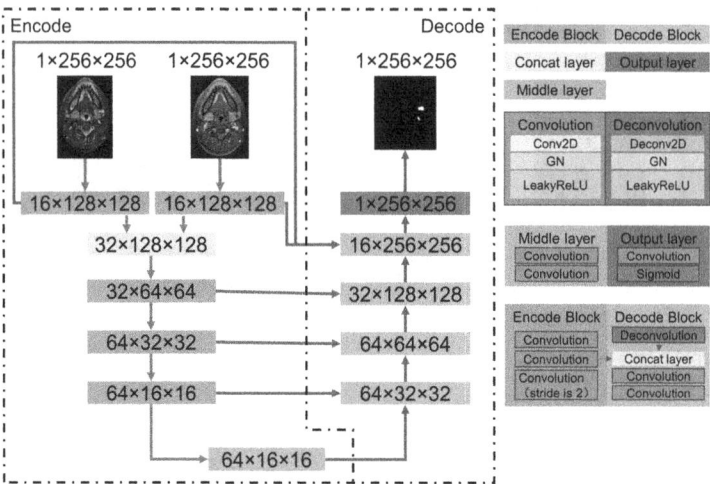

Fig. 2. Structure of the proposed segmentation network. The left diagram gives an overview of the network's structure, with 'C × N × N' notation, where 'N × N' is the feature map size and 'C' is the number of feature maps. Blue, gray, and brown arrows indicate data flow in encoding, decoding, and skipping connection, respectively. The top five operations within the network are represented, along with the internal structure of these operation blocks at the bottom. 'Conv2D' is the 2D convolution layer, 'Deconv2D' is the 2D deconvolution layer, 'GN' is the group normalization layer, and 'LeakyReLU' denotes the leaky rectified linear unit. (Color figure online)

transformation are found in the supplementary section titled '*Image Transformations*'.

2.3   Comparison Experiments

We assessed the efficacy of this approach through a comparison of ten-fold cross-validation results derived from 44 labeled datasets and UOM, alongside outcomes reported in previous studies. Here, UOM denotes the model pretrained using HR on 86 unlabeled datasets. Further details of these experiments can be found in the supplementary section, '*Comparison Experiments*'.

2.4   Evaluation Metrics

The divergence between the results and the ground truth was gauged using the Dice Similarity Coefficient (DSC). The formula for DSC is defined as

$$DSC = 2\,A \cap B|/(|A| + |B|) \tag{1}$$

where A and B are different images.

We designed comparison experiments involving oncologists to validate the assistive role of this method when applied clinically. We utilized this method on

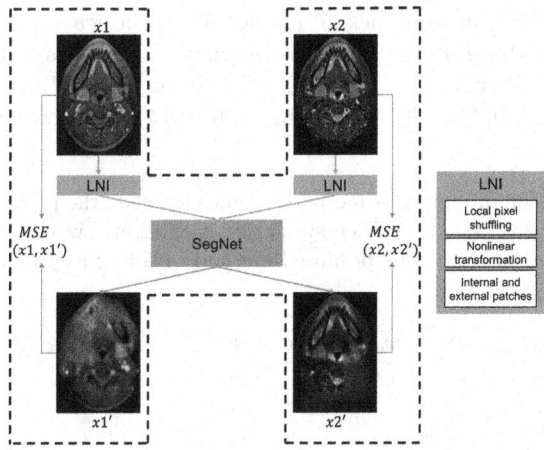

Fig. 3. Flowchart of the HR. $x1$ and $x2$ indicate the pair of dual-sequence MRI images. $x1'$ and $x2'$ indicate the pair of dual-sequence MRI images. The green boxes refer to the transformations. The blue box refers to the dual-way network as SegNet. The orange arrows refer to the original image input to the LNI module, the green arrows refer to the transformed image input to reconstruct the SegNet, the blue arrows refer to the reconstructed image output from the SegNet, and the gray arrows refer to the calculation of the difference between the original and reconstructed images by MSE loss. (Color figure online)

22 cases of unlabeled datasets to obtain segmentation results and then handed these results over to two experienced oncologists with over ten years of practice for modifications. We then calculated the DSC between the modified results and the outputs of our method to quantify the magnitude of the oncologists' revisions, which we define as

$$Magnitude = 1 - DSC \tag{2}$$

The extent of revisions required was stratified into five levels, each differentiated by 20%. Additionally, we computed the average DSC of the 22 cases to illustrate the overall effectiveness of our approach in clinical practice. The results produced by our method were provided to one of the two oncologists for refinement. Two months later, a second round of modifications was made by the original two oncologists, who were unaware of the initial and each other's modifications. Finally, we determined the Intraclass Correlation Coefficient (ICC) for both intra-observer and inter-observer measures to evaluate the reproducibility of the oncologists' revisions.

3   Results

As demonstrated in Table 1, when UOM was applied to the 44 patients, it yielded a mean DSC (median DSC) of 0.75(0.76), exhibiting a 0.04 gap with the U-net. The semi-automatic method by Lin et al. [10] had a median DSC of 0.79.

Neither Ye et al. [26] nor nnU-net [5] managed to produce segmentation results as remarkable as those of the proposed method. The average DSCs (and the corresponding gaps with U-net) of studies by Ke et al. [6], Tang et al. [21], and Tao et al. [22] were 0.77, 0.80 (0.04), and 0.80 (0.14) respectively.

Table 1. Comparison of segmentation performance between the proposed method and reported studies. DSC refers to Dice similarity coefficient, sw to a single path, dw to a dual path, and UOM to our proposed method optimized by the extra unlabeled pretraining dataset.

Dimension	Method	Mean (Median) DSC	Labeled data size (patients)	Gap with U-net
3D	nnU-net [5]	0.73(0.76)	44	0.02
	Lin [10]	(0.79)	1021	–
2D	Ye [26]	0.72(0.74)	44	0.01
	Ke [6]	0.77	4100	–
	Tang [21]	0.80	60	0.04
	Tao [22]	0.80	596	0.14
	U-net-sw [17]	0.71(0.74)	44	0
	U-net-dw	0.72(0.76)	44	0.01
	UOM	**0.75(0.76)**	**44**	**0.04**

Based on expert criteria, our method's segmentation was satisfactory in most cases (16 out of 22, or 72.7%), as Table 2 shows. Oncologist 1 required 0 to 20% revisions in 16 cases, and 20 to 50% in 6 cases; Oncologist 2 needed 0 to 20% revisions in 20 cases, 20 to 50% in one case, and 100% in one case. The average DSC reflects the overall clinical impact of our method. The intra-observer ICC for Oncologist 1 was 0.732, and the inter-observer ICC between Oncologist 1 and Oncologist 2 was 0.830.

Table 2. Assessment of the revision magnitude by oncologists. Comparison of the magnitude of intra- and inter-observer oncologist revisions. Oncologist1-1 and Oncologist2-1 means the same results from our method were modified by two different oncologists. Oncologist1-1 and Oncologist1-2 means the twice revisions by Oncologist 1. For N (M, R), N is the number of cases, M is the median of the DSC, and R is the DSC range. ICC indicates intraclass correlation coefficient, and DSC is calculated between the network segmentation results and oncologist modification results.

Magnitude of oncologist revision	Oncologist1-1	Oncologist1-2	Oncologist2-1
> 0–20%	16 (0.94, 0.82–0.98)	16 (0.95, 0.88–0.99)	20 (0.88, 0.83–0.97)
> 20–50%	6 (0.74, 0.49–0.77)	6 (0.77, 0.62–0.79)	1 (0.77)
> 40–100%	0	0	1 (0)
Mean DSC	0.86	0.89	0.84
ICC	–	0.732	0.830

4   Discussion

We created HR to utilize dual-sequence MRI and unlabeled data, improving UOM for NPC segmentation. It addressed gray value discrepancies, extracted consistent features from dual-sequence MRI images, and overcame registration challenges between different sequences by treating partial registration deviations as transformations.

We analyzed the situation where gaps with U-net reduced inter-study variation, comparing our method's results with those deficient in a gap with U-net. As demonstrated in Table 1, Ye et al. [26] used the same dataset, but our result surpassed Ye's. We also outperformed state-of-the-art techniques like nnU-net [5], and our result was close to Ke et al. [6] with 4100 cases when 86 unlabeled cases were used, highlighting our method's efficient use of unlabeled data. Tang et al. [21] had the same gap with more samples. Although Tao et al. [22] had a gap more than three times ours using additional sequences, this supports our conclusion that more sequences yield better results. Lin et al. [10] achieved superior performance with a 3D dataset and smaller slice thickness at 3T, but their method segmented lesions in ROIs from specific templates, limiting generalizability, and their mean result for 1021 cases wasn't reported.

Two radiation oncologists refined the automated contouring. Our method achieved DSCs of 0.86 and 0.84, showing minimal need for modifications to satisfy clinical needs. High intra-observer reproducibility was observed with an ICC of 0.732 (Oncologist 1), and inter-observer reproducibility had an ICC of 0.830. Our method's automatic outcomes could reduce oncologists' subjectivity and enhance confidence in delineation.

This study has several limitations: our dataset was small and from a single center, but intra- and inter-observer oncologist revision results demonstrated the method's stability and effectiveness. To further validate, gathering more data from multiple sites is needed. The small amount of unlabeled data used made exploring the relationship between unlabeled and labeled data difficult, limiting our method's potential to enhance segmentation. The association between pretrain and downstream tasks also needs more investigation for efficient pretraining.

In this study, we introduced UOM, a fully automatic segmentation method for NPC lesions, utilizing unlabeled data on dual-sequence MRI images to initialize the model's pre-weights through self-supervised learning. Post-processing eliminated false positives. This method may streamline oncologists' delineation of NPC lesions, minimize errors due to subjective factors, and enhance radiotherapy planning efficiency.

Conflict of Interest. No relevant conflicts to disclose.

References

1. Chen, L., Bentley, P., Mori, K., Misawa, K., Fujiwara, M., Rueckert, D.: Self-supervised learning for medical image analysis using image context restoration. Med. Image Anal. **58**, 101539 (2019)
2. Feyjie, A.R., Azad, R., Pedersoli, M., Kauffman, C., Ayed, I.B., Dolz, J.: Semi-supervised few-shot learning for medical image segmentation. arXiv preprint arXiv:2003.08462 (2020)
3. Huang, B., et al.: Fully automated delineation of gross tumor volume for head and neck cancer on PET-CT using deep learning: a dual-center study. Contrast Media Molecular Imaging 2018 (2018)
4. Huo, Y., Xu, Z., Bao, S., Assad, A., Abramson, R.G., Landman, B.A.: Adversarial synthesis learning enables segmentation without target modality ground truth. In: 2018 IEEE 15th international symposium on biomedical imaging (ISBI 2018), pp. 1217–1220. IEEE (2018)
5. Isensee, F., Jaeger, P.F., Kohl, S.A., Petersen, J., Maier-Hein, K.H.: nnU-Net: a self-configuring method for deep learning-based biomedical image segmentation. Nat. Methods **18**(2), 203–211 (2021)
6. Ke, L., et al.: Development of a self-constrained 3D DenseNet model in automatic detection and segmentation of nasopharyngeal carcinoma using magnetic resonance images. Oral Oncol. **110**, 104862 (2020)
7. Kim, S., An, S., Chikontwe, P., Park, S.H.: Bidirectional RNN-based few shot learning for 3D medical image segmentation. In: Proceedings of the AAAI Conference on Artificial Intelligence, vol. 35, pp. 1808–1816 (2021)
8. Lahiani, A., Gildenblat, J., Klaman, I., Navab, N., Klaiman, E.: Generalizing multistain immunohistochemistry tissue segmentation using one-shot color deconvolution deep neural networks. arXiv preprint arXiv:1805.06958 (2018)
9. Li, Q., et al.: Tumor segmentation in contrast-enhanced magnetic resonance imaging for nasopharyngeal carcinoma: deep learning with convolutional neural network. BioMed Res. Int. 2018 (2018)
10. Lin, L., et al.: Deep learning for automated contouring of primary tumor volumes by MRI for nasopharyngeal carcinoma. Radiology **291**(3), 677–686 (2019)
11. Ma, Z., Wu, X., Song, Q., Luo, Y., Wang, Y., Zhou, J.: Automated nasopharyngeal carcinoma segmentation in magnetic resonance images by combination of convolutional neural networks and graph cut. Exp. Ther. Med. **16**(3), 2511–2521 (2018)
12. Ma, Z., et al.: Nasopharyngeal carcinoma segmentation based on enhanced convolutional neural networks using multi-modal metric learning. Phys. Med. Biol. **64**(2), 025005 (2019)
13. Mattes, D., Haynor, D.R., Vesselle, H., Lewellyn, T.K., Eubank, W.: Nonrigid multimodality image registration. In: Medical Imaging 2001: Image Processing, vol. 4322, pp. 1609–1620. SPIE (2001)
14. Men, K., et al.: Deep deconvolutional neural network for target segmentation of nasopharyngeal cancer in planning computed tomography images. Front. Oncol. **7**, 315 (2017)
15. Mondal, A.K., Dolz, J., Desrosiers, C.: Few-shot 3D multi-modal medical image segmentation using generative adversarial learning. arXiv preprint arXiv:1810.12241 (2018)
16. Peng, H., et al.: The current status of clinical trials focusing on nasopharyngeal carcinoma: a comprehensive analysis of ClinicalTrials. gov database. PLoS One **13**(5), e0196730 (2018)

17. Ronneberger, O., Fischer, P., Brox, T.: U-Net: convolutional networks for biomedical image segmentation. In: Navab, N., Hornegger, J., Wells, W.M., Frangi, A.F. (eds.) MICCAI 2015. LNCS, vol. 9351, pp. 234–241. Springer, Cham (2015). https://doi.org/10.1007/978-3-319-24574-4_28
18. Ross, T., et al.: Exploiting the potential of unlabeled endoscopic video data with self-supervised learning. Int. J. Comput. Assist. Radiol. Surg. **13**, 925–933 (2018)
19. Roy, A.G., Siddiqui, S., Pölsterl, S., Navab, N., Wachinger, C.: Squeeze and excite guided few-shot segmentation of volumetric images. Med. Image Anal. **59**, 101587 (2020)
20. Taleb, A., Lippert, C., Klein, T., Nabi, M.: Multimodal self-supervised learning for medical image analysis. In: Feragen, A., Sommer, S., Schnabel, J., Nielsen, M. (eds.) IPMI 2021. LNCS, vol. 12729, pp. 661–673. Springer, Cham (2021). https://doi.org/10.1007/978-3-030-78191-0_51
21. Tang, P., et al.: DA-DSUnet: dual attention-based dense SU-et for automatic head-and-neck tumor segmentation in MRI images. Neurocomputing **435**, 103–113 (2021)
22. Tao, G., et al.: SeqSeg: a sequential method to achieve nasopharyngeal carcinoma segmentation free from background dominance. Med. Image Anal. **78**, 102381 (2022)
23. Tao, X., Li, Y., Zhou, W., Ma, K., Zheng, Y.: Revisiting Rubik's Cube: self-supervised learning with volume-wise transformation for 3D medical image segmentation. In: Martel, A.L., et al. (eds.) MICCAI 2020. LNCS, vol. 12264, pp. 238–248. Springer, Cham (2020). https://doi.org/10.1007/978-3-030-59719-1_24
24. Wang, H., et al.: A collaborative dictionary learning model for nasopharyngeal carcinoma segmentation on multimodalities MR sequences. Comput. Math. Methods Med. 2020 (2020)
25. Wang, Y., et al.: Automatic tumor segmentation with deep convolutional neural networks for radiotherapy applications. Neural Process. Lett. **48**, 1323–1334 (2018)
26. Ye, Y., et al.: Fully-automated segmentation of nasopharyngeal carcinoma on dual-sequence MRI using convolutional neural networks. Front. Oncol. **10**, 166 (2020)
27. Zhao, A., Balakrishnan, G., Durand, F., Guttag, J.V., Dalca, A.V.: Data augmentation using learned transformations for one-shot medical image segmentation. In: Proceedings of the IEEE/CVF conference on computer vision and pattern recognition, pp. 8543–8553 (2019)
28. Zhou, Z., Sodha, V., Pang, J., Gotway, M.B., Liang, J.: Models genesis. Med. Image Anal. **67**, 101840 (2021)

MetaRegNet: Metamorphic Image Registration Using Flow-Driven Residual Networks

Ankita Joshi[1] and Yi Hong[2(✉)]

[1] Department of Computer Science, University of Georgia, Athens, GA 30602, USA
[2] Department of Computer Science and Engineering, Shanghai Jiao Tong University, Shanghai 200240, China
yi.hong@sjtu.edu.cn

Abstract. Deep learning based methods provide efficient solutions to medical image registration, including the challenging problem of diffeomorphic image registration. However, most methods register normal image pairs, facing difficulty handling those with missing correspondences, e.g., in the presence of pathology like tumors. We desire an efficient solution to jointly account for spatial deformations and appearance changes in the pathological regions where the correspondences are missing, i.e., finding a solution to metamorphic image registration. Some approaches are proposed to tackle this problem but cannot properly handle large pathological regions and deformations around pathologies. In this paper, we propose a deep metamorphic image registration network (MetaRegNet), which adopts time-varying flows to drive spatial diffeomorphic deformations and generate intensity variations. We evaluate MetaRegNet on two datasets, i.e., BraTS 2021 with brain tumors and 3D-IRCADb-01 with liver tumors, showing promising results in registering a healthy and tumor image pair. The source code is available at https://github.com/ankitajoshi15/MetaRegNet.

Keywords: Pathological Image Registration · Image Metamorphosis · Diffeomorphisms · Residual Networks

1 Introduction

Deformable image registration (DIR) establishes dense pixel/voxel correspondences between 2D/3D images using a deformation that transforms images into a common space for fusion or comparison [33]. Existing DIR methods include classical registration models, e.g. SyN [5], Large Deformation Diffeomorphic Metric Mapping (LDDMM) [7,10], Stationary Velocity Fields (SVF) [4], and recent deep-learning-based methods, e.g., QuickSilver [36], VoxelMorph [13], SYM-Net [27]. These methods focus on registering image pairs with no missing correspondences, i.e., all pixels or voxels in the source image are matched with those in the target image using a bijective mapping function. Such assumptions limit their

© The Author(s), under exclusive license to Springer Nature Switzerland AG 2023
W. Qin et al. (Eds.): CMMCA 2023 (MICCAI Workshop), LNCS 14243, pp. 160–170, 2023.
https://doi.org/10.1007/978-3-031-45087-7_17

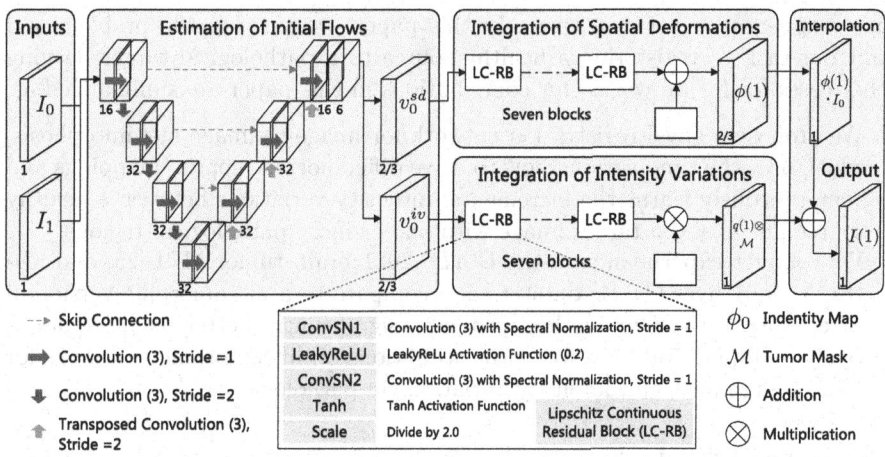

Fig. 1. Overview of our metamorphic image registration network, MetaRegNet.

ability to tackle registration between image pairs with appearing or disappearing structures, e.g., developing brain scans during myelination, a healthy image and a tumor one, etc. These image pairs have both spatial deformations caused by the movements of shared structures and intensity changes caused by missing correspondences between unshared ones. Such intensity changes challenge existing methods, including diffeomorphic image registration that provides smooth transformation with a smooth inverse to preserve topology between image pairs.

To capture spatial and intensity changes simultaneously, we turn to metamorphic image registration [34], which introduces a source term to simulate the intensity changes in the diffeomorphic image registration framework [20]. The model complexity of traditional metamorphic image registration makes them impractical for handling large-scale and high-resolution images. To reduce the computational cost of existing methods, researchers propose some deep learning based solutions to handle pathological image registration, a special case of deep metamorphic image registration, e.g., the existence of tumor regions as in [24,28]. Existing methods use either a cost function masking (CFM) strategy, which completely separates deformations and intensity changes in the pathological and non pathological regions, or a clean/healthy source or target image where a tumor is simulated to match with the other one with tumor. These methods ignore the deformations of healthy regions affected by pathological regions, which cause large artifacts within and surrounding the pathological regions.

To address this challenge, we reformulate traditional metamorphic image registration and propose a deep metamorphic solution MetaRegNet, see Fig. 1. Based on the Lipschitz continuous ResNet blocks proposed in [21], MetaRegNet consists of two pathways to jointly integrate spatial deformations and intensity changes along the trajectory from the source to the target image. That is, MetaRegNet produces diffeomorphic deformations to account for spatial deformations between images and jointly learns intensity changes to account for the tumor appearance between them. In this paper, we simplify the problem and limit our task to registering a healthy source to a pathological target, leaving other cases for future work. Our contributions in this paper are summarized as:

– We propose a novel registration network for image-to-image metamorphosis, which uses the time-varying flow to drive diffeomorphic spatial mappings and simultaneously learns the incremental intensity variations between a healthy source image and a target image with one or more pathological regions.
– We conduct experiments on the BraTS 2021 brain tumor MRI [25] and 3D-IRCADb-01 liver CT [1] datasets and compare to a metamorphic version of VoxelMorph [13]. Our method produces significantly better results qualitatively and quantitatively, for both estimations of diffeomorphic mappings for spatial alignment and intensity variations in pathological regions.

1.1   Related Work

Mask-Based Methods. This category assumes that pathological masks are available for learning; so that, the healthy and pathological regions can be treated separately. In [9], masks exclude the pathological regions from measuring the image similarity loss. The geometric metamorphosis [29] uses masks to separate the foreground and background deformation models for capturing intensity and spatial changes separately. Similarly, masking strategies are used in [12,28]. Joint registration and segmentation approaches are also proposed in [11,16,28,35], but these methods fail to have good appearance matching or smooth deformations. Differently, our method automatically learns the amount of intensity variation and balances it with spatial deformations. The mask *softly* restricts the estimated intensity changes within the pathological regions, resulting in continuous spatial deformations and greatly reduced artifacts surrounding the pathological regions.

Reconstruction-Based Methods. Another choice for metamorphic image registration is to reconstruct a pathological image into a clean quasi-normal one before registration [8,18,19]. A variety of techniques have been proposed, such as image in-painting [31], Variational AutoEncoder (VAE) based approaches [8], and a low-rank decomposition model to learn a normal image appearance [23]. These approaches do not require masks of pathological regions; however, their registration quality is limited by the imperfect or over-smoothed reconstructions. Also, these methods require extra healthy image scans for training and work well only if the size of the pathological region, like tumor or lesion, is relatively small.

Other Methods. In [8,24,32], researchers disentangle the shape and appearance changes of an image when performing registration. In [15,17], a biophysical model is adopted to introduce a growing tumor into a healthy image and perform image registration with another tumor image; however, modeling the growth of a tumor is a non-trivial task. In [14], a semi-langrangian scheme is proposed to carry out registration for each pair but has limited ability to handle a large-scale dataset.

The model in [24] is the closest one to ours. It also uses residual networks and deforms a pathological source image into a fixed healthy atlas, which is a special case of ours, since we allow choosing different healthy images, not limited to the atlas. More importantly, unlike them, we do not need a hyper-parameter to balance spatial deformations and intensity changes, which is not practical since it varies with different inputs and datasets.

2   Background and Reformulation

In the LDDMM framework [7], diffeomorphic image registration is formulated as a minimization problem, which estimates a smooth deformation field $\phi : \Omega \to \Omega$, where $\Omega \subseteq R^{n_x \times n_y \times n_z}$ (i.e., the size of a 3D image). The formulation is given as

$$E(v) = \frac{1}{2} \int_0^1 \|v\|_L^2 \, dt + \frac{1}{\sigma^2} \|I_1 - I(1)\|_2^2, \quad s.t. \ I_t + \nabla I^T v = 0, I(0) = I_0. \quad (1)$$

Here, v is the time-dependent velocity field, L is a spatial regularizer to ensure the smoothness of v; I_0 and I_1 are the source and target images, $I(0)$ and $I(1)$ are the deformed images at $t = 0$ and $t = 1$, respectively; σ controls the influence of the regularization term and the image matching term. This formulation is an image-based version of LDDMM, where the image intensity is driven by the velocity field v. We can also use map-based implementation, which uses a deformation ϕ that is driven by the velocity field and then used to warp the source image.

Metamorphic registration can be formulated based on the diffeomorphic LDDMM model [20], by introducing a control variable q in the image transport equation, as shown in Eq. (2). This introduced variable q simulates an intensity source term and models intensity changes caused by appearing or disappearing objects in the image. The new optimization function is formulated as

$$E(v, q) = \frac{1}{2} \int_0^1 \|v\|_L^2 \, dt + \rho \|q\|_Q^2 \, dt \ s.t. \ I_t + \nabla I^T v = q, I(0) = I_0, I(1) = I_1, \quad (2)$$

where ρ is a constant value to balance the intensity variations introduced by the control variable q, Q is a smooth operator applied on q. Different from LDDMM, metamorphic registration moves the image matching term into the constraints and can achieve a *perfect matching* between warped image $I(1)$ and the target image I_1, due to the introduced q. The solution in [20] presents a tight coupling of velocity fields that drive spatial deformations and additive intensity changes.

Reformulation. In the deep learning framework, we use the map-based image registration and disentangle the velocity fields into two parts, i.e., v_t^{sd} that drives the spatial deformation ϕ and v_t^{iv} that drives the intensity variation q. Hence, we replace the transport equation in Eq. (2) with a reformulation of two separate dynamics, using the following two ordinary differential equations (ODEs):

$$\frac{d\phi}{dt} = v_t^{sd} \circ \phi(t), \phi(0) = id \quad and \quad \frac{dq}{dt} = v_t^{iv} \cdot q(t), q(0) = 0, \quad (3)$$

where id is the identity map, the spatial deformation ϕ lies in a vector space that has the same size as the velocity field v, and the scalar intensity variation q has the same size as the image I. The final transported image $I(1)$ is the combination of the deformed source image $\phi(1) \cdot I_0$ and the total intensity changes $q(1)$.

3 Deep Metamorphic Image Registration

Based on the above reformulation, we propose a metamorphic image registration network (MetaRegNet) to jointly model spatial deformations and intensity changes. Overall, MetaRegNet adopts a UNet network to estimate two initial velocity fields v_0^{sd} and v_0^{iv}, which drive the spatial deformation ϕ and the intensity variations q over time. The combination of the deformed source image and estimated intensity changes matches the target image. The proposed architecture is presented in Fig. 1, with each component described below.

Estimation of Initial Flows. To obtain spatial deformations and intensity variations, we first estimate their initial driven flows. We adopt a UNet [30] to estimate the initial values v_0^{sd} and v_0^{iv} from an image pair. As shown in Fig. 1, the network includes a non-probabilistic U-Net architecture, which directly outputs the flow estimation, without sampling from the mean and variance as done in [13]. This non-probabilistic approach is simple and works well in our experiments.

Integration of Spatial Deformations and Intensity Variations. To solve Eq. (3) with the estimated initial flows, we utilize Lipschitz Continuous ResNet Blocks (LC-RB) proposed in [21]. These LC-RB blocks are used as numerical integration schemes for solving ODEs. We use the version without sharing weights among seven blocks, which models time-varying velocity fields and produces diffeomorphic deformations. That is, we obtain the diffeomorphic deformation $\phi(1)$, which captures the spatial transformations between the source and target images and deforms the healthy source image to generate parts of the final image.

   Another branch with the same number of LC-RB blocks produces incremental residual mappings of additive intensity changes between the input pair, starting from q_0. Intensity variations produced at the end, $q(1)$, are added to the deformed source to approximate the target image I_1. Naively, if $q(1)$ was a simple pixel-/voxel-wise subtraction of the input pair, it would perfectly reconstruct I_1; however, this solution fails to meet the anatomical matching constraint of image registration. To address this, we add a regularization similar to [24], which restricts the learned intensity variations within the pathological region of the target image, i.e., missing correspondences only happen within the pathological regions. We assume the availability of the binary mask $\mathcal{M}$ of the pathological region, like a tumor, and use it to mask out the intensity variations in the non-pathological regions, i.e., $q(1) \otimes \mathcal{M}$. When the mask $\mathcal{M}$ is empty like registering two healthy images, our model is downgraded to standard image registration. That is, the standard diffeomorphic image registration is a special case of our metamorphic image registration.

Interpolation and Output. In this step, we generate the final output to approximate the target image I_1. Firstly, with $\phi(1)$ we generate the deformed source image using a differentiable interpolation layer. For each voxel p in the target image, this layer computes its location given at $\phi(p)$ in the source image and obtains its intensity value using linear interpolation. Upon this, we produce our final metamorphic output by adding the generated intensity variations, which performs a pixel-wise addition of $q(1) \otimes \mathcal{M}$ to the deformed image $\phi(1) \cdot I_0$, i.e., the final output is calculated as $I(1) = \phi(1) \cdot I_0 + q(1) \otimes \mathcal{M}$.

Loss Function. Similar to metamorphic image registration formulated in Eq. (2), we have the image matching between our metamorphic output and the target image, and the regularization on the spatial deformation and the intensity variation. The overall loss function is formulated as

$$\mathcal{L} = \lambda_1 \mathcal{L}_{sim}(\frac{1}{|\Omega|} \|I_1 - (\phi(1) \cdot I_0 + q(1) \otimes \mathcal{M})\|_2^2) + \lambda_2 \mathcal{L}_{reg}(\nabla(q(1) \otimes \mathcal{M})$$
$$+ \lambda_3 \mathcal{L}_{Jdet}(0.5(|\mathbb{J}(\phi(1))| - \mathbb{J}(\phi(1))))), \tag{4}$$

where Ω is the image spatial domain and $|\Omega|$ indicates the number of pixels or voxels in an image, and λ_1, λ_2 and λ_3 are the balancing weights, which are set to $[1.0, 1.0, 0.001]$, respectively, in our experiments. We use mean squared error (MSE) as the image similarity metric $\mathcal{L}_{sim}$ to measure the goodness of image matching. We also discourage dramatic intensity changes within the learned intensity values by using a diffusion regularizer $\mathcal{L}_{reg}$ on the estimated intensity changes, where ∇ is the spatial gradient operator. Besides, to restrict the learned deformations to be diffeomorphic we use $\mathcal{L}_{Jdet}$, where we penalize the total number of locations where the Jacobian determinants $|\mathbb{J}(\phi(1))|$ are negative.

4 Experiments

Datasets. *(1) BraTS 2021* [6,22,26]. This dataset includes image scans collected from 1251 subjects. Each scan is pre-processed by skull-strpping, co-registering to a common anatomical template, and being interpolated to the same resolution of $1 \times 1 \times 1\,\mathrm{mm}^3$, which is followed by an intensity normalization between 0 to 1. We select 120 slices with no tumor as our healthy image set and 120 slices with tumors as our pathological set, by checking their corresponding tumor masks. We keep aside 20 images from each set for testing and 5 for validation. As a result, we have 240 random image pairs for training, 5 pairs for validation, and 20 pairs for testing. *(2) 3D-IRCADb-01* [1]. This database is composed of 3D CT scans of 20 different patients with hepatic tumors. Each image has 74~260 slices with size of 512×512, which is resampled to a pixel

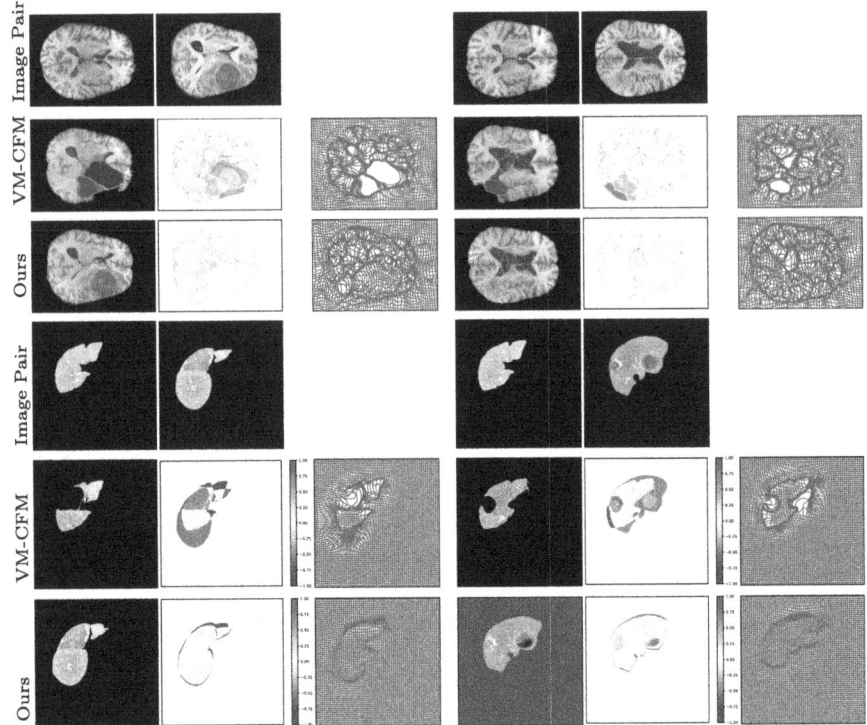

Fig. 2. Qualitative comparison between VM-CFM and our MetaRegNet on brain and liver datasets. Given an input pair on the top, the final output, its intensity difference to the target, and the spatial deformation are shown from left to right for each sample.

spacing of 1 mm. Since the pixel values are in Hounsfield and in the range of $[-1000, 4000]$, we perform a color depth conversion using the mapping as in [3]: $g = \frac{h - m_1}{m_2 - m_1} \times 255$. Here, g is the converted gray level value, h is the Hounsfield value in the raw image, and m_1 and m_2 are the minimum and maximum of the Hounsfield range, respectively. Then, we crop the liver region using the provided liver mask and normalize the image intensity to $[0, 1]$. We collect 20 slices that contain healthy liver regions and 6 slices that have a pathological regions in the liver. We take 12 slices from the healthy set and 3 slices from the unhealthy set to make our training set, resulting in 36 image pairs, and take 3 healthy slices and 1 unhealthy slice to make 3 pairs for validation, and 5 healthy slices and 2 unhealthy slices to make 10 pairs for testing. Due to the limited training samples, we extend the training set to 144 pairs, via rotating each image by 90, 180 and 270°. For both datasets, we have *subject-wise* splitting for training, validation, and test sets.

Baseline Methods. For comparison, we choose the diffeomorphic version of VoxelMorph [13], a deep-learning-based image registration model, as our baseline. Since VoxelMorph cannot handle the metamorphic image registration problem, we modify it and adopt the cost-function-masking (CFM) strategy [9] to exclude the similarity measure of the tumor regions using their masks during training. This modified VoxelMorph is denoted as VM-CFM.

Implementation and Settings. We implement our MetaRegNet using Keras and TensorFlow and train it in an end-to-end fashion, with the Adam optimizer and a fixed learning rate of $1e^{-4}$. Both our architecture and the baseline model VM-CFM have been deployed on the same machine with an Nvidia TITAN X GPU. We build our method on top of the R2Net implementation with default parameters reported in [21]. All models are trained from scratch.

Evaluation Metrics. We measure the average Sum of Squared Distance (SSD) between the deformed source and target images, including the whole image (SSD-total) and the healthy region only (SSD-healthy). To measure the number of foldings in the estimated spatial deformations, we report the number of voxels with negative Jacobian determinants. Also, we measure the segmentation Dice score by using estimated deformations and the inference time as well.

Table 1. Comparison between VM-CFM and our method on brain and liver datasets. The Dice of brain segmentation is not reported since we do not have brain masks.

Data	Method	SSD (e^{-1}) SSD-total	SSD (e^{-1}) SSD-healthy	Dice	#Foldings (per img. pair)	Time (ms)
Brain	VM-CFM	$0.13_{\pm0.003}$	$0.1_{\pm0.002}$	–	$88.585_{\pm76.63}$	21
	MetaRegNet	$\mathbf{0.08}_{\pm0.002}$	$\mathbf{0.07}_{\pm0.002}$	–	$\mathbf{3.62}_{\pm6.34}$	23
Liver	VM-CFM	$1.5_{\pm0.004}$	$0.07_{\pm0.003}$	0.88	$23.16_{\pm34.56}$	22
	MetaRegNet	$\mathbf{0.40}_{\pm0.012}$	$\mathbf{0.04}_{\pm0.002}$	$\mathbf{0.95}$	$\mathbf{1.00}_{\pm4.90}$	24

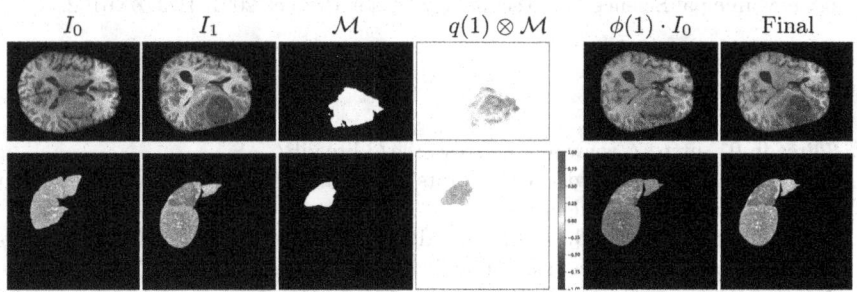

Fig. 3. Image appearance separation learned by MetaRegNet. Left to right: clean source image I_0, pathological target image I_1, tumor mask $\mathcal{M}$, learned intensity changes within the tumor region $q(1) \otimes \mathcal{M}$, the deformed source image $\phi(1) \cdot I_0$, and the final output.

Experimental Results. Table 1 reports our quantitative results. Compared to VM-CFM, our model provides a better matching, not only in the healthy region but also in the whole image, for both brain and liver datasets. Figure 2 presents the visual improvement, showing better matching in both tumor and healthy regions, for images with either large or small tumors. Our deformations are much smoother, as demonstrated by the much fewer foldings reported in Table 1 and smoother maps within tumors and their surrounding regions in Fig. 2. Unlike VM-CFM, we have spatial deformations going under the tumor regions, and the rest appearance changes are contributed by the intensity variance, indicating the appearing tumors from a healthy source to a pathological target, which is also observed in Fig. 3. To further evaluate the effectiveness of MetaRegNet, we use deformation maps to transfer the segmentation mask of the source image to match the target one. Since only liver masks are available, we apply our method on liver segmentation and obtain a mean Dice score of 0.95, compared to 0.88 produced by VM-CFM. And we only takes 2ms more for registering one pair.

5   Conclusion and Future Work

In this paper, we propose a metamorphic image registration framework, MetaRegNet, which utilizes LC-ResNet blocks as flow integrator and allows for joint estimation of spatial deformation and intensity variation between a healthy source image and a pathological target image. Although we work on 2D images, our method is general and straightforward to apply on 3D images. In the future work, we will work on the BraTS-Reg challenge [2], which provides 3D images and landmarks for evaluation. One limitation of our method is the need of using tumor masks. We can fully leverage existing tumor segmentation networks and use them to produce the required masks or integrate them into our network, which is left as our future work. Another extension of our work is registering any pairs of healthy and pathological images, including the registration between two pathological image scans, which is also our future work.

Acknowledgments. This work was supported by NSFC 62203303, NSF 1755970, and Shanghai Municipal Science and Technology Major Project 2021SHZDZX0102.

References

1. 3dircadb-01. https://www.ircad.fr/research/3dircadb/
2. Brain tumor sequence registration (brats-reg) challenge. https://www.med.upenn.edu/cbica/brats-reg-challenge/
3. Almotairi, S., Kareem, G., Aouf, M., Almutairi, B., Salem, M.A.M.: Liver tumor segmentation in CT scans using modified SegNet. Sensors **20**(5), 1516 (2020)
4. Arsigny, V., Commowick, O., Pennec, X., Ayache, N.: A log-Euclidean framework for statistics on diffeomorphisms. In: Larsen, R., Nielsen, M., Sporring, J. (eds.) MICCAI 2006. LNCS, vol. 4190, pp. 924–931. Springer, Heidelberg (2006). https://doi.org/10.1007/11866565_113

5. Avants, B.B., Tustison, N.J., Song, G., Cook, P.A., Klein, A., Gee, J.C.: A reproducible evaluation of ants similarity metric performance in brain image registration. Neuroimage **54**(3), 2033–2044 (2011)

6. Baid, U., et al.: The RSNA-ASNR-MICCAI BraTs 2021 benchmark on brain tumor segmentation and radiogenomic classification. arXiv preprint arXiv:2107.02314 (2021)

7. Beg, M.F., Miller, M.I., Trouvé, A., Younes, L.: Computing large deformation metric mappings via geodesic flows of diffeomorphisms. Int. J. Comput. Vision **61**(2), 139–157 (2005)

8. Bône, A., Vernhet, P., Colliot, O., Durrleman, S.: Learning joint shape and appearance representations with metamorphic auto-encoders. In: Martel, A.L., et al. (eds.) MICCAI 2020. LNCS, vol. 12261, pp. 202–211. Springer, Cham (2020). https://doi.org/10.1007/978-3-030-59710-8_20

9. Brett, M., Leff, A.P., Rorden, C., Ashburner, J.: Spatial normalization of brain images with focal lesions using cost function masking. Neuroimage **14**(2), 486–500 (2001)

10. Cao, Y., Miller, M.I., Winslow, R.L., Younes, L.: Large deformation diffeomorphic metric mapping of vector fields. TMI **24**(9), 1216–1230 (2005)

11. Chitphakdithai, N., Duncan, J.S.: Non-rigid registration with missing correspondences in preoperative and postresection brain images. In: Jiang, T., Navab, N., Pluim, J.P.W., Viergever, M.A. (eds.) MICCAI 2010. LNCS, vol. 6361, pp. 367–374. Springer, Heidelberg (2010). https://doi.org/10.1007/978-3-642-15705-9_45

12. Clatz, O., et al.: Robust nonrigid registration to capture brain shift from intraoperative MRI. IEEE Trans. Med. Imaging **24**(11), 1417–1427 (2005)

13. Dalca, A.V., Balakrishnan, G., Guttag, J., Sabuncu, M.R.: Unsupervised learning for fast probabilistic diffeomorphic registration. In: MICCAI. pp. 729–738. Springer (2018)

14. François, A., Gori, P., Glaunès, J.: Metamorphic image registration using a semi-lagrangian scheme. In: Nielsen, F., Barbaresco, F. (eds.) GSI 2021. LNCS, vol. 12829, pp. 781–788. Springer, Cham (2021). https://doi.org/10.1007/978-3-030-80209-7_84

15. François, A., Maillard, M., Oppenheim, C., Pallud, J., Gori, P., Glaunès, J.A.: Weighted metamorphosis for registration of images with different topology. In: 10th International Workshop on Biomedical Image Registration (2022)

16. Gooya, A., Pohl, K.M., Bilello, M., Biros, G., Davatzikos, C.: Joint segmentation and deformable registration of brain scans guided by a tumor growth model. In: Fichtinger, G., Martel, A., Peters, T. (eds.) MICCAI 2011. LNCS, vol. 6892, pp. 532–540. Springer, Heidelberg (2011). https://doi.org/10.1007/978-3-642-23629-7_65

17. Gooya, A., et al.: GLISTR: glioma image segmentation and registration. IEEE Trans. Med. Imaging **31**(10), 1941–1954 (2012)

18. Han, X., et al.: Brain extraction from normal and pathological images: a joint PCA/image-reconstruction approach. Neuroimage **176**, 431–445 (2018)

19. Han, X., et al.: A deep network for joint registration and reconstruction of images with pathologies. In: Liu, M., Yan, P., Lian, C., Cao, X. (eds.) MLMI 2020. LNCS, vol. 12436, pp. 342–352. Springer, Cham (2020). https://doi.org/10.1007/978-3-030-59861-7_35

20. Hong, Y., Joshi, S., Sanchez, M., Styner, M., Niethammer, M.: Metamorphic geodesic regression. In: Ayache, N., Delingette, H., Golland, P., Mori, K. (eds.) MICCAI 2012. LNCS, vol. 7512, pp. 197–205. Springer, Heidelberg (2012). https://doi.org/10.1007/978-3-642-33454-2_25

21. Joshi, A., Hong, Y.: Diffeomorphic image registration using lipschitz continuous residual networks. In: Medical Imaging with Deep Learning (2021)
22. Kuzilek, J., Hlosta, M., Zdrahal, Z.: Open university learning analytics dataset. Sci. Data **4**(1), 1–8 (2017)
23. Liu, X., Niethammer, M., Kwitt, R., McCormick, M., Aylward, S.: Low-rank to the rescue – atlas-based analyses in the presence of pathologies. In: Golland, P., Hata, N., Barillot, C., Hornegger, J., Howe, R. (eds.) MICCAI 2014. LNCS, vol. 8675, pp. 97–104. Springer, Cham (2014). https://doi.org/10.1007/978-3-319-10443-0_13
24. Maillard, M., François, A., Glaunès, J., Bloch, I., Gori, P.: A deep residual learning implementation of metamorphosis. In: 2022 IEEE 19th International Symposium on Biomedical Imaging (ISBI), pp. 1–4. IEEE (2022)
25. Menze, B.H., et al.: The multimodal brain tumor image segmentation benchmark (brats). IEEE Trans. Med. Imaging **34**(10), 1993–2024 (2014)
26. Menze, J., et al.: A comparison of random forest and its Gini importance with standard chemometric methods for the feature selection and classification of spectral data. BMC Bioinf **10**(1), 213 (2009)
27. Mok, T.C., Chung, A.: Fast symmetric diffeomorphic image registration with convolutional neural networks. In: Proceedings of the IEEE/CVF Conference on Computer Vision and Pattern Recognition, pp. 4644–4653 (2020)
28. Mok, T.C., Chung, A.: Unsupervised deformable image registration with absent correspondences in pre-operative and post-recurrence brain tumor MRI scans. arXiv preprint arXiv:2206.03900 (2022)
29. Niethammer, M., et al.: Geometric metamorphosis. In: Fichtinger, G., Martel, A., Peters, T. (eds.) MICCAI 2011. LNCS, vol. 6892, pp. 639–646. Springer, Heidelberg (2011). https://doi.org/10.1007/978-3-642-23629-7_78
30. Ronneberger, O., Fischer, P., Brox, T.: U-Net: convolutional networks for biomedical image segmentation. In: Navab, N., Hornegger, J., Wells, W.M., Frangi, A.F. (eds.) MICCAI 2015. LNCS, vol. 9351, pp. 234–241. Springer, Cham (2015). https://doi.org/10.1007/978-3-319-24574-4_28
31. Sdika, M., Pelletier, D.: Nonrigid registration of multiple sclerosis brain images using lesion inpainting for morphometry or lesion mapping. Tech. rep, Wiley Online Library (2009)
32. Shu, Z., Sahasrabudhe, M., Alp Güler, R., Samaras, D., Paragios, N., Kokkinos, I.: Deforming autoencoders: unsupervised disentangling of shape and appearance. In: Ferrari, V., Hebert, M., Sminchisescu, C., Weiss, Y. (eds.) ECCV 2018. LNCS, vol. 11214, pp. 664–680. Springer, Cham (2018). https://doi.org/10.1007/978-3-030-01249-6_40
33. Sotiras, A., Davatzikos, C., Paragios, N.: Deformable medical image registration: a survey. IEEE Trans. Med. Imaging **32**(7), 1153–1190 (2013)
34. Trouvé, A., Younes, L.: Metamorphoses through lie group action. Found. Comput. Math. **5**(2), 173–198 (2005)
35. Wang, J., Xing, J., Druzgal, J., Wells III, W.M., Zhang, M.: MetaMorph: learning metamorphic image transformation with appearance changes. In: Frangi, A., de Bruijne, M., Wassermann, D., Navab, N. (eds.) Information Processing in Medical Imaging. IPMI 2023. Lecture Notes in Computer Science, vol. 13939, pp. 576–587. Springer, Cham (2023). https://doi.org/10.1007/978-3-031-34048-2_44
36. Yang, X., Kwitt, R., Styner, M., Niethammer, M.: Quicksilver: fast predictive image registration-a deep learning approach. Neuroimage **158**, 378–396 (2017)

Author Index

W. Qin et al. (Eds.): CMMCA 2023 (MICCAI Workshop), LNCS 14243, pp. 171–172, 2023.
https://doi.org/10.1007/978-3-031-45087-7

Printed in the United States
by Baker & Taylor Publisher Services